ADVERTISING MEDIA PLANNING

Advertising Media Planning blends the latest methods for digital communication and an understanding of the global landscape with the best practices of the functional areas of media planning. Taking a unique brand communication approach from an agency perspective, the textbook is organized into four key parts, walking the student through the foundations of brand communication, communication planning, the different media channels available, and the process of preparing, presenting, and evaluating a media plan.

This fifth edition has been fully updated to include:

- An emphasis throughout on digital and global media planning
- New chapters on the role of brand communication, media planning and data analytics, paid media, mobile media, influencer marketing, and B2B media
- New mini-case studies and innovation-focused call-out boxes throughout, showcasing media examples from Europe, the United States, and Asia
- Discussion questions to foster engagement and understanding

A highly regarded new edition, this practical and integrated textbook should be core reading for advanced undergraduate and postgraduate students studying Media Planning, Advertising Management, Integrated Marketing Communication, and Brand Management. Instructor resources include: PowerPoint slides, a test bank, and an instructor manual.

Larry D. Kelley is Professor of Advertising at the Jack J. Valenti School of Communication at the University of Houston, USA.

Kim Bartel Sheehan is Professor Emerita at the University of Oregon, USA.

Lisa Dobias is Associate Professor of Practice who has been teaching full-time at the University of Texas-Austin, USA, since 1996.

David E. Koranda is Professor of Practice Emeritus at the University of Oregon, USA.

Donald W. Jugenheimer is an author, researcher, consultant, and educator. He has authored or co-authored 20 books.

Advertising Media Planning

A Brand Management Approach

FIFTH EDITION

Larry D. Kelley
Kim Bartel Sheehan
Lisa Dobias
David E. Koranda
with
Donald W. Jugenheimer

Routledge
Taylor & Francis Group

NEW YORK AND LONDON

Cover image: MF3d

Fifth edition published 2023
by Routledge
605 Third Avenue, New York, NY 10158

and by Routledge
4 Park Square, Milton Park, Abingdon, Oxon, OX14 4RN

Routledge is an imprint of the Taylor & Francis Group, an informa business

First edition published by Prentice Hall of India 1980
Fourth edition published by Routledge 2015

ISBN: 978-1-032-19217-8 (hbk)
ISBN: 978-1-032-19215-4 (pbk)
ISBN: 978-1-003-25816-2 (ebk)

DOI: 10.4324/9781003258162

Typeset in Times New Roman
by KnowledgeWorks Global Ltd.

Access the Support Material: www.routledge.com/ 9781032192154

Contents

Preface

This is the fifth edition of *Advertising Media Planning: A Brand Management Approach*, a book that will benefit anyone making advertising and brand communication decisions. Media planning is a crucial part of the brand communication process, yet little has been written on the topic. Our goal with the first four editions was to fill this void in the market and provide a resource on how brand management can impact media decisions. The initial two editions focused on the media planning process from the viewpoint of media planners as well as brand managers who ultimately will approve how advertising dollars are allocated. The third edition expanded on the concept of media planning to consumer engagement reflecting the ever-expanding array of media choices for connecting a brand with the consumer. In the third edition, we provided much more detail regarding media alternatives. We added or expanded on digital media, social media, in-store media as well as ethnic and alternative media. To provide a more holistic view of media, we included chapters on sponsorships, promotion, and publicity.

The fourth edition built on the holistic viewpoint of the third edition to provide an overall media framework for media planners and brand managers. The fifth edition expands on the idea of a holistic view of brand communications in an ever-expanding array of communication platforms driven by the digital revolution.

Brand communication used to be largely confined to paid media. Today's brands communicate with their own media and encourage conversation with consumers through earned media. The paid, owned, and earned framework for brand communication is now the industry standard. By adopting this framework, we are rapidly moving from advertising media planning to brand communication planning. This edition is built on this changing paradigm. New chapters have been added to that capture this evolution from media planning to communication planning. There is a chapter describing media framework. Other chapters include how to develop a communication idea and communication strategies. Because media convergence is here to stay, we have broadened our viewpoint on media categories. Video and audio replace older definitions of media distribution channels. We have added a chapter on gaming, which has carved out a major niche in the media landscape. The topic of international media is included for the first time as the business of media is certainly global. Chapters on social media, digital media, print, out-of-home, television, and radio have all been updated to reflect the constant change in the media marketplace.

Like our previous books, this edition of *Advertising Media Planning* ties into the new, fifth edition of *Advertising Media Workbook and Sourcebook*, also published by Routledge. For students and instructors of media planning courses, the workbook offers a detailed perspective on each facet of media and the strategic media planning process. Practical exercises offer students the opportunity to put sometimes-abstract concepts into real-world situations.

Within the dynamic field of media, there are more reasons than ever to have a "go-to" source that any level of communication decision-maker can use to help make crucial decisions that affect a brand's value. Brand managers who have little formal training in communication planning, students of advertising, integrated marketing communication and marketing programs, and other practitioners such as agency account managers, junior media personnel, and media salespeople can benefit from this book's content and practical application.

Acknowledgments

The authors wish to thank Sophia Levine, our editor, as well as the entire Routledge publishing team. We also thank our spouses and families for all their support, without which this project would not have been possible.

CHAPTER 1

The changing role of media planning in brand support

....

MEDIA PLANNING IS ALL ABOUT CONTENT, CONTACT, AND ULTIMATELY, CONNECTION

Brand communication boils down to two fundamentals. One is content – what the brand communicates. The second is contact – how the communication connects to its intended audience. Media planning is the art and science of making that connection.

Making that connection is crucial to the success of the brand. Whether you are a brand manager, an advertising account manager, or even a top-level executive seeking profits for the entire company or corporation, you need to understand the impact of brand communication and the role that media planning plays in delivering the message.

The importance of effective media planning is a central ingredient to that success. Media ultimately connects the business of the brand to the consumer. Imagine a planning schematic. At the top is the business problem. Marketing develops a plan to solve that problem by analyzing the various levels of its discipline. The classic four are known as the four Ps (4Ps): product, price, place, and promotion. Brand communication – the communication of the brand to its audiences or public – is a capstone of the promotion category of the 4Ps.

Advertising is a significant aspect of brand communication. Historically, the media planner's role had been to connect the advertising message to the audience through various paid media channels. While this role is important, it left out numerous other communication considerations. What role – if any – should earned media such as public relations play in the communication mix? And how does owned media, such as the brand's social media platforms or the brand's website, contribute to consumer engagement? All these aspects of brand communication must be considered in developing a plan in today's global and digital communication landscape.

DOI: 10.4324/9781003258162-1

TABLE 1.1 Evolution of media planning to communication planning

From	To
Advertising support	Brand support
Reaching	Influencing
Multimedia strategy	Multichannel strategy
Placing ad units	Impacting multiplatform content

It is not enough to just plan advertising media in today's communication world. That's why this book approaches media planning from an *integrated brand communication perspective.* The media plan should consider all consumer brand touchpoints regardless of their origin. In this text, we call the media planner a *communication planner* to ensure that we address all potential aspects of a brand's communication platforms.

Media planning has evolved to brand communication planning. Table 1.1 provides an overview of the four key ways this shift has occurred. The first is the evolution from advertising support to overall brand support – a move that gives the planner a broader role. The second is reaching versus influencing. In today's dialogue media, it is not enough to think about simply reaching the right audience; you need to understand how your actions will influence them. The third component is moving from a multimedia strategy to a multichannel strategy, and the fourth and final major shift is from placing just paid advertising units to impacting multiplatform content.

One other point is the increasing need for media professionals to understand communication from a global perspective. Many companies and brands operate in a global environment. Some forms of communication are also global. As we move forward in this text, it is important to keep that in mind.

BRAND COMMUNICATION VERSUS ADVERTISING SUPPORT

A fundamental change in the planning of media revolves around the notion of brand planning support versus advertising support. Advertising media planning has been the historical role of media planners, those professionals charged with crafting the best possible delivery for an advertising message. Traditionally, advertising media planners assessed the strengths and weaknesses of various classes of paid media to determine the optimum approach for a given product or service. The limitation on this approach was that it did not consider alternatives outside of the broad paid media classes.

The standard media classes considered by advertising media planners include television, radio, magazine, newspapers, out-of-home, search, digital display, social, and cinema. Table 1.2 provides a list of two types of areas where a brand may invest its funds. They are Above the Line (ATL) and Below the Line (BTL), which are terms used by accounting departments to categorize long-term versus short-term expenses. This is a common term in many areas of communication including the movie industry. ATL refers to paid media that is designed to reach a large audience, which can

TABLE 1.2 Above the Line (ATL) versus Below the Line (BTL) advertising examples

ATL		
	• TV	• Online Display
	• Radio	• Search engine marketing (SEM)
	• Print	• Paid Social
	• Out-of-Home	
BTL	• Direct Marketing	• Brand Website
	• Sales Promotion	• Brand Social Media
	• Events	• Other Brand Media
	• Public Relations	
	• Consumer	

be considered a long-term investment in awareness and brand building. Television – which includes network, cable, syndication, streaming, and local support – and the Internet – which includes search or pay-per-click ads, display, social media, and online video – are the two largest paid media areas.

BTL encompasses activity that is not mass media related. This includes items such as direct mail, telemarketing, sales promotion, public relations, event sponsorship, and influencer marketing (see Table 1.2). BTL activities are considered a current expenditure and are largely executed by companies that are not advertising agencies (although many are owned by advertising agencies or advertising agency holding companies). Owned media such as a brand's website or social media platforms also fall into the BTL designation.

Integrated brand communications is a Through the Line (TTL) activity. In a brand communication plan, media planners are not restricted to ATL activities. Rather than approaching the communication from the perspective of media type, a brand communication plan looks at how the consumer engages with the brand and the brand with the consumer.

CHANGING NATURE OF MEDIA

The need to move to an integrated brand communication planning perspective is driven by the rapidly changing world of media. Advertising media have evolved in previously unforeseen ways over the past ten years, led principally by the digital media revolution.

The past decade has certainly seen the rise of new kinds of advertising media, and digital media has led the way. Search engine marketing (SEM), the largest aspect of digital advertising, is almost as old as the Internet. Other advertising media spawned online include banner ads that paved the way for more engaging online advertising such as rich media or video. And new channels of communication, from smartphones to tablets to video games to satellite radio and virtual and augmented reality, have extended the rise.

In the more recent past, social media platforms have provided a new level of engagement for brands and consumers. Through social media, the ascent of consumer-generated media is helping to redefine the media landscape. Now, anyone with a smartphone or video camera can shoot commercials or footage and post them on the Internet. Blogs, shorthand for weblogs, or digital personal journals allow everyone the freedom to comment on whatever they want. All of this consumer-generated media can be linked to your favorite social media network for viewing by thousands and sometimes millions of consumers. Fundamentally, anything can become a medium these days – for better or worse.

Existing media have evolved as well. The area of point-of-sale advertising has been transformed with opportunities in seemingly every venue. Shopping malls have digital signs that not only show television commercials but can also serve relevant ads based on facial recognition of passers-by. In some markets, buses contain television sets that are programmed to show a retail ad within a block or two of the advertised establishment. Ads are popping up in elevators, on escalators, inside fortune cookies, and even on celebrity or wannabe-celebrity body parts.

CHANGING NATURE OF THE CONSUMER

As media have evolved, so have consumers. There was a time when network television programs were called appointment television – consumers actually listed the time their favorite program aired on their appointment calendars. Those days have come and gone. In today's media environment, consumers are in control of how they use media. They can consume it when they want, where they want, and through whatever method or device they want. This represents a huge change in an industry where advertisers controlled when consumers received media messages. If you scheduled your media on Thursday to support a Friday sales event, you expected the targets of your message to see it on Thursday; that expectation no longer holds up. In the past, if you scheduled an ad to appear online, you expected the consumer to view it on a computer; now, consumers might view it from a tablet or, even more likely, from a smartphone.

Digital technology has reshaped how consumers use media. With the rapid penetration of tablets, smartphone devices, and wearable technology such as wristwatch smartphones, consumers are increasingly attached to some form of media machine. Because consumers have so many media consumption choices and have largely mastered the ability to multitask, the use of media has skyrocketed. A variety of studies indicate that people consume more hours of media in a day than they are awake.

The rapid rise of social media has changed the course of consumer brand engagement from a distant link to a one-on-one connection. Marketers no longer communicate in a one-sided conversation. The consumer is now talking back and even initiating brand-related discussions. Once a marketer's dream, this trend toward extreme engagement can, it seems, turn into a nightmare when consumers hijack the brand's message. Media professionals now must go beyond finding the right media to reach the consumer. They must understand users and learn how to influence them once they are engaged with the medium and the brand.

The nature of data and consumer privacy is at the forefront of public debate. With digital communication, the opportunity for media companies to capture very detailed personal behavior grows every day. While brand communication planners relish the idea of targeting content on a micro level, those data points represent real people. Those people have rights. The intersection of commerce using Big Data and consumer privacy is a major area confronting planners going forward.

CHANGING NATURE OF MEDIA EFFECTIVENESS

Media plans and media buys have long been judged by their reach, frequency, and efficiency. The stalwart measures of media effectiveness answer questions like: How many people were exposed to a given message? How many times? Was the media buy cost efficient? And did it deliver the desired results?

Reach, frequency, and efficiency remain key components in media planning and buying. However, the quest to achieve reach is rapidly giving way to a goal of achieving *influence*, with a growing emphasis on understanding how consumers use media, how media impact the creative content, and when consumers are most susceptible to a given message.

Let's tackle the area of susceptibility first. Psychologists have long debated whether primacy or recency is more important in advertising. Is it more important to be the first brand message seen or heard in a product category, or is it better to be the last impression seen or heard before the consumer makes a purchase decision?

For example, if you know that most consumers make a meal decision an hour or two before they eat, you may want to load up your food-related messaging to intercept them at that point. This involves looking at media through the eyes of the consumer. In the past, media planners used syndicated research to determine what consumers watched, read, or listened to, and then they constructed a media plan that brought together the most efficient combination of those elements.

Today, media planners continue to look at syndicated data, but they are more likely to conduct their own brand research. They may observe how consumers use media, or how various media influence consumers' decisions about the brand. A recent study showed marked differences in consumers' views of media for impulse items versus planned purchases. So, effectiveness in certain cases might mean finding media that fit best with impulse-purchase decisions. This type of thinking is much more in line with consumer behavior theory than media theory, and the idea has led to a number of studies regarding the role of media in the creative message. For example, if a brand's success is based on a high degree of trust, you would be better off associating your brand's message with media that are deemed trustworthy, or should you just look for the most efficient media regardless of the trust factor? Media effectiveness is certainly an evolving aspect of the media landscape.

Media are also evaluated from a return-on-investment perspective. In fact, media can act as sales channels for many brands. Retailers may have a combination of stores, website sales, social media, apps, catalogues, and kiosks. They may know exactly what their Sunday newspaper insert or their Twitter promotion does for their business. Most service and business-to-business brands track the source of their leads, which might stem from SEM, a blog, a print ad, or a series of seminars.

Brand marketers conduct rigorous analyses to determine the lift that each medium and media vehicle or activity gives to incremental brand sales.

These recent changes and future developments in media make it mandatory for marketing professionals to have a working knowledge of how media operate and the role they play in the overall marketing effort.

CHANGING INDUSTRY STRUCTURE

The media industry has also undergone major structural changes. It seems quaint to think that at one time in the not-too-distant past, media ownership was a mom-and-pop business. Individual families owned local newspapers, radio, or television stations. But family-owned, community-based media outlets have largely disappeared. Media ownership has been massively consolidated. Large media conglomerates such as Alphabet, Comcast, Disney, and Facebook manage a host of media properties. Despite the existence of thousands of online media properties, Google controls more than two-thirds of search volume and about 70 percent of online video through its ownership of YouTube. Facebook controls more than 80 percent of all social media traffic and is constantly adding to its portfolio through acquisitions such as Instagram and WhatsApp. Disney produces content for television, cable, streaming services, and movies as well as owning theme parks, cruise lines, and a huge content library.

Given that the growth of the media universe is accompanied by the consolidation of ownership power, *multichannel media strategies* are on the rise. Instead of focusing on multimedia strategies, media companies are taking a lesson from packaged-goods brands. For example, CNN is not only a popular cable news channel but also a leading content provider with a huge presence that includes airport television networks, radio networks, mobile apps, and a worldwide online news portal. Media content is being delivered in a variety of forms – and not within a single medium.

As the media industry landscape has changed, so has the process of planning, buying, and supplying ad content. The advertising industry has followed the same pattern of growth and consolidation as the media industry: At one time, there were thousands of locally owned advertising, public relations, and sales promotion agencies. Now, the industry largely belongs to eight holding companies. Within that set, the three most dominant global holding companies are Omnicom, WPP, and Publicis; the balance is made up of either Japanese networks like Dentsu and Hakuhodo or Western-based networks such as Interpublic, MDC, or Havas. These companies own hundreds of marketing services companies specializing in advertising, media buying, digital, public relations, and sales promotion.

As large holding companies acquired advertising agencies, they found it more efficient to consolidate their swelling media planning and buying operations into firms devoted solely to that function. Fundamentally, this approach split the advertising function, with an agency devoted to message strategy and creative on the one hand and a large media company devoted to media planning and buying on the other. Large media agencies such as Starcom, MediaCom, and Mediaedge now control a significant amount of global paid media spending.

On an individual company basis, the agency business continues to specialize. Some agencies focus solely on SEM or social media or events and promotions. Others have carved out a niche in a specific business area such as health care. Within this consolidated landscape is a very diverse cottage industry of agencies of different sizes, makeups, and areas of expertise.

WHO CONNECTS THE DOTS?

The biggest question brand managers wrestle with concerns unity: Who connects the dots? Who develops an integrated brand communication plan that considers all channels, whether it is paid, owned, or earned media?

The answer seems straightforward enough: Just have one of the large media planning and buying companies develop the plan; their specialists can cover every area of a brand communication plan. But it's important to consider that these individual companies have their own profit and loss to worry about, and they may or may not want their compensation dictated by a single media company. Going directly to the brand or company may get them a bigger share of the pie. Another drawback is the possible loss of continuity in the overall brand communication strategy, with lots of moving pieces and parts to manage and coordinate.

An alternative is to go to an independent agency or an agency that has a variety of internal resources. Again, there are potential problems: The issue with this approach is that the agency may lack the appropriate resources to meet every need. It is difficult, after all, to be an expert in every facet of the communication world.

Very large advertisers such as General Motors are developing their own agency models, taking resources from the big holding companies to ensure control of the entire process. But the typical brand doesn't have this type of financial clout. For smaller companies, then, connecting the dots typically becomes a task shared by the brand and the agency.

SUMMARY

Media planning is a dynamic and ever-changing field of study. Its emphasis has shifted from allocating dollars to media in order to reach consumers to understanding consumer behavior and matching it with a brand's benefits. All brands view media planning as an integrated brand communication effort. The trick is to figure out how best to connect the dots in the most opportune way.

CHAPTER 2

Role and importance of data in planning

....

DATA AND INSIGHTS ARE THE FUEL FOR BRAND SUCCESS

Since its beginning as a discipline, media has been the function formally charged with getting the right message to the right people at the right time. Although media as a field has drastically changed and increased in importance, as discussed in Chapter 1, these fundamental responsibilities of media planning could never be more valid than in today's disruptive environment.

Implied here is the need to better understand at the deepest level possible what the right message actually is, who the right people genuinely are, and when the right time really is. As we move from mass to niche channels, and from customized to now personalized outreach, finding these insights and providing this fuel for brand success is not only much more possible, but also exponentially more expected.

Imagine if you could have a personal chat with each member of your brand's community or those who you would like to bring into that community. What if you could ask each of these individuals questions about their likes, dislikes, preferences, and needs with regards to the brand. What if you could ask them about when or how they bought your product last? Imagine you could also talk with them about how they spend their time. What media channels are they most engaged with? Where do they get their news? What are the biggest influences on their purchasing decisions? Can you imagine how much more productive and focused your outreach planning would be if this were all feasible? Well, this seemingly fantasy world is actually a reality in a sense via the world of Big Data.

BIG DATA AND THE INTERNET OF THINGS

The reality is that information is being gathered 24/7/365 about all consumers both actively and passively while we use digital platforms, make cashless purchases both online and off, and just go about living our daily lives. Anywhere there is a digital connection, there is information created that can be connected. Think about it. From

DOI: 10.4324/9781003258162-2

using our phones, to our computers, cars, refrigerators, ovens, washers and driers, even our digital home thermostats or doorbells, we are all generating virtual transactions almost all day long via a digitally connected network of physical devices called the *Internet of Things* (IOT). IOT information can be stored, cleaned, organized, aggregated, anonymized, autonomized, and analyzed to create an informed path forward. This information can be used to make our individualized healthcare more accurate, our shopper user experiences more personal, and our workout routines more productive.

All of this information generated every day around the world creates enormously large and complex datasets that are referred to as *Big Data*. What officially makes any data big? According to World Advertising Research Center (WARC), to officially be considered Big Data, information must exhibit extremes of *Volume, Velocity, Variety, and Veracity*. WARC provides retail transactional databases and web tracking as two perfect examples of Big Data.

DATA THEN AND NOW

The truth is that good media planning has always been grounded in data even before Big Data was our reality. Information has been the cornerstone of media from both the planner/buyer and seller side. Planners and buyers of media have always needed information to determine who, how, when, and where to reach people as well as how much to value and pay for the media options they chose, while media publishers have always needed information to justify and sell their ad inventory to brands and show their value.

The difference today is because the volume of information available with the advent of digital platforms is so much greater that data can now be used to drive and optimize strategic planning on both a macro and micro level.

Data in media can be both *deterministic* and *probabilistic*. Deterministic data is information that can tell planners what is happening. This type of information helps us better understand the various influences currently happening within the marketplace. By comparison, probabilistic data is information that is predictive in nature. Computer models can be created using probabilistic data to forecast what will happen in the future.

The influx of data-powered decision making is one of the biggest reasons media planning has been elevated as one of the primary competitive tools in the marketplace. Media professionals are looked to as key navigators in the world of data insights, which makes them more integral in all aspects of brand planning.

TYPES OF DATA

When looking at data information, it is often broken into three larger categories based on the origin source of information.

First-party data is proprietary data that brands collect and have private access to via their own customer relationship management (CRM) systems, e-commerce platforms, mobile or online apps, customer feedback surveys, or owned media platform analytics. This is information the brand "owns," meaning that it is not in the public domain and can continue to be analyzed or added to for future insights. An example would be an outdoor equipment brand creating customized email marketing campaigns to retarget customers who have purchased camping gear via their mobile app with messaging promoting other complementary camping accessories.

Second-party data is information that brands can gain access to via their strategic partner alliances. Often brands create working relationships with other brands who have shared objectives and or an interest in the same target audiences. Both brands involved have a relationship with the consumers about which data is being collected. Under these agreements, brands can borrow or even exchange their first-party data for the benefit of both brands. An example of using second-party data would be a movie theater chain borrowing information about specific entertainment purchasing behaviors from a major credit card company or online ticket retailer to place more geographically relevant messaging for potential movie-goers. This is information the movie theater brand has limited or temporary access to and does not "own" indefinitely.

Finally, third-party data is information from outside providers who do not have a direct relationship with the consumers about which data is being collected. This type of information is purchasable on a small scale for a single project, to a large, on-going scale via online subscriptions. Third-party data is the most available and scalable, but also lacks transparency, which means it should be used even more cautiously. Third-party data can be "stitched together" to generalize media strategies. An example of using multiple third-party data sources would be a loan consolidation company using information provided by local city governments to establish which ZIP codes have the highest home ownership in tandem with other information on per capita family debt in neighborhoods to determine the best target areas for messaging regarding potential home loan consolidation services.

ADDING MORE PRIMARY AND SECONDARY RESEARCH TO THE CONVERSATION

In conducting research for planning, brands often determine information that would be inspiring. One large category of purchasable information that brands have access to is secondary, often referred to as syndicated data. This is data that brands can purchase from research providers via ongoing online database access or in smaller customized reports. Syndicated data is gathered, organized, and made available to any subscriber. By definition, it is generated externally from brands and is not private or proprietary to any one brand. Because of this, secondary research is not customized, can be less accurate, and is often a lower cost investment for brands than primary research.

Beyond syndicated research, most brands may decide to participate in a number of other primary research gathering techniques. Activities can be overt, such as focus groups, in-depth interviews, and surveys, or they can be covert, such as other observational studies. Primary research can be conducted internally or hired out via research vendors. This type of research is proprietary to the brand that conducted or commissioned the study, is highly customizable, and can be a significant cost investment.

It is an industry best practice for planners to exhaust secondary research avenues prior to deciding to undergo primary research studies. Doing so can make the results of primary research much more precise and intentional. In general, while secondary research should be conducted first to find out *what* is happening, primary research can then be carefully crafted and conducted to look more into *why* things are happening.

QUANTITATIVE DATA VERSUS QUALITATIVE DATA

When looking for information to help planners better understand the people in their brand's community, it is important to look at all types of data. While seeking out data, most think of information that is quantitative or numerical in nature. This includes specifics such as facts, figures, and statistics that describe important characteristics and behaviors. An example of using quantitative data might be for a company considering the click-through rate (CTR) of their most recent search ad campaign when optimizing their investments. This means looking at how many people numerically clicked on their ads from each keyword placed to better understand which message and word combinations were most productive.

Another often undervalued or even overlooked type of data to be included when looking at a brand's community is qualitative data. This type of information looks more at attributes or characteristics that reflect the beliefs, values, sentiments, or perhaps even motivations of individuals. An example would be a brand using the comments provided in their customer service follow-up surveys to carefully craft the most relevant future editorial calendar for their social media content.

THE DATA GATHERING PHASES IN PLANNING

To best foster an environment where creative insights thrive, particularly at the onset of a new campaign effort, it is important to approach the process of data collection in two separate, sequential phases. The hunting and gathering of information should always begin first as open-ended, and then later become intention-driven.

The first phase of conducting research and seeking out data is considered the discovery stage. It is important here that planners maintain neutrality and pursue information of all types with an open mind to finding new things. In this phase, the planner acts resourcefully as a detective gathering evidence with curiosity. Predetermined beliefs or other bias can significantly limit or even taint this process as planners look for what is expected rather than what is possible.

The second phase of conducting research and seeking out data is considered the confirmation stage. The time needed to move from the discovery stage to the confirmation stage varies depending on the scope of work as well as the time available. The key is to be certain that enough discovery research has been conducted to begin creation of insights. Once hypotheses on unique insights are formed, confirmation research can begin to create validation of and further support for the insights being honed. Confirmation research may also disprove and or alter the initial insights in new or more valid directions. This process can also bring to light the need for more discovery research to take place. Regardless, it takes skilled planning with the right combination of discovery and confirmation research to create outcomes that are both creatively inspired and valid.

BEYOND PLANNING TO OPTIMIZATION & MEASUREMENT

As just described, data is an essential part of the planning process, but its use does not stop there. Because information is the fuel for good decision-making, leaning into data is important at all stages of media. Now that we have information in near real-time, it is important to use that information as our media campaigns unfold to update, shift, and otherwise change our plans. This process of modifying media as it plays out is called *optimization*. For example, a brand may have multiple search engine marketing (SEM) keywords within an ad group simultaneously active in a campaign. As the campaign gets up and running, media planners can note the performance of each keyword and choose to phase out words that are underperforming, allowing them to put more money behind, or optimize, the words that are most successful.

Data should also be used after the campaign is over to course correct any future plans based on this new input. New benchmarks, test-and-learns and other predictive tools can be used to help keep the brand's plans current and in-step with the marketplace. However, one very big point to remember is that data is never to be used blindly or to create over-reactive knee-jerk responses. Although a very powerful tool, data is never to be used instead of good human decision-making. Data can tell is what is happening as well as predict what might happen in the future, but it does not necessarily tell us *why* things are happening. By its nature, human nature can be highly unpredictable and well... human.

THE DIFFERENCE BETWEEN DATA AND INSIGHTS

In better understanding the role of data in planning, it is critical to distinguish the difference between data and insights. By definition, data is nothing more than facts, statistics, or other types of information that has been collected. Capturing data alone cannot inspire decisions. It is in the analysis, understanding of, and acting on the stories found in data where insights are born. Data sets are the building blocks of insights. Where data provides planners with the basic ingredients for decision-making, it is the mining of data insights found that provides them with new direction.

A critical reminder here is to never forget that the data we are working with is the voice of our community. Just as we would respect individual people talking with us and sharing their personal stories, we need to respect the data they provide us as we analyze it and turn it into insights. We must never allow ourselves to make unsubstantiated generalizations, compromise consumer privacy, or act in any otherwise unethical way when listening to our community talk to us via their data.

It is also important to note that no two strategists may see the stories in the data in the same way. Harvesting insights from data is one of the most creative skills in media today. The portions of data a planner chooses to be primary, the way they seek out and combine the information they have access to, and the methodologies they employ for understanding that information are unique and inspired. Hence, the role of finding strong insights for planning is both an art and a science.

DATA OWNERSHIP, COMPLIANCE, AND REGULATION

As evidenced in the daily news, few things are more highly debated today than who owns the private information that constitutes the Big Data available in the media marketplace. Unquestionably, consumers have the right to protect themselves from financial or other compromise they can be subjected to based on brands using their personal data, including the digital information they both knowingly and sometimes unknowingly generate. While it is true that this information is exploited by brands to market their goods and services, the use of personal and behavioral information can make the individual media user experience better. For example, by keeping track of consumer preferences via tracking pixels, brands can make sure that the most relevant messaging gets to the most likely targets at the right time, reducing the waste of brand resources, but also helping consumers enjoy both ad and editorial content that is most appealing to them.

In addition to brands and publishers collecting consumer and audience information during online sessions, there are a plenitude of other third-party companies tracking online communities and their behaviors. The largest groups operating in this space are *Data Management Platforms* (DMPs). DMPs are large organizations that aggregate and anonymize vast data sets that can be sold to others for implementing campaigns. For example, Facebook has one of the world's largest DMPs based on their billions of users. The personal information of those users fuels the Facebook DMP and generates significant revenue for the company who sells this information when serving paid advertising.

Across the globe, landmark legislation has been increasingly passed to help protect consumers and their private information. In 2018, the European Union (EU) began enforcing the first sweeping laws known as the *General Data Protection Regulation* (GDPR). The GDPR was put into place to generally provide consumers more control over their personal information by requiring all companies that conduct business in the EU to follow standard data compliance policies. Since that time, countries around the world have increased regulation and requirements to affect the ways in which companies can capture, store, and use consumer information. For example, in addition to phasing out the use of tracking cookies, the United States has tightened the rules and subsequent penalties for the ways personal identifiable information (PII) must be handled.

Consumers have benefited from the new privacy laws that demand more corporate transparency and have increased their choices to opt-in or opt-out of having personal data collected. This evolving legislation has impacted the practices of companies and expedited the growth of data collection referred to as *Zero-Party Data*. Rather than using tracking or other hidden, intuitive measurements and analytics, zero-party data is information intentionally solicited and openly shared by consumers with brands regarding their preferences, motivations, and even purchase intentions. Creating deeper brand community relationships and heightened brand trust is pivotal to generating quality zero-party data, which many believe will be the key to the future of brand success via personalized outreach planning in the years to come.

SUMMARY

Information about people, their purchasing and media audience behaviors, and trending situations has always been the bedrock of solid media planning. The vast and relatively recent influx of Big Data into the process of media planning and buying via digital platforms has added complexity and challenge to the process. With more robust information comes more opportunity, but also more responsibility. It is up to each brand to use data in the most inspiring but ethical manners possible. It is important that strategists remember that data in the media space is the voice, beliefs, and motivations of their consumers as expressed via their actions, behaviors, comments, and time spent. As such, media data must be treated with the same respect and diligence that each individual represented in the data would be.

Facial coded out-of-home

In 2002, Tom Cruise starred in a movie called *Minority Report* where advanced intelligence could tell in who was going to commit a crime before the crime ever happened. One of the most talked about scenes in this science-fiction thriller featured Cruise's character, John Anderton, walking into a retail store where a voiceless robot asked him if he enjoyed the pants he had purchased the previous week. This ten-second scene was invented by scientists at MIT who thought it could never occur in real life, yet the future depicted in *Minority Report* may be much closer than we think.

In-store marketing, a type of out-of-home advertising, has always had media professionals questioning the ability to use this medium for micro targeting. Micro targeting is a type of marketing that analyzes large amounts of personal data, gathered online, to create and distribute messages that reflect an individual's preferences and personality. Social media sites like Facebook and Instagram are expert in micro targeting, as these sites have access to all kinds of information users leave in their digital footprints while using those sites.

A large Japanese company, NEC, has changed that game. NEC makes a variety of home electronics including both hardware and software. Recently, the company developed a proprietary piece of facial recognition software that can be used to unlock smartphones and help doctors recognize patients in masks. This code can also be embedded into electronic advertising displays. NEC placed this software into ad messaging in airports around the world so that advertising messages change on the billboard based on facial recognition. So, a man may see a different ad than a woman or an older adult may see a different ad than someone in their 20s. Amazing.

What are some other uses for facial recognition technology that you can imagine?

CHAPTER 3

Establishing a media framework

....

LET'S BUILD A STRONG FOUNDATION FOR BRAND MESSAGES

Historically, media planning involved allocating dollars to single types of paid media. For example, a television station sold airtime, a newspaper sold ad space on a page or a portion of a page, or an outdoor company leased space on a billboard. That model of media planning no longer exists.

From a brand perspective, looking solely at paid media is a bit naïve. The challenge is recognizing how to use *any* communication method to help promote the brand. Paid media is one of those options – but certainly not the only one. Media types have undergone striking changes that mirror the evolution of technology. Television programming can now be viewed on a television, a laptop, or a mobile device. Newspapers can be accessed through print and/or digital devices. Even outdoor, the world's oldest medium, can provide digital messages. These changes make the historical ways of approaching media obsolete. This chapter offers media planners an updated framework for looking at the world of media.

BRANDS AS MEDIA AND MEDIA AS BRANDS

The marketplace is abuzz with the media convergence movement – providing content in a variety of forms. Established forms of media such as television, radio, newspaper, magazine, and outdoor are doing it. They are providing their content in digital formats and with new functions.

Media convergence goes well beyond just providing content in new ways. It is the convergence of content, branding, and consumer engagement. In essence, brands are now media, and media are now brands. It used to be that brands did something and the media provided a forum for brands to say something. Now both media and brands do something, say something, and engage with consumers directly.

DOI: 10.4324/9781003258162-3

For example, Red Bull is a manufacturer of energy drinks. Red Bull also has the Red Bull Media House. This aspect of the Red Bull brand focuses on sports, culture, and lifestyle content across television, digital, audio, and print media as well as produces and licenses a broad selection of global events. Is Red Bull an energy drink, a media company, or a lifestyle? Red Bull is a classic case of taking advantage of today's media world to become a brand platform for living life to its fullest.

On the other hand, media have changed from being just a conduit for brands to tell their story; media are becoming brands themselves. *Better Homes and Gardens* (BH&G) is a venerable magazine that provides content in a variety of forms. Just like Red Bull, it has broadened its brand by licensing it (in BH&G's case, to the real estate and retail market). Now there are Better Homes and Gardens real estate agents and house wares and furniture exclusively for Walmart. And BH&G engages consumers through a variety of digital and physical sponsorships and events.

Brands are acting like media companies and media companies are acting like brands. It's no wonder that the historical way of looking at media needs a new framework.

PAID, OWNED, AND EARNED MEDIA FRAMEWORK

Suppose you have determined that Facebook should be a big part of your brand communication plan. The question becomes how to use it. You have a variety of options. One is to purchase ads that are posted on the Facebook newsfeed. The second is to create a Facebook page dedicated to your brand. The third is to devise a contest where consumers share their most unforgettable brand stories. Or you can do a combination of all three.

This example helps explain how the media landscape is changing. Media used to be a channel where you purchased advertising to promote your brand. Now media is a brand platform. Instead of determining the role various media play in your plan, you need to explore the role your brand plays in various media.

Facebook is a great example of the media framework that is based on a brand's integrated brand communication plan. The framework is paid, owned, and earned media, sometimes referred to as POE. Table 3.1 provides a definition of each media type.

The first media type is *paid media*. This is the history of media planning. In this case, the brand pays to leverage a media channel. It could be buying an ad on Facebook, a pre-roll video on YouTube or a television schedule across a variety of networks. Regardless of the purchase, the key to paid media is that the brand is directly paying

TABLE 3.1 Paid, owned, and earned media framework

Media type	Definition
Paid media	Brand pays to leverage a channel
Owned media	Brand controls the channel
Earned media	Brand has consumers/companies become the channel

a media company for access to their audience in the hopes of turning that audience into brand buyers. This is Advertising 101.

The second media type is *owned media*. In this case, the brand controls the channel. Brands have become a medium in today's marketplace. Most companies and brands have their own website. This channel is totally controlled by the brand. In many cases, a brand's website becomes a consumer hub where customers can comment on a brand, get promotional discounts, and engage in contests or other promotional events. In our Facebook example, a brand can create its own Facebook page to interact with consumers. Brands have many opportunities to create their own media. Later in this textbook, we devote a complete chapter to owned media.

The third media type is *earned media*. This is where consumers and/or companies become a channel for the brand. Earned media has become a quest for many brands, since the benefit of earned media is a lot of brand exposure for little to no money. Earned media includes publicity that is initiated by the brand. It may include an influencer program. The broader area of earned media also includes any activity regarding the brand stimulated by the consumer and/or other companies. In our Facebook example, the brand is developing or initiating a contest to stimulate consumer-shared stories. The goal is to seed a conversation that grows on its own. Brands have embraced this media type. Just as we devote an entire chapter to owned media, we also dedicate one to earned media as well as a special chapter that deals with influencer programs for a more extensive view of how marketers are using this media type.

PAID MEDIA CLASSIFICATIONS

Advertisers and media planners have segmented paid media into a variety of subclasses. A common typology is *traditional media, nontraditional media*, and *new media*. Others classify media as *traditional, digital*, and *nontraditional*. These classifications are largely a result of media's digital revolution. In terms of advertising, any medium that was developed prior the Internet is considered a traditional medium.

This type of classification is misleading. Television is a highly digital medium with content accessible via laptop, tablet, or phone and offers over-the-air, cable, and streaming options. While its origins predate the Internet, it has adapted to the times. Radio, print, and out-of-home have digital components as well. Digital media have moved into so-called "traditional" spaces. For instance, Spotify, an online radio service, purchased a radio station so it could adjust its costs for purchasing content.

The convergence of media forms is rendering these simple classifications a moot point. If social media is new media, then what is television programming that contains a built-in social media platform? Is it traditional media or new media or new traditional media?

When does a new medium become an old or traditional medium? Many digital or online media are ten or more years old. Google has been around for more than a decade. Is it really that new? There are many new methods of providing an existing service. Pandora is a self-programmable radio station accessed online. Flipbook is a digital print product that allows the consumer to aggregate the content they want from a variety of media sources. While digital is rapidly changing the landscape of how consumers can get content, the content itself is much the same as in the past.

The paid media world boils down to two broad categories: One is advertising-supported consumer content. The second is advertising that provides content or items that can be connected to advertising.

ADVERTISING-SUPPORTED CONSUMER CONTENT

The majority of paid media falls into this category, providing content to consumers with a revenue model that is based primarily on advertising. The original media in this category include television, radio, magazines, and newspapers.

Social media companies such as Facebook and Twitter provide a platform for consumer content with an advertising-supported revenue model. They create content and allow consumers to create content on their media platform. While the content may differ from other media, the idea is the same. More eyeballs equals more advertising revenue. That's what drives the needs of the advertising community.

Google and Yahoo! are portals that provide either access to information or unique information and/or services. Just like other media companies, they are dedicated to advertising as their revenue model.

Whether the medium is new or old, the similarities are that they provide consumer content in exchange for advertising revenue.

ADVERTISING CONNECTIONS THAT PROVIDE CONTENT OR ITEMS CONNECTED TO ADVERTISING

A growing number of advertising connections provide content or items connected to advertising. The largest category in this type is out-of-home advertising. Whether it's outdoor billboards, bus benches, or mall advertising, out-of-home is an opportunity for a brand to connect its message to its audience. Media such as out-of-home are advertising-supported structures with no consumer content other than the advertising message itself.

Besides the large out-of-home advertising, there are other types of media – typically called nontraditional – that fall into this category. Like out-of-home, they usually carry no consumer content other than the advertising message. Some examples are ads on items such as coffee sleeves, shopping carts, escalators, and dry cleaning bags. All of these items have functional uses other than advertising, yet they carry advertising.

Guerrilla advertising also falls into this category. Guerrilla advertising is using unconventional means to get your message across. An example is KFC, the chicken restaurant chain that purchased manhole covers for the city of Louisville in exchange for making the covers look like buckets of chicken. Another example is the cable network TNT, whose marketers staged a "drama" in a Belgian city square to promote their channel to the market.

What do both of these types of paid media have in common? The brand is purchasing something in exchange for providing its message.

FRAMEWORK FOR STRATEGY

POE media capture the essence of today's media marketplace. The lines between them can sometimes be blurry. Rather than looking at POE as a classification system, a media planner can use the framework as a strategic tool.

For example, suppose that a brand wants to extend its campaign through earned media. One way to do this is to pay a group of bloggers to promote their brand. Is this paid media (since the bloggers are being paid), or is it earned media (since the bloggers are interacting with their respective audiences who are furthering the brand discussion)? Does it really matter? The point is that the brand is leveraging one media type to gain another.

Red Bull's Extreme Mountain Bike Race is a great example of an event that extends the boundaries of the brand. Red Bull is the creator and sponsor of the event. In essence, it pays for the content and owns the event. The event itself is extended through earned media in a number of facets. The event is publicized. Other brands participate in the event, which extends its reach even further. Participants and attendees carry on a conversation about the event.

You can ask yourself if your media purchase can result in "owning" that medium or creating earned media. The POE framework helps guide that discussion and sets the stage for a broader view of connecting the consumer to the brand in a relevant manner.

SUMMARY

POE media provide a framework for developing a brand communication plan. This framework comes at it from an integrated brand communication perspective. It is used to help media planners establish how the consumer comes into contact with the brand. Each media type has its role in the communication plan. It is the job of the media planner to weigh each broad type to meet the brand's objectives. Hopefully, the media planning team will work to leverage its media selection to extend the brand's consumer connection.

CHAPTER 4

Dynamics of paid media

....

PAID MEDIA: WHAT MOST PEOPLE THINK OF WHEN THEY THINK ABOUT ADVERTISING

When you think of advertising, many people think of paid media. You surely have seen a commercial on television, cable, or a streaming service. Perhaps you have seen an advertisement in your Facebook news feed or a text sponsored ad when you search the Internet. All of these are examples of paid media.

Paid media consists of messages that are paid for by the company/organization/ brand to a media company. Messages are paid for either at a negotiated rate, as is the case with media such as television, print, or radio, or through some type of bid system, such as search engine marketing. Regardless of the payment method, the exchange in paid media is dollars for reaching a specific audience. The cost for media is largely based on the number of people or audience size that is potentially exposed to the message.

Traditionally, paid media has been associated with advertising agencies. The term advertising agent comes from those who represented an advertiser to purchase media with the reward of a commission (typically 15%) from the media as an incentive. In today's strategic communication landscape, the purchasing of media can be the responsibility of an advertising agency, media specialist agency, public relations agency, marketing consultant, or by the advertiser themselves.

The larger role of paid media in our society is one of providing the revenue to help fund content development and distribution. Paid media helps fuel the world of public entertainment, news, and culture. Without paid media, the consumer cost to purchase this content would be prohibitive.

Worldwide advertising or paid media is approximately $750 billion with the United States leading the world in paid media with roughly 30% of total spending. The paid media industry is huge by any standard. At its current size, the paid media

DOI: 10.4324/9781003258162-4

industry would rank in the world's top 25 country's GDP, larger than Belgium, Austria, or Thailand. We will be discussing all types of paid media in detail later in this book. The following summarizes strengths and weaknesses of paid media as a category.

STRENGTHS AND WEAKNESSES

With so many dollars invested in paid media, there are some obvious benefits. Companies would not invest such large amounts of dollars if there was no return. Paid media has historically been the catalyst for introducing new products, services, and ideas to the public for many years. The following are the key strengths of paid media:

- **Reach/Frequency:** Scheduling advertising in paid media offers the brand the opportunity to reach a significant audience. For example, one Super Bowl advertisement historically has had nearly 50% viewership of all US adults.

    The other side of paid media is the opportunity to generate significant message frequency among the desired audience. Together, the ability to reach a large audience combined with the opportunity to have that audience see/hear the message provides the advertiser with the tools to effectively deliver a campaign message.
- **Audience Targeting**: Paid media offers the opportunity to place your message in front of a specific audience. Through a variety of research tools, the ability to define an audience demographically, behaviorally, or psychologically provides precision in message delivery.
- **Media Mix/Messaging:** Through paid media channels, there is the opportunity to have your message on different media types, platforms, and properties. This offers the message flexibility to tailor messages by size and by channel.
- **Content Association:** By associating the brand's message within desirable content provides a positive halo effect. For example, if you find a publication that you associate with luxury, the advertising in the publication will also be associated with being of a very high quality.
- **Accountability:** Paid media provides a high level of accountability where there is an audit of costs and delivery that is reconciled on a periodic basis, depending upon the medium. This accountability ensures that the advertiser gets what they have paid for.

While paid media offers a lot of opportunities, it does have some downsides. Here are a few weaknesses to consider:

- **Cost:** There can be a significant cost to funding paid media. The cost to purchase media channels can be extremely high. For example, one: 30-second commercial in the Super Bowl may cost upwards of $5 million. The other cost implication is production of content. The cost to produce video, audio, digital, or print content can run into the millions of dollars. To be a large investor in paid media on a national or global scale requires tens of millions of dollars.

- **Clutter:** Your brand is typically not alone when purchasing paid media. Many other brands are shown across all paid media, which can make for a cluttered marketplace. This competitive clutter can have a diminishing effect on your brand's message.
- **Control:** There is an increasing lack of control over when a consumer may be exposed to your message and the content that your message is within. The latter is particularly true of large-scale digital purchases on the Internet.

Paid media is the cornerstone of many strategic communication campaigns. Over time, the landscape of paid media has greatly changed. The following summarizes a few of the key changes that have impacted paid media.

EVOLUTION OF PAID MEDIA

The evolution of paid media has changed based on a number of factors. There are three key factors that impact the business.

- **Consolidation of Media Companies:** There was a time when much of the media landscape was owned by individuals. It was not uncommon up until 1990 for a wealthy family to own a television station, a newspaper, or a magazine. Media ownership was much diffused within our society. Those days are gone. Today, ownership of media is concentrated in the hands of very few publicly traded corporations. For example, Comcast, Disney, Viacom/CBS, 20th Century Fox, and AT&T control the vast majority of television programming in the US. Google and Facebook control over half of all digital advertising both in the US and beyond. While US conglomerates lead the world in content development, Sony in Japan, Bertelsmann in Germany, Liberty in the UK, Televisa in Mexico, and Grupo Global in Brazil are all examples of large, diversified global media giants.

  The impact of these media conglomerates is that they have size, scale, and operate on a multi-platform basis. This means that they have a wide variety of media assets under their control. For example, Disney owns ABC, ESPN, Marvel, Pixar, Lucasfilm as well as a host of cable and radio stations, theme parks, and cruise lines. This concentration of media/entertainment ownership gives them great leverage when it comes to securing favorable pricing for their products.
- **Consolidation of agencies and advertisers:** On the buyer side of the media equation, there has also been considerable consolidation in the advertising agency space. Five publicly traded holding companies such as WPP, Omnicom, Dentsu, Publicis, and Interpublic own the vast majority of all the strategic communication companies such as advertising agencies, public relations agencies, research companies, and other consultancies in the world. In a bid to gain economies of scale and leverage, many of these holding companies, combined the media purchasing power of their individual advertising firms into mega-media agency

firms. These media-only agencies use their large scale to attempt to leverage pricing concessions from the media.

The paid media business, or seller versus buyer, is in a large part a dance among the elephants. Fewer larger media companies control access to content creation, and fewer larger buyers work to chase that content.

- **Digital technology:** In the midst of the media and agency consolidation came the disruptive force of digital technology. The Internet has fundamentally altered the media landscape. People use the Internet to find and learn about everything. Google is the dominant search engine in the world capturing over 80% of the world's search volume according to multiple sources. And Google's sister company, YouTube, is second in terms of global search volume and the leading search engine for video content. Large tech companies, such as Alphabet, the owner of Google and YouTube, now dominate the media landscape. Facebook dominates the social media landscape with its Facebook and Instagram platforms. Other large tech companies such as Amazon are entering into the media and entertainment world by purchasing content makers. These tech companies have placed pressure on traditional media companies to respond.

As a result, digital technology has expanded the media portfolios of traditional media companies to include websites, podcasts, streaming services, digital publications, and more. As technology advances, there are increasingly more options for media companies to engage with the consumer. The big keep on getting bigger.

SUMMARY

In summary, paid media is any form of content where an advertiser pays to have their message placed within that content. Paid media continues to be the dominant method for marketers to promote goods and services. The landscape of paid media has rapidly changed in the past 50 years in size, scale, dimension, and type of media. Technology will continue to push new boundaries for this area. As you read further in this text, we will highlight a broad array of media categories and specific media channels that are considerations for any media plan.

CHAPTER 5

Dynamics of owned media

....

YOUR BRAND'S OWN MEDIA ARE GREAT ASSETS

When most think of a media plan, their thoughts immediately are directed to pur-chasing media or developing a great public relations or social media plan. Yet, for many brands, you need to look no further than the brand itself for terrific media opportunities.

In fact, media planners should look to leverage the existing brand assets first *before* considering other media. Why wouldn't you take advantage of consumer touchpoints that you already control? It is the best way to maximize cost efficiency. If you already own it, you don't need to repurchase it. Building a brand that engages with the con-sumer is all about developing and building owned media assets.

Owned media are items such as a company or brand website, packaging, company employees, and events and sponsorships. These are assets that the company or brand has developed or that are a part of doing business. Since all of these items or people touch consumers, you can consider them a media opportunity. Owned media fall into three camps. There are physical assets, digital assets, and created assets, which include events and sponsorships. Before we review each area, let's discuss the overall strengths and weaknesses of this media area.

STRENGTHS/WEAKNESSES OF OWNED MEDIA

Owned media are an underappreciated area in media. Yet, this asset offers the brand so much promise. Unlike any other media alternative, you are not confined to any pre-existing requirements. You have a blank canvas.

Owned media are especially powerful in building a long-term relationship with existing customers. That is a role that this area of media can play for the brand. Owned media have real strength to influence the lower end of the brand purchase

DOI: 10.4324/9781003258162-5

funnel – the areas of repeat purchase and brand loyalty and advocacy. This role is supported by the benefits of owned media.

- *Control*: Owned media allows you to control the message. There is no other media filter or context, so the message you deliver is a pure brand message.
- *Timely*: Owned media can be very timely. You can respond to a situation or consumer at any moment. You can be very topical and relevant.
- *Lasting*: Owned media allows you to have a lasting message. Unlike other media, where you message is fleeting, you can maintain the same message for a long period of time.
- *Personal*: Owned media can be very personal and flexible. You can develop different messages for different targets. It offers the opportunity to be highly targeted and relevant to your consumer base. You can speak to consumers on a one-to-one basis.
- *Cost efficient*: Owned media can be highly cost efficient. Owned media typically doesn't involve paying for media, so costs can be relatively low compared to other media choices.

There are a lot of benefits to developing a strong owned media portfolio. This should be a goal for the majority of brands in today's crowded communication marketplace. While owned media offer a lot of opportunities, it does have some downsides. Here are a few weaknesses to consider.

- *Not trusted*: Owned media obviously provides a company or brand message. Consumers know this, so they may be skeptical of the message. This is particularly true when brands engage directly with consumers. If the brand says one thing and behaves differently, there is the potential for trouble.
- *Time consuming*: Owned media may not cost a lot in terms of media outlay, but it can be time consuming. Time is money. It can take a lot of personnel hours to effectively manage a strong owned media portfolio. This is especially true of manning digital assets such as a Facebook page or Twitter feed. Developing continuous content takes time and dedicated people to do it.
- *Lack of consistency*: Owned media can have many owners. That can lead to a lack of consistency in the brand's voice. For example, a company website may report to the IT director. A blog may report to the corporate communication director. And a brand microsite may be developed independently for a specific brand manager.

The more owned media, the more potential problems it can create. Most problems with owned media can be summed up as departmental coordination challenges. Getting everyone aligned and working together to develop a consistent brand voice is the top challenge for maximizing owned media. Although there may be challenges, owned media offers the brand some great opportunities. Let's discuss the three broad areas of owned media, beginning with physical assets.

PHYSICAL ASSETS

If you are marketing a consumer packaged-goods brand, the package that contains your brand may be your biggest media asset. Think about it. Wouldn't you want a medium at the point of sale that consumers see every day? Of course you would. The outside of the package is a daily billboard that can be refreshed with new messages or offers. The inside of the package offers an opportunity to reward and/or engage the buyer. It is a great medium. Simple packaging changes can make a huge difference in sales.

Imagine that you are a fast-food restaurant with the need to communicate a limited-time offer. You can purchase television or radio airtime to communicate this or you can paint your windows with the message. Which is less expensive? If you don't have the money for broad-based media, a simple message on your window can help drive sales. Restaurants using window messaging have seen sales increase by as much as 15%. Not bad for some paint, a little time, and some elbow grease.

To introduce its environmental "Think Green" message, Waste Management used its fleet of garbage trucks as rolling billboards. Messages were affixed to the side of the truck touting its environmental stewardship. Rather than buying a billboard in every market in North America, Waste Management produced messages for their own truck fleet at a fraction of the cost.

People can become a media asset. Polo shirts embossed with a company logo worn by your company's associates are an easy way to get name recognition in the market-place. Plus, associates can hand out flyers, business cards, or promotional items. All of these can be effective consumer touchpoints.

Physical assets from packaging to plants and trucks to people can all become a part of an effective media campaign. Make a list of all the physical assets your brand and/or company have to offer, and you will likely be amazed at the number of media choices you already own.

DIGITAL ASSETS

Just about every company has a website. Many times, your brand's website is the face of the brand. Company websites are used for all types of purposes. Usually, a company will tell its story, profile its management, provide customer information, and have a place for consumers to contact them. If the company is publicly traded, it will have an investor relations tab. Depending upon your relationship with the customer, your website can take on great importance. For example, if you are marketing in a business-to-business environment, your website is a crucial new business tool. Case studies and white papers can be posted to the website. Interactive videos can be used to demonstrate your company's expertise. The website can be constructed to tailor messages to a variety of potential needs.

If you are marketing a consumer brand, then you may use the corporate website for corporate activities and rely upon other digital assets to engage the consumer. Social media platforms such as Facebook and/or Twitter can become valuable consumer engagement platforms. The current rise in upscale food trucks has been driven by

Twitter. Food trucks use Twitter to announce their lunch locations and engage with consumers over menu items. Facebook is an engagement platform to offer incentives, games, and other interactive content. YouTube is another platform that provides an opportunity for business marketers to tell their story and for consumer brands to provide content that is outside normal media channels. Other social media platforms such as Instagram, Snapchat, TikTok, and Pinterest offer opportunities for a brand to provide their message to specific sets of consumers.

Tablet and mobile applications provide a brand with a mechanism to engage with consumers on the go. Tablet applications offer the opportunity for a deep dive or immersive experience, while mobile applications can provide quick reference or incentives for the consumer. For example, Nike offers a series of training applications for a variety of sports such as soccer, tennis, basketball, and track. These applications allow you to customize your workouts. The mobile application allows the user to input real-time training information to get feedback and analysis. Applications such as these provide an immersive experience that just isn't possible through other forms of media.

Digital assets are becoming a mainstay of the brand experience. For those consumers who want to engage with a brand, this is their opportunity. Digital assets provide a way for the brand to develop a customer relationship that is ongoing and meaningful.

CREATED ASSETS: EVENTS AND SPONSORSHIPS

Brands can create their own events or sponsorships. For example, McDonald's created the McDonald's All American Games team that highlights high school athletic achievement. There is a McDonald's All American list for basketball, football, and soccer. McDonald's also extends this by creating televised all-star games with the McDonald's All Americans. The sponsorship has become a part of America's popular culture, especially in basketball. Many college teams refer to how many McDonald's All Americans they have recruited.

McDonald's also has invested in the Ronald McDonald House, which provides temporary housing for parents with children who are hospitalized with severe medical conditions. The Ronald McDonald House charity has houses across the country that help parents stay close to their children during treatment. Just like the McDonald's All American program, the Ronald McDonald House is an example of a company that created a program to help society and to extend their brand.

Created events and sponsorships are different from just sponsoring a cause or a sports team: The event or sponsorship wouldn't exist if the brand hadn't created it. If Capital One decided not to sponsor the Orange Bowl (which is not a created event), the Orange Bowl would find another title sponsor. The same is true of causes such as the Susan G. Komen Race for the Cure. Every year, a variety of sponsors associate themselves with this event.

Created events can be a large part of a business-to-business media plan. By creating a branded seminar or event that is relevant to the audience, a brand can elevate its position in the marketplace. Brands can create their own training or certification programs that position the brand as an expert in the field. Google is famous for its Google certification program that provides extensive training in search engine marketing. Oracle provides a certificate program in becoming an expert in their software. By providing these programs, Google and/or Oracle become a part of that customer's life. Their value extends beyond the services they provide; they actually add value to their customers.

Created events and sponsorships can be a very valuable brand platform. They allow the brand to gain publicity in a relevant context. Events and sponsorships can be extended through other owned media channels.

SUMMARY

Owned media offer an opportunity for a company or a brand to stake its claim to proprietary media channels. In today's over-communicated world, having a strong owned media program can set the brand apart from its competition. Whether it is physical, digital, or created events and sponsorships, owned media should be at the forefront of a brand's media plan.

CHAPTER 6

Dynamics of earned media

....

LET'S GIVE 'EM SOMETHING TO TALK ABOUT

The third part of the "paid, owned, and earned" (POE) strategic communication model is earned media. We have discussed that advertising consists of a paid placement, such as a print ad, a TV commercial, or an ad in a Facebook newsfeed. Owned media are those communication assets that are controlled directly by the brand. These include items such as a website, a Facebook page, or brand-specific assets such as packages, people, or buildings.

Earned media consist of *branded messages* that another entity distributes for your brand. Publicity or public relations has historically been associated with earned media. Generating publicity through the media by engaging journalists has been the traditional avenue for earned media. Social media has been the game changer for this important area of strategic communication. Social media has magnified the role that earned media can play in helping to promote a brand in the global digital marketplace.

Today, earned media refers to a mix of brand mentions on news pickups, shares on social media sites, and through the engagement of influencers. Earned media are the natural result of ad campaigns, events, and the content that brands create. This is not a new concept. Brands have long hired public relations firms to reach out to the media in order to get them to write stories about the brand. The new aspects of earned media are influencers such as popular bloggers, individuals on Facebook with large numbers of friends, and Tweeters with lots of followers. Additionally, positive reviews on social media sites like Yelp can be considered "earned media." The strength of earned media is that third-party endorsements garner lots of trust. Who hasn't looked at restaurant reviews on Yelp or product reviews on Amazon to determine where to eat or what to purchase. Third-party messages can be a very powerful part of any strategic communication campaign.

DOI: 10.4324/9781003258162-6

Agencies sometime refer to a campaign *going viral*, when a large number of third-party people write, post, like, or tweet about it. For example, the global brand Dove produced a video where a sketch artist drew pictures of women based on their own self-images, as well as pictures of the same women based on impressions by others. The video was featured on the homepage of Reddit, a news website where online users contribute the content. The video was then featured on blogs and news sites and two days after it was posted, it was featured on the *Today* show. Plus, millions of people liked, commented, and shared this content. It has been estimated that a successful campaign can convince up to 5% of viewers to share the campaign with the people in their networks. Dove exceeded this number handily. This is an example of a strategy called *flare and connect*, which suggests that an agency has to "light a flare" underneath a piece of media content and then make as much noise as possible online to promote the content. For the Dove campaign, this earned media aspect of the campaign was crucial to not only gaining awareness but to generate large numbers of advocates for the brand.

PROS AND CONS OF EARNED MEDIA

Earned media has a number of advantages. It's "free" in the sense that clients are not "billed" for the earned media placement. Unlike paid media where each impression has an associated cost, earned media impressions have no cost. The other key advantage of earned media is that many consumers trust earned media more than they trust paid advertising messages. In particular, people trust the recommendations of their friends and acquaintances much more than a traditional television ad.

Earned media does have some drawbacks, though. Earned social media relies on consumer participation, and there are no guarantees that all consumers will love your brand all the time. Consumers can be fickle. And a negative comment on social media can suddenly spread just as quickly as a positive message. Although earned media impressions are free, earned media has many hidden costs that sometimes the client is challenged to recognize. Creating earned media takes time and effort as well as investment in internal and external social media content generation and development. To continue the conversation on social media can require a fulltime team of people. Once many of these conversations are in the works, the brand may be committed to the effort for longer than they would like.

Many agencies, including advertising, media, and public relations, now hire an earned media director (EMD). This individual assists brands to strategically plan earned media campaigns, ensuring broad reach of content through paid media buys, public relations programs, and free social distribution strategies. Agencies measure the impact of earned media on bottom-line sales and brand reach. An EMD's job is to guide the creation and execution of earned media campaigns – and then provide clear metrics showing the impact these earned media campaigns have on brand reach, sales, and marketing return on investment (ROI). In particular, they are tasked with finding all earned media channels to ensure campaigns achieve the greatest impact. At media agencies, EMDs help clients better understand which social platforms will produce the most sharing for which campaigns, and how to strategically use paid media to increase the reach of earned media campaigns. At creative agencies, EMDs help direct the full creative process from concept to execution, ensuring that campaigns incorporate the right social triggers and content to generate maximum earned media. The EMD is actually a bridge position between creative and media, as earned media becomes strategically woven into the brand strategy.

QUANTITY VERSUS QUALITY

One of the challenges of earned media is measuring its results. One way to measure is quantity – for example, the number of Facebook fans and Twitter followers. This is analogous to the media reach of a brand. However, getting these fans and followers to share the content created by the brand is an indication of the quality of the results. Some of the people who share content are the people who are most likely to influence others, making them valuable fans and followers for brands.

There are several ways that an earned media campaign can help audiences share content. The brand message must match the channel, and the brand personality must come through. If a brand message is somewhat complex, for example, it might not work well on Twitter and may work better on a blog or through a video. A brand that is social or entertainment-oriented may work best on social media like Instagram, since users are often there to be social. Brands should also find out what kinds of opportunities their target audience enjoys. If members enjoy contests, the brand should sponsor a contest. If they like quizzes, the brand should create fun quizzes. Clearly, this requires a depth of knowledge of the target audience that goes beyond simple demographic information.

There should also be a plan to reward audience members who share information. Most influential people did not become that way because they spammed their friends with information, and so they are often highly conscious of not creating clutter. Understand what users do and do not see as shareable information. Think about the benefit that the influencer will get from sharing the content. For example, people share their quiz results when the result is consistent with their own self-image. If an individual finds content highly entertaining, their friends might find it entertaining as well.

It is important to note that there is a difference between messages that influence consumers to interact with brands and messages that are heavily shared. For example, people are less likely to share that they've entered a sweepstakes or giveaway, since sharing it decreases their chances of winning. That's why many brands offer an additional entry if the sweepstakes information is shared. On the other hand, a brand that has a socially relevant message or is advocating for a cause may be the type of message that helps enhance the image of the influencer. If this is the case, the influencer may be more than willing to share it.

SUMMARY

The bottom line is that an earned media plan, like every other media plan, must have specific goals in mind. Earned media should attract audiences to the brand, and should complement, not replace or compete, with paid messages. To that end, think about the following areas when developing your earned media plan.

- Create a positioning statement that distinguishes your business from others in the industry. This will provide your competitive benefit and is a way to make sure that the content that is built refers back to what you want consumers – both influencers and their friends and fans – to think and feel.
- Match the goals of the earned media plan to the goals of the overall brand strategic communication plan.
- Work with others in the agency to develop content that actually delivers solutions to people and reflects the brand. A good earned media director will be able to track and assess the type of content that is shared most often by members of the brand's target audience in order to have the best opportunities for a message to go viral.

Earned media can be a very powerful part of the overall POE brand strategic communication plan. In fact, if properly executed, earned media can take the leading role in driving brand awareness and engagement.

CHAPTER 7

Components of a brand strategic communication plan

....

FAILING TO PLAN IS PLANNING TO FAIL

Every brand strategic communication plan should begin with an outline. Outlining what is contained in the plan is an efficient way to begin the brand strategic communication planning project. Of course, all plans are unique depending upon the company, brand, or organization. However, there are fundamentals that should be part of any plan.

Exhibit 7.1 contains an outline for a brand strategic communication plan. It covers ten broad areas, beginning with an executive summary and ending with ways to measure the results of your plan. Other than the executive summary, each component of the plan builds on the prior component. For example, marketing objectives/strategies lead into the role that communication plays in solving the marketing challenge. This leads to brand communication objectives, which then lead to brand communication strategies and tactics. Each brand communication plan is not unlike a book. It tells a story. In this case, the story is how you plan to solve the brand's marketing challenge.

BRAND STRATEGIC COMMUNICATION PLAN VERSUS ADVERTISING MEDIA PLAN

A brand strategic communication plan and an advertising media plan have very similar components. The key difference is the approach they take to solving the marketing problem. In an advertising media plan, it is assumed that advertising is the solution to the marketing problem. Therefore, a paid media plan is necessary to convey the advertising message to the appropriate target market.

In a brand's strategic communication plan, advertising is one of the myriad alternatives to solving the marketing challenge. It may or may not be the solution, or it may be a part of the solution in combination with other communication alternatives. A communication plan then assesses advertising, promotions, public relations,

DOI: 10.4324/9781003258162-7

EXHIBIT 7.1 COMPONENTS OF A COMMUNICATION PLAN

1. Executive Summary
   a. Summary of marketing objectives/strategies
   b. Summary of communication objectives/strategies
   c. Budget summary
2. Situation Analysis
   a. Marketing
   b. Communication
   c. SWOT
3. Marketing Objectives/Strategies
   a. Business
   b. Brand
4. Role of Communication
   a. Message
5. Communication Objectives
   a. Target segment
   b. Geography
   c. Seasonal/Timing
   d. Reach/Frequency/Continuity
6. Communication Strategies
   a. Mix
   b. Scheduling
7. Communication Tactics
   a. Vehicle
   b. Rationale
   c. Costs
   d. Impressions
8. Communication Budget
   a. Dollars by communication channel
   b. Dollars by month
9. Communication Flowchart
   a. Weekly schedule
   b. Recap of dollars
   c. Recap of impressions
   d. Reach/Frequency
10. Testing and Evaluation
    a. Test programs
    b. Evaluation methods

a brand's owned media assets, and any other form of communication. It embraces the paid, owned, and earned framework. The brand strategic communication plan should be strategy neutral. It should not be assumed that one method of communication is better than another going into the planning process.

COMPONENTS OF A BRAND STRATEGIC COMMUNICATION PLAN

There are ten components to the brand strategic communication plan, as highlighted in Exhibit 7.1. The following are brief descriptions of each element.

Executive summary

An executive summary focuses management on the link between the marketing objectives and strategies and the communication objectives and strategies. From a management viewpoint, it is crucial to understand how communication is tied to the business goals of the brand. Management will also want to understand the strategic nature of the plan and the budget necessary to implement it. All of that information is contained in the executive summary.

Situation analysis

The situation analysis forms the context for the plan. It should contain a marketing/brand analysis as well as a communication analysis. A marketing analysis for a good or service would contain a review of pricing, distribution, resources, and product differentiation compared with competing brands in the category. A brand analysis may contain measures of brand awareness, brand usage, and perceptions of the brand. A communication analysis contains message, copy, and communication channel comparisons with competing brands in the category. All of these analyses should be rolled up into a summary of strengths, weaknesses, opportunities, and threats, better known as a SWOT analysis.

Marketing objectives/strategies

All communication plans derive from a marketing strategy. It is paramount to recap the marketing objectives and strategies in your plan. These objectives and strategies typically have two focal points: (1) business-related aspects, typically defined by number of customers and sales, and (2) brand-related aspects, which may be defined by specific brand attributes such as awareness levels, perception of the brand, and attributes closely associated with the brand.

Role of communication

The role of communication defines how communication is going to solve the marketing challenge or meet the objectives – in other words, how the brand will communicate with its intended audience. Some typical roles of communication are to increase awareness, change perceptions, announce "new news," and associate the brand with quality perception. Within this section is the overall communication idea that leads into the creative strategy. This is the foundation for the communication plan.

Communication objectives

The Big Four communication objectives are target audience, geography, seasonal/timing, and reach/frequency/continuity, which respectively address: (1) the target audience for your message, (2) where you are targeting, (3) when you are targeting, and (4) how much pressure you plan to apply.

Communication strategies

Communication strategies are the methods you'll use to achieve your objectives. Each objective should have a corresponding strategy. There are two major strategies for a communication plan. The first is the communication mix – the blend of communication channels you plan to use. This is where you address the weight given to paid, owned, and earned media. The second is scheduling – when you plan on deploying each channel.

Communication tactics

Communication tactics reflect the details of the strategies. For example, if a strategy to support a specific local market contains local radio, out-of-home, and publicity, then the tactics would be which radio formats or stations to recommend, what type and location of out-of-home, and specifics about a publicity approach. Tactics are the specifics of the plan that include supporting rationale. For example, paid media tactics may address each vehicle recommended, the creative unit, costs, and the impressions that the vehicle will deliver. Owned media may address the use of individual brand media assets and earned media may address an influencer program.

Communication budget

The communication budget is a recap of the dollars allocated to each communication channel and not to the specific vehicle. The starting point is the allocation for paid, earned, and owned media. The latter two media areas may include agency fees or salaries. Within paid media, funds are allocated by media category. For example, keyword search or paid social media. Communication budgets include dollars by channel and also a recap of dollars by month.

Communication flowchart

A communication flowchart is a schematic of the plan on a single page. It contains a weekly schedule of activity, a recap of dollars by vehicle and category, a recap of impressions by vehicle and category, and a reach/frequency analysis. The communication flowchart is a summary of all activity, scheduling, and costs. Depending upon the brand, a flowchart may contain production dollars necessary to develop content for the plan as well as any fees associated with content development.

Testing and campaign measurement/evaluation

Testing is an optional aspect of a communication plan. Many communication plans have test programs. A test program may be used to see how an increase in media pressure might impact a specific market, or it may be a way to try out an emerging medium. Any test would be covered in this section. The other aspect of this section is how to evaluate the success of the plan. This may involve a recap of a research method or a recap of the measure and methods to ensure that the communication plan meets the overall campaign objectives. A second part of the evaluation process measures whether the overall plan and each tactic reach their impression objectives.

SUMMARY

Before exploring a particular brand strategic communication plan, it is important to outline its components. Doing so will provide the best and most efficient method for developing the plan. It is vital that each section of the plan build on the prior section. A brand strategic communication plan provides a road map for how communication can help solve marketing challenges.

CHAPTER 8

How marketing objectives affect communication planning

....

DON'T SAY WE DIDN'T WARN YOU!

Here's the warning: Never, under any condition, should you begin an advertising media plan without first establishing your objectives. But even before establishing those objectives, there's something else you need to do.

Of course, it makes perfect sense to set forth your objectives before you begin your planning effort, whether in media or any other aspect of your marketing program. But media objectives for the brand rely on other brand objectives, and those must be established prior to laying out your media objectives.

OBJECTIVES: MARKETING, COMMUNICATION, ADVERTISING, THEN MEDIA

Always begin by establishing your overall brand objectives, followed by the marketing objectives that will help achieve some of the brand objectives. These can be set together with the brand marketing department and the full account team. Then, with the advertising team, set separate advertising objectives, which must be in concert with and derived from the overall marketing objectives. Finally, set the communication and media objectives, which are based on the advertising objectives (which, as we just saw, are based on the marketing objectives). Again, the communication and advertising media objectives will be stated separately from the other objectives, but they will derive from and support both the advertising objectives and the marketing objectives. Advertising media do not operate in a vacuum; they must be part of the overall plan. Of course, not everything goes as intended, which is why contingency plans are also necessary (see Exhibit 8.1).

Along with media objectives, you are likely to include specific advertising message objectives and perhaps research, production, or other types of objectives for your advertising campaign.

DOI: 10.4324/9781003258162-8

EXHIBIT 8.1 CONTINGENCY PLANS

A contingency is a future event or circumstance that cannot be predicted with certainty. For example, you know you will have to do taxes next year. Perhaps the best time to prepare for next year's taxes is right after you finish this year's taxes. That way, you'll have all your documents and figures gathered, and most importantly, you will know what you wish you had done better for the current year.

Similarly, the best time to do a contingency media plan is right after the proposed media plan has been completed. That way, you have all your documents and figures, and you are well aware of the other options that came to mind that you didn't implement and might wish to consider in the upcoming year.

A contingency plan is not the same as a reserve fund. A reserve takes part of the advertising media budget and sets it aside for unanticipated emergencies. While many brands have such funds, a reserve indicates two negative ideas: you are not confident about your proposed plan and you don't need your entire budget.

A better strategy is to have a contingency plan, which is an alternative to the plan that has been proposed. Rather than setting aside budgeted monies, it allows for transfers among media choices.

Contingency plans usually answer three questions, all of which start with the same phrase: What will you do during the year if …? The questions are these:

1. What will you do during the year if sales expectations are not being met?
2. What will you do during the year if sales expectations are being exceeded?
3. What will you do during the year if a competitor takes some unexpected action?

If the campaign proposal is for some period other than a year, substitute "during the campaign period" for "during the year."

The more complete and accurate you can make your contingency plans, the better. If they are actually needed, it will likely be an emergency situation, so you will not have time to re-do media plans or to finalize details. You need contingency plans that you can put into action on short notice.

BASED ON RESEARCH

Ideally, all objectives will be based on research. Be wary if someone proposes using advertising media, or using advertising at all, without first doing research. Some people seem to have an innate feeling or sixth sense about advertising and media, but they are not really operating without research foundations; instead, they are using their own experience and expertise, which qualify as a type of research – one based on the results of past efforts.

Most people, though, must make their research efforts clear. You draw up a list of questions that need answers, and then design or contract for research that will provide insights into those answers.

Perhaps surprisingly, the research may not include such questions as, "What advertising media should we use in the upcoming campaign?" Instead, questions may focus on the best kinds of people to target or the best kinds of locations in which to market. The answers to these questions will help you derive your target markets and target groups – and, then, your media selections.

Utilizing research makes the task much easier when it is time to establish the marketing, advertising, communication, and media objectives.

OBJECTIVES AS A ROAD MAP

Imagine that you are in Kansas City and you want to drive to Tulsa. Unless you are familiar with the route, you would likely consult a GPS road map.

When you look at the map, you first find Kansas City, then you find Tulsa, and on the map you might work your way back from Tulsa to Kansas City. If you just start out driving from Kansas City, you have no idea which way to go: north, south, east, west, or, in this case, southwest. So knowing where you already are is important, but that knowledge alone is not enough. You need to know your destination, too.

If you track back from Tulsa to Kansas City, you are working from your objective back to your starting point. That is not the way you will drive it, but you might find it helpful to plot your course from your intended destination back to the point of origin.

That's the way you make your marketing plan, advertising plan, communication plan, or media plan work, too. You know your point of origin, and then you set up your objectives, but first you work backward from your destination to find out what is needed to meet your goals.

OBJECTIVES, STRATEGIES, AND TACTICS

So far, we have used the term *objectives* for the place you wish to go. Sometimes the term *goals* will be used. In advertising, objectives are what you want to accomplish in the long term and goals are what you want to accomplish in the short term. In business, the short term is usually within the coming year, and the long term applies to things beyond the coming year. Use this vocabulary consistently with your coworkers.

Most of the time, you will have a five-year plan, which is the long term, with details for the coming year, which is the short term. Each year, you will update the short-term goals and plans, and then extend the long-term plans and objectives for another year, always working about five years ahead. Whether the timeframe is three years, five years, or ten years does not matter as much as the fact that you always have short- and long-term achievements and plans, and that they are updated regularly – because things often change rapidly in advertising. The long-range plans may be for a shorter period, and the updating may occur more often.

So objectives and goals are what you want to achieve. The plans you establish to meet these objectives and goals are called *strategies*. The actual implementation or execution of those plans are the *tactics*. Remember that distinction and use Exhibit 8.2 to remind yourself. Tactics put the plans into action.

ADVERTISING MEDIA ARE STRATEGIES, NOT OBJECTIVES

Even though you will eventually establish media objectives and goals, the advertising media themselves are not objectives or goals. Media are strategies.

EXHIBIT 8.2 RELATIONSHIPS AMONG GOALS, OBJECTIVES, STRATEGIES, AND TACTICS

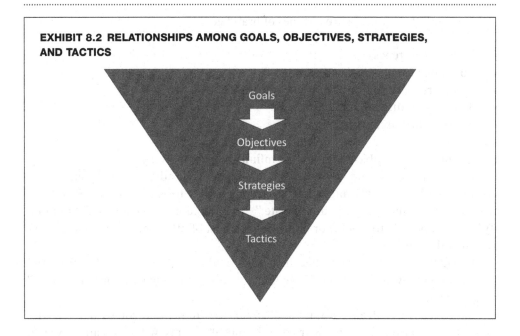

Your advertising media goal may be to reach a certain number of consumers, with a certain frequency, with some impact. The media goal is not to use newspapers or television or outdoor billboards. Rather, the media are the ways that you plan to achieve those goals of reach, frequency, and impact, and maybe even continuity, cost efficiency, and creative considerations.

Keep this distinction in mind. Media are strategies, not goals or objectives. Do not establish goals to use certain media. Instead, establish goals of things that you hope to accomplish with your advertising media, and leave the actual media selection to the strategy stage.

Why make this differentiation? Because if you establish the use of certain types of media as part of your goals, you are setting out on your trip without knowing where you want to go. It would be like driving in any direction from Kansas City, on any highway, without having the vaguest sense of where Tulsa is located. If you spell out the media as goals, you are likely to overlook some good alternatives because your mind is already made up.

Make this a three-stage process. First, set your media goals and objectives, without detailing which actual media might be used. Then plan how to achieve the goals and objectives using the best types of media. Finally, implement the plan and execute the actual advertising campaign.

SETTING GOOD OBJECTIVES

We've already established that good goals and objectives are crucial to success because they help you determine where you want to go with your marketing, advertising, communication, and media efforts.

In general, there are five broad types of brand goals:

- To build awareness
- To create an emotional connection
- To differentiate your brand from competitors
- To create credibility and trust
- To motivate purchasing

To compose good objectives, use the infinitive form of a verb, as in "to do" something. Note that the brand goals above do just that. Your advertising objectives that grow out of brand goals might be "to accomplish," "to sell," "to convince," "to change," "to increase," "to communicate," "to eliminate," "to compete," "to modify," "to promote," "to reach," or to do any of a host of other things, or some combination of these things.

Note that the advertising media themselves could not possibly be objectives and goals because they are not verbs. You could not have "to newspaper" or "to outdoor" as a media goal.

Good objectives will also be quantifiable. It is easy to say that you wish to increase sales. But by how much? If this year you sell 3,000,000 items, will you really have met your goal if next year you sell 3,000,001? It is more helpful to state quantifiable terms such as, "Next year, we will increase our sales by 2.2%," or "Next year, we will increase sales by 60,000 units." Then you will know for sure whether you have increased your sales, and you will know for sure whether you have met your goal.

CONSISTENCY WITH MESSAGE STRATEGIES

It is also important for your media goals and objectives to be consistent with other goals and objectives, as well as with other strategies. We have already seen that advertising media goals must be consistent with marketing and advertising goals. The same goes for message strategies. If, for example, the copy and art teams have already decided that they must use demonstrations to make the advertising campaign effective, then the media goals must reflect the need for media that allow for demonstrations. Such media include television and cinema, but it is too early to state what media type will be used; in the goal-setting stage, it is enough to state that the eventual media selection must include media that permit ease of demonstration.

A long-standing controversy exists over which should be decided first: the advertising message or the advertising media. It makes sense for media to come first, because it would be silly and wasteful for the message and creative strategies to develop messages for, say, billboards if outdoor advertising is not included in the schedule. However, more often than not, message dictates media. If the creative, message, or copy staff needs certain capabilities, it is usually up to the media goals and plans to accommodate them. In the best case, both media and message will be developed alongside each other – simultaneously – so that each can draw upon the expertise and capabilities of the other. Because of the time constraints involved in advertising, this situation is more of an ideal than a reality. Exhibit 8.3 provides examples of categories that might be used for objectives in marketing, advertising, communication, and media.

EXHIBIT 8.3 EXAMPLES OF MARKETING, ADVERTISING, COMMUNICATION, AND MEDIA OBJECTIVES

Marketing objectives	Advertising objectives	Communication objectives	Media objectives
Sales levels (in dollars and in units)	Merchandising support Creative	Message Points of recall	Efficiency CPP and CPM –
Sales shares (in percentages and in competitive indices)	considerations Media considerations: Flexibility Contingency	Major stressed items Order of items Target audiences	Then, TAI and GRP targets can be derived Reach
Product position	Timing:	Need for	Frequency
Geographic distribution	Flights Hiatus periods	awareness, knowledge	Impact Continuity
General consumer profile	Sustaining periods Budget considerations:	Product or service strengths	Targets: Groups
Competitive goal	Allocations to:	Geographic	Regions
Timing during year	Regions	distribution of	Markets
Timing by seasons	Markets	messages	Audiences
Packaging	Media functions	Formats	Creative
Pricing	Targets	Audience	considerations
Types of store or other outlets	Target markets:[a] Areas or regions	calculations Size	and support Media capabilities
Relative needs for awareness, knowledge, interest, desire, and sales	Target groups[a] Target audiences[a] Levels of awareness, Circulation numbers desire, and	Composition	Flexibility Merchandising support Competitive strategies
Distribution knowledge, preference, considerations	purchase Competitive prospects numbers Show package?		Audience sizes[b] Matched with Media mix versus media
Tell price?	Concentration[c]		
Coupons	Advertising units		

a   Target markets, target groups, and target audiences are often left to the strategy stage, rather than included as objectives.
b   All given in audience terms, not simply in demographics.
c   Note that media types to be used are usually considered strategies rather than objectives.

SUMMARY

So there you have the outline of how to establish goals and objectives, whether for marketing, advertising, communication, media, or any other phase of the marketing effort. You also have an understanding of the process: first, goals and objectives, then strategies, and finally, tactics. You can see how the various phases must work together and support each other.

Good objectives and goals are essential in every phase of your work, and advertising media work is no exception.

In some cases, the campaign targets are established as part of the goals and objectives, but more often, targets are part of the strategies. In the next chapter, you will learn more about setting up and reaching your advertising media targets.

CHAPTER 9

The role communication plays in brand support

....

THE BRAND IS THE STAR, BUT THE MEDIA PLAN IS AN IMPORTANT SUPPORTING PLAYER

A media plan is part of a larger marketing communication program. It isn't, nor should it be, crafted in isolation from other parts of the marketing plan. Media planners are valuable members of the brand team since they are part marketers, part behavioral scientists, part researchers, and part negotiators. They must have exceptional critical thinking skills and knowledge of a variety of disciplines. Finally, they must clearly understand what communications can and can't do for brands.

THE ROLE OF COMMUNICATION

A media plan is part of the overall communication plan. The role that communication plays in supporting the marketing strategy is where the media plan resides. As with the need to align the marketing mix with the marketing strategy, a media planner must understand the broader context of how the media plan fits into the overall communications plan.

Communication problems are somewhat different from marketing problems. An example of a marketing problem is a brand being priced too high or low in the market. The communication problem may be that consumers who should be part of the target audience believe the brand is too expensive or too cheap. Communication problems are an outgrowth of a broader business challenge. Communication may or may not be the solution to the business problem. That's why it's important to understand what communication can do.

The following are basic roles that communication can play with a brand:

1. Communication can help to increase awareness of a brand. This might include raising brand awareness, informing consumers about "new news," or informing consumers about what the brand has to offer.

DOI: 10.4324/9781003258162-9

2. Communication can help to change the perception or overall attitude toward the brand. This typically involves persuading consumers to rethink their feelings about the brand.
3. Communication can help to associate the brand with a specific image.

Informing, convincing, and *associating* are three key functions of any communication plan. While this is not an all-inclusive list, each of these roles dictates how a media planner would approach developing a plan.

For example, if the charge was to increase brand awareness among a specific target market, you might consider media such as television – one of the best for generating immediate awareness. Or the communication task may be to reach out and inform a different audience about "new news" that would be relevant. This could dictate a complete change in the media approach going forward. For example, print in beauty publications may be used to introduce a new cosmetic brand or ads on tech websites may be used to introduce a new software product.

Changing brand perception or attitudes toward a brand is very different from merely increasing awareness. Awareness for the brand can be increased rapidly. Consider brands that launch with commercials that air during the Super Bowl. Those commercials reach nearly 50% of the adult population in the United States. If the message is relevant and powerful, generating awareness can be done in relatively short order. On the other hand, it can take time to change deep-seated perceptions and/or attitudes about a brand. Consider the attempts that JCPenney has made to change its brand perception from that of a discount seller of fundamental clothing to that of a bolder, more fashion-forward retailer. Their struggles to do this have gone on for many years. The implication for a media planner is that brand media support must recognize the need for continued pressure over a long period of time. A media planner who allocates all of the available dollars in a one-month period to change a deeply engrained perception will likely fail.

One central role of communication is to help associate a brand with a specific image. This might be achieved by targeting a particular group. For example, Mountain Dew has positioned itself as a soft drink for consumers who go to the extreme. They target extreme sports such as the X Games and other high-profile events. This brand is focused on a specific image and audience. Even though this target group may also like tennis, an association with that sport may not be appropriate for the brand. When the central role of the communication is to establish or reinforce the brand's image, the context within which any message appears is paramount. Context may be the driving force behind the media selection for the brand with reach or cost as a secondary consideration.

There are a few things that brand communication can't do. Clearly, communications cannot fix performance issues within a brand. If a brand doesn't have the basic performance needed in a category, a great media plan might get people to buy the product once, but it is likely they won't buy it again. Similarly, ads can't correct bad customer service or fix delivery issues. However, brand communication can help to build credibility and trust so that any type of performance issue can be addressed and hopefully overcome.

Media planning is a crucial part of the overall communication strategy. The communication strategy is a key component of the marketing plan. The marketing plan is a key element of the business strategy. They all need to work hand in glove. One supports the other.

The business of a brand is to deliver revenue and profit to the company, so a firm knowledge of profitability is crucial to media planning. The secret to growing a brand is to ensure that its growth generates money. Typically, media (and particularly advertising media) take up a large portion of the communication budget as well as the overall marketing budget.

Media time and space can be expensive. It is not uncommon for media to account for 80% or more of the total communication budget. The remaining 20% may be allocated to cover research, production, evaluation, and agency fees. Because media can be such a large expenditure for a brand, financial managers at the brand's parent company will scrutinize these figures. They will be asking questions such as, "If you allocate $10 million to media, what will be the return on investment?"

We will cover return on investment (ROI) in a later chapter in this text. It's a vital component to any plan. No brand is going to invest millions of dollars in anything without understanding what it's trying to get.

As a media planner, there are a couple of lessons here. One is that you need to understand how the brand makes money and how your plan fits into that equation. Second, understand there is always a trade-off when spending money. A company could invest millions of dollars in advertising, or they could use that money to upgrade their manufacturing plant. In many cases, monetary resources (or a lack thereof) become a much larger issue in a company than a media planner might realize. Finally, it is important to know that media is only a portion of the total brand's activities. It is always difficult to isolate which message really pushed the needle to achieve goals. At the same time, brand managers will want to understand whether the message and the media were successful, and why.

PART OF THE MARKETING MIX

You may recall the four Ps (4Ps) mentioned in a basic marketing class. The 4Ps – *product, price, place*, and *promotion* – are the broad definition of the marketing mix. In contemporary brand planning, we often also consider an extension of the 4Ps to include people, process, and physical environment. People are the employees and other workers associated with the brand who serve as brand ambassadors. Process is the delivery of an excellent customer experience. And physical environment is where customers engage with the brand, whether it be a brick and motors store or a digital space.

Media planning is the coordinated effort behind promotion. Within the traditional 4Ps, the term *promotion* is used in its broadest sense to mean anything that is a part of brand communication. We typically use it to describe a type of communication rather than a class of activity. The extended 4Ps include multiple parts of customer engagement. Together, this suggests that the media plan must include the following types of media:

- Paid media: Brand content that agencies create and that brands pay to place in front of an audience, such as television commercials and digital billboards.
- Owned media: Brand content that the brand creates and controls, such as a brand website or Facebook page.
- Earned media: Brand content that others create and control, such as reviews or Instagram posts.

The media plan is a part of this overall marketing mix. From a brand perspective, in a perfect world, paid, owned, and earned media all work together. A poorly designed media plan can actually sabotage an entire brand effort.

Let's first consider a misalignment in paid media: The effect of not aligning with price. Suppose that you are marketing an $80,000 automobile. It's a luxury car by almost anyone's standards. The message strategy is to position this car as the ultimate luxury experience. The media team places advertising in the *National Enquirer.* The message and the media audience are obviously a bit of a disconnect. In this case, the media team should be looking for media properties with which they can better associate this upscale auto brand.

The greatest risk of misalignment comes with earned media, as the brand has no control over the content that people not affiliated with the brand will post. However, the brand can have plans in place with regards to its owned media placements to track and respond to problematic earned content in order to address any misalignments that occur.

Media advertising may play a role in the timing of a brand being able to raise its price. Media timing may also be affected by pricing. Suppose a cola company wants to raise its price in the next few months. Research shows that if you have strong brand communication that leads into a price increase, the consumer will be more willing to accept it. Understanding of the pricing impact of the brand will be helpful in crafting a solid media plan.

Changes to the product also have an impact on media planning. If a brand develops a "new and improved" feature, a certain level of media support will be needed to announce this "new news." Increased social media presence, perhaps through teaser ads, may be necessary as well. A brand's specific features may help dictate certain media support. A hybrid auto might suggest a different media approach versus a muscle car.

Place or distribution is a crucial component to media planning. Where the brand is actually sold can dictate media strategies and tactics. Suppose you are selling canned soup and you find that the brand doesn't have distribution in Walmart. That would have a big impact on how you approached supporting the brand since a large percentage of consumers may not have access to the brand. Or perhaps the brand is gaining distribution in the convenience store arena. Or maybe the brand is placing soup vending machines in college dorms. All of these initiatives would have an impact on media planning.

The point is that media planning is interwoven with the other Ps of the marketing mix. As a media planner, you need to understand the brand's entire marketing mix so that you can ensure that your efforts are aligned.

At the same time, paid, owned, and earned media must be integrated. Let's say you want to gain new users to the brand and category. This means that you are reaching out to consumers who don't know your brand. Using intrusive media such as television (a paid media) might be a good way to get your point across. On the other hand, if your charge is to get current users to use your brand more often, you may elect to develop a strong social media program (owned media) that encourages current brand users to share tips about the different uses for the brand (earned media).

PART OF THE MARKETING STRATEGY

Media planning is a part of the overall marketing mix. It is driven by the overall marketing strategy, or how the brand will achieve its business goals. The brand has a goal of increasing sales and/or market share along with a profit contribution.

To gain sales and/or market share requires the brand to plot a course of action. There are a few fundamental strategies that brands pursue.

1. A brand can switch competitive brand users to its brand.
2. A brand can get new users (outside the category) to try its brand.
3. A brand can get its current user base to increase its purchase frequency of the brand.

Brand marketing strategies boil down to increasing brand penetration or buy rate. Brand penetration means getting more users into the fold. Brand buy rate deals with increasing the frequency of usage of the brand. Brands can elect to have programs that increase penetration and buy rate. These two paths are not necessarily mutually exclusive.

For example, to convince competitive consumers to switch to your brand in a given product category, you may elect to use targeted incentives directed solely at those brand users. Or you may scrutinize the competition's paid media plan and social media presence to ensure that your media investment trumps them on a macro or micro basis. You might also investigate the earned media of competitors to see if consumers are sharing weaknesses of your competition that could be addressed by your brand.

Regardless of the marketing strategy, the media plan must follow suit. The marketing strategy will largely dictate the target market for the media plan. Focusing on the brand's existing user base is radically different than attempting to convince a new market to try the brand. It's like comparing apples and oranges. Convincing competitive brand users to switch to your brand also sets into motion a specific set of objectives for the media plan.

It should go without saying that the media planner must clearly understand the marketing strategy for the brand. The marketing strategy dictates the target market that the plan must address. If the media plan is not aligned with the marketing strategy, it will greatly hamper marketing efforts.

SUMMARY

Media planning is a part of a larger brand effort. It begins with the overall business goals of the brand. The media plan is how the brand delivers on its promotional support. This part of the marketing mix needs to be executed in concert with the rest of the 4Ps. The brand's marketing strategy may dictate which audience the brand targets. The role that communication plays in supporting the brand provides the overall context for how a media planner delivers the communication strategy. The media plan is interwoven with all of these facets of the brand. As a media planner, you need to understand how your piece of the plan works with the total brand support plan.

CHAPTER 10

Working with a situation analysis

....

WHAT'S SWOT? YOU'RE ABOUT TO FIND OUT!

Before providing a strategic recommendation for an advertising media plan, assess the situation. That's the first step in the planning process. A properly constructed situation analysis should provide you with the necessary information and insights to construct a communication plan that will meet the brand and marketing objectives.

SWOT ANALYSIS

The situation analysis is typically called a SWOT analysis. SWOT stands for *strengths, weaknesses, opportunities*, and *threats*. Exhibit 10.1 shows the SWOT analysis and its components.

Strengths

Strengths are something that the brand has that will be helpful in achieving the marketing objectives. For example, Frito-Lay has a sophisticated and highly developed distribution network for providing its products to all types of retail outlets, including grocery stores, convenience stores, and big box stores. When Frito-Lay is introducing a new product, this is a great asset as it is simple to get the new product in front of customers.

Weaknesses

Weaknesses are elements of the brand that might prove harmful to achieving the marketing objectives. For example, Buick might be viewed as having an old and stodgy reputation that must be addressed in order to appeal to younger consumers.

DOI: 10.4324/9781003258162-10

EXHIBIT 10.1 SWOT ANALYSIS

	SWOT analysis	SWOT analysis
Strengths today	You are poised to take advantage	You are strong to defend against threats
Weaknesses today	You are not positioned well to seize opportunities	Your survivability is threatened

---

Opportunities

Opportunities are external forces that will aid the brand in reaching its objectives. For example, if birth rates are rising by 5%, that is a good trend for baby brands like Pampers to sell more products. Or if the US government decides to tax soft drinks, that could be an opportunity for bottled water brands to increase sales and market share.

Threats

Threats are external forces that will be harmful or will get in the way of a brand's ability to achieve its objectives. If, for instance, Pepsi increases its marketing budget by 50%, that could have a negative impact on Coke and other brands in the soft drink category. Another threat to the entire beverage industry would be the government banning soda machines from all public schools. The Covid-19 pandemic that began in 2020 was an external threat that no brand saw coming, and it had a huge effect on many brands.

PUTTING SWOT IN CONTEXT

It is important to construct a SWOT analysis with a clear goal in mind; otherwise, the SWOT becomes a mere listing of unrelated items that have no impact on the future strategy of the brand. So, if the brand's objective is to grow sales by 5%, and the strategy for doing this is by expanding the brand's user base, then the SWOT analysis should be done within that context.

In this case, it means looking at consumers who are not currently using the brand. A brand's strength may be that it is easy for new users to find and purchase. But a weakness may be that it is perceived as being too expensive. An opportunity could be that purchasers want higher quality products within the category. A threat could be that another brand completely dominates this sector of the market, or that your competitor's purchasers are highly brand loyal.

The key to an effective SWOT analysis is thinking about how each item will either help or hurt the brand's cause. That's what makes your SWOT analysis more powerful and actionable.

BRAND COMMUNICATION SWOT

As you develop a SWOT analysis for a brand communication plan, you should identify marketing elements and communication elements that can influence the brand. The third category – consumer trends – has an impact on both areas. Next, we discuss examples of marketing and communication items that should be considered for the SWOT analysis.

Marketing

Marketing elements include distribution, pricing, and product comparisons between the brand and each of its competitors. Marketing can also include factors such as how financially strong the company is, how experienced its management is, the quality of its customer service, and whether the company has any patents or other proprietary items of value. Additionally, it takes into account brand perceptions by the consumer and other perceptual items related to the brand.

Communication

Communication elements include message, copy platforms, digital assets, and communication outlet comparisons between the brand and each of its competitors. Communication can also include perceptual elements such as how strong the creative message is and if there are any media or sponsorships associated with the brand. Cost and consumer trends in media consumption figure in this mix as well.

The aforementioned examples do not make up an exhaustive list of items for either marketing or communication. The key to success is identifying all the elements relevant to the brand and its competitive set. It is also important to view the brand from the consumer's viewpoint. How the consumer sees the brand is crucial in determining how to tackle the marketing challenge. All of this information should be captured in the SWOT analysis.

SUMMARY

The SWOT analysis is a tremendous tool for determining future communication strategy. Remember that the best SWOT analyses start with an objective in mind. This puts the process in proper context. Media planners must consider both marketing and communication elements when preparing a SWOT analysis. These suggestions and a thorough review of consumer trends will aid in developing a meaningful analytical tool.

CHAPTER 11

Defining the audience

······························

THE AUDIENCE IS YOUR NEXT DOOR NEIGHBOR, YOUR MOM, OR IT MIGHT EVEN BE YOU!

Nothing is more important in building an effective media plan than properly defining the market and audience. An efficient execution of an improperly targeted media plan is not going to produce results. As brand manager, you need to ensure that the media plan and the creative execution are working together. If the agency's creative group is crafting commercials for affluent, suburban soccer moms, while the media group is working on an efficient media plan to reach college students on a shoestring budget, then your advertising program is likely to be ineffective and may even come off as offensive.

Honing in on the right audience appears on the surface to be a simple exercise, but it takes careful crafting and tremendous coordination to get the most out of your marketing budget. The audience you choose for your brand's messages must make sense from a business perspective, a marketing perspective, a media perspective, and a creative perspective. Unless all your stars are aligned, your spaceship will likely hit an asteroid.

In the mid-2000s, Burger King was on a roll. They worked with Crispin Porter + Bogusky (CP + B) to create a number of award-winning campaigns directed at the frequent fast-food user, young men ate fast food many days each week. For the first few years, sales soared. The "King" was an icon, even making an appearance as a video game. While things seemed to be going smoothly for Burger King, there were some underlying consumer trends that didn't bode well for the future of the brand. By relying primarily on young men as their audience, Burger King was losing other consumers. Moms, in particular, switched from Burger King for other alternatives. When the economy took a downturn and resulted in double-digit unemployment for young men, Burger King sales quickly dropped. Young men weren't eating out, no

DOI: 10.4324/9781003258162-11

matter what the marketing effort; they simply didn't have the money to eat at Burger King. So, what started out as a brilliant audience strategy turned into a real dilemma for Burger King.

Another example of the business impact of audience selection is Chef Boyardee. In the late 1990s, Chef Boyardee changed its emphasis to teenage boys, who made up the largest consumer category of the brand. Message strategy was crafted and tested, and a media plan was fully developed. The program resulted in a double-digit decline in brand sales for Chef Boyardee. But doesn't directing your messages to your best consumers make sense? The answer is, only if they are buying the product. In this case, the teenager's parents still bought the brand and, although kids were the ultimate consumers, the parents were making the purchase decision. When the audience was subsequently changed to focus on mothers, brand sales began to rise. The moral is that you must start with the right objectives before moving toward a proper audience.

START WITH THE RIGHT OBJECTIVES

Isn't getting the proper audience as simple as finding out who is using the brand and getting your message to them? As we saw in both the Burger King and Chef Boyardee situations, just finding the consumer who uses the brand may not be enough. Obviously, understanding who uses your brand is paramount to the targeting process, but it is not always the best place to begin.

The first thing to note is that the word "audience" can refer to a variety of different groups. Brands have multiple external audiences, or audiences from outside your company. These can include consumers (people who might buy your brand), customers (people who have bought your brand), and advocates (people who spread your message). Other external audiences include suppliers (such as those who provide the raw materials to make the brand) and regulatory authorities (such as the Food and Drug Administration, who reviews food and prescription drug advertising in the United States). There can also be overlaps between these three groups: for example, an advocate can become an advocate because they bought your brand, liked it, and want to tell others about it. Someone who supplies the metal for an automobile may also be an owner of that automobile.

Brands also have internal audiences, which are people who work for the brand organizations. These include new employees who need to understand the nuances of the brand, sales representatives who need to understand competition and external threats, scientists who are involved in research and development, remote works, and a variety of other people. There is also likely to be overlap between internal and external groups. For example, many employees can be consumers of the brand.

The place to begin to define the audience is with the behavior you want to change. This behavior may be included in the creative brief but is often left out of the media discussion. For example, you may have a marketing objective of increasing the user base of your brand. To do this, the strategy may suggest that you need to attract new users. However, if your media plan focuses on heavy users of the brand, are you going to meet that goal? Of course not – they're already using your brand.

It is important to outline the specific objective that your marketing plan seeks to accomplish before evaluating the appropriate media audience. As we will see, the media planning group should be right in the midst of defining the audience, but it is more than strictly a media exercise.

Let's take a look at the soup category. Campbell's Soup dominates the US soup market and is also the fifth largest soup brand in the world. In the United States, then, the company must try to expand the category in order to attain growth. Campbell's can do this either by getting non-users to purchase the brand or by getting current users to use it more frequently, such as by using soup in recipes. Outside of the United States, though, Campbell's strategy could be to convince users of brands such as Progresso and Maggi to switch to Campbell's.

As brand manager, you need to assess the strengths and weaknesses of the brand in question. If your charge is to grow the brand by 5%, then you have a number of ways to get there.

One of the most likely ways to accomplish this goal is to get your current users to use your brand more often. In this case, you would focus on your current user base. You may also have to attract new users away from other brands (stealing share) or grow the category. This would lead to an audience that might not necessarily be your brand's existing audience. Perhaps there is an ethnic niche that hasn't been reached. Or there may be a purchase influence dynamic at play, where the influencer, rather than the actual purchaser, drives the business.

Again, all your goals must align. Start with the business goal, which is typically growing the business at X%. Then ask yourself how you are going to get there. From this point, you should assess your brand versus the category and the competition. Is the product category growing at the same rate as the brand? Is there a gap between your brand and the category that could lead to a potential source of business? Or is there some sort of competitive threat or opportunity that would lead to a growth opportunity for the brand? Once these issues are raised with both the agency and the brand group, you can begin to define the proper audience.

TOOLS FOR DEFINING THE AUDIENCE

A number of secondary research tools can aid in defining the media audience. Over the years, there have been several improvements in linking actual brand purchase data to media behavior. These have led to a recent rise in the ability to model schedules and to determine the sales impact potential of various media alternatives.

Historically, the two nationally syndicated research studies used by media planners have been those of Mediamark Research Inc. (MRI) and Simmons Market Research Bureau. Both annual studies were initially designed to support the magazine industry with sales and audience data. The companies have merged, and MRI-Simmons now provides consumer data on demographics, psychographics, attitudes, and behaviors on both a local and a national level for the US market.

MRI-Simmons also provide in depth studies on magazine readership. Nielsen and IRI are the two services that track manufacturers' brand movements through grocery store chains. Both have powerful databases of purchase behavior, which are used in helping media planners to understand the purchase dynamics of a multitude of brands and categories.

As a syndicated source of secondary data, MRI-Simmons reports on more than 600 categories and 6,500 brands. Data are collected through a constantly fielded annual sample consisting of 40,000 adults aged 18 and older (18+), so it is highly reliable. They investigate more than 60,000 elements, including multicultural variables addressing acculturation, identity, and media usage. Their data can also help identify a variety of consumer segmentation schemes, including looking at consumer buying styles, green attitudes, and technology adoption.

To find out actual purchasing information, research companies Nielsen and Spectra have developed a tool that bridges the gap between retail tracking and consumer targeting. This tool connects actual product purchase behavior with Spectra's lifestyle segmentation grid, which allows the brand manager to analyze consumer behavior not only for media but for consumer promotion. With this segmentation scheme becoming very popular for brands, Spectra has become much more important in the media planning process with its link to MRI-Simmons data.

Using this system, the media planner can get actual brand purchase data that can be linked to media behavior. Until this time, media planners used MRI-Simmons for both media and marketing data. Now media planners can confirm MRI-Simmons marketing data and use the same MRI data for media planning.

There are two local market tools available primarily for local retail planning. Scarborough Research, a service in joint partnership with the Nielsen Company and Arbitron, Inc., measures local media markets for the leading 75 US markets. The Media Audit is a competitive product that offers a deeper market list at 86 markets, but not quite the level of detail in terms of advertisers measured. Both are excellent sources for analyzing local market activity and can be manipulated to include custom regions.

Those are the key secondary resources used in broad-based media planning. Once a plan is developed, media buyers use specific audience measurement tools for negotiation purposes. The key broadcast sources in the United States are Nielsen for television and cable and Arbitron for radio. Recently, there has been a move toward primary research studies for the brand that can be geocoded by either a PRIZM or Spectra database and linked back to other studies such as MRI.

For analyzing and measuring global audiences, some of the top sources include:

- Euromonitor, a syndicated source that provides detailed data and analysis on industries and consumers in 1,200 cities and 210 countries.
- Statista, another syndicated source examining 11,500 brands in more than 50 countries around the world.
- GWI, a large global survey on the digital consumer, collecting data from consumers in 40 countries on about 40,000 brands.
- Nippon Research Service, an annual omnibus survey of Japanese consumers.

AUDIENCES

Keep in mind that not every audience can be reached by media. For example, if you are selling dog food, you'll obviously want to reach dog owners. But there is no advertising medium that reaches all dog owners and only dog owners. Even media aimed at dog lovers, such as *Modern Dog Magazine* and its website, moderndogmagazine .com, reach some people who do not have a dog but (1) would like to adopt or buy one in the future; (2) have recently lost a pet and are not quite ready to get another; or (3) are not in a position to be a pet parent due to lack of space or an erratic schedule that involves a lot of travel. But these people may still read the magazine or visit the website. Of course, even *Modern Dog Magazine* doesn't reach all owners of dogs – maybe you have a dog and you've never heard of it! And there may be people who buy dog food who do not have a dog; perhaps they donate the food to a local shelter. The bottom line is that while it is important to have a target group like dog owners, you also need to identify a specific audience: a group that can be reached by media and that can be clearly defined.

At the same time, you also want to identify a communication audience. Again, if you want to reach dog owners, that's your audience: people in households with dogs. But it's unlikely that the entire household is buying food for their dog. The principal purchasing agent is the communication audience: the person who actually goes to the store to buy dog food.

THE HEAVY-USER DEFINITION

Now that you have the right tools, how do you go about defining an audience? There are a number of ways to look at an audience. We have identified some of these from the marketing objectives. An important way to look at your audience profile is in terms of consumption.

The Pareto principle states that 20% of any given audience represents 80% of the consumption. There is a heavy-user segment for nearly every brand. The heavy user may not represent 80% of consumption, but there is a strong ratio – typically in the 2-to-1 range – for usage-to-users ratios. The procedure of looking at the heavy, medium, and light users of a brand is an excellent analysis tool and a viable way to target (see Tables 11.1 and 11.2).

TABLE 11.1 Tomato sauce category usage analysis

Sauce category range	Users		Volume		
	(000)	%	(000)	%	Avg.
Heavy 6+	3,587	17	40,030	50	11.2
Medium 3–5	5,892	28	22,208	28	3.8
Light 1–2	11,395	55	17,359	22	1.5
	20,874	100	79,597	100	3.8

Source: MRI Doublebase

TABLE 11.2 Diced tomato category usage analysis

Diced category range	Users		Volume		
	(000)	%	(000)	%	Avg.
Heavy 6+	1,867	14	15,406	41	80.0
Medium 3–5	2,481	18	8,487	22	3.4
Light 1–2	9,456	69	13,970	37	1.5
	13,804	100	37,863	100	2.7

Source: MRI Doublebase

Let's look at a hypothetical example for several different products from Hunt's. As Table 11.1 shows, a heavy user of Hunt's tomato sauce is defined as someone who uses six or more cans per month. This group represents 17% of the user base but accounts for 50% of the usage. This might suggest that Hunt's must not lose the heavy-user group because it is a small yet vital part of the category. But the real opportunity may be in targeting those other 83% of the users to get them to use the brand more often.

Another gap to analyze is the gap between competitive brands. For example, there may be a difference in usage between Hunt's and other large tomato sauce brands like Classico and Prego. After assessing the reason for this difference, the brand can determine if this gap is something that advertising can alter or if it is the result of a product trait. For example, Classico may be purchased by people in smaller households, and Hunt's by people in larger households. Reaching purchasers in smaller households might be one way to grow the brand.

The heavy-user concept is certainly one that packaged-goods brand managers use regularly. In addition, retail and business-to-business brand managers can use this theory to segment their audiences.

For example, a grocery retailer knows that a mom with kids is likely to spend more on groceries than a single retired adult. The grocery retailer may use basket size (how many products a person is buying from the store, which translates into how many dollars a person is spending at the store) as a barometer of a heavy user. So, a shopper who spends $200 on an average visit is worth more than the one who spends $50 per visit. With sophisticated retail databases so prevalent in today's retail landscape, this type of analysis is relatively easy to conduct.

External audiences also include those who may be reached by business-to-business marketing, even though these transactions aren't usually as frequent as in retail or packaged goods. Nevertheless, there is still a size dimension that relates to heavy usage. One way that business-to-business marketers can evaluate their sales database is to see how large the sales are in rank order, or to have their financial department help them assess the profitability of each customer in terms of sales versus customer support required to service that customer. Each of these methods can be used to arrive at some form of ranking of heavy to light usage or of profitable to less profitable customer.

TABLE 11.3 PAM cooking spray

	Life stage						
Spectra lifestyle	18–34 w/kids	18–34 w/o kids	35–54 w/kids	35–54 w/o kids	55–64	65	Total lifestyle
Upscale suburbs	105	53	112	104	136	154	116
Traditional families	73	55	93	107	130	178	111
Mid/upscale suburbs	62	60	108	82	122	142	108
Metro elite	78	34	88	71	121	130	83
Working-class towns	77	45	94	86	145	157	104
Rural towns and farms	48	44	86	103	127	145	99
Mid-urban melting pot	48	38	83	73	108	148	89
Downscale rural	49	35	90	86	119	162	103
Downscale urban	56	30	85	71	97	148	87
Total	65	42	94	87	124	151	100

Sources: AC Nielsen and Spectra/Media*PLAN*. Reprinted with permission

LIFESTYLE AND LIFE STAGE SEGMENTATION

Beyond the usage method of targeting, there are a number of lifestyle and life stage assessment methods that affect media targeting. It is possible to gain insight into your audience by looking at their lifestyles and life stages. We noted that the key tools for assessing lifestyles and life stages are PRIZM and Spectra. Both of these research tools define lifestyle largely by where you live and how affluent you are. For example, the lifestyle of a consumer who lives in an upscale suburb of a large metropolitan area is very different from that of a consumer living in a small, rural farming community. This type of analysis helps put a face on your audience and may suggest that you need different media approaches to reach various lifestyle groups.

Another way to look at your audience group is by their life stage. Consumer patterns of behavior are sometimes dictated by where you are in your life. There is a huge difference between a 25-year-old mother of two and a 25-year-old working woman with no kids. In many cases, life stages serve as marketing milestones that require different media approaches. For example, if you are a senior in college, it is likely that credit card companies have been soliciting you because they know you will be getting a job soon and establishing credit. Similarly, new parents receive all sorts of coupons for various baby products as well as banking products to save for their children's education.

Let's look at an example of lifestyles and life stages of users of PAM cooking spray (Table 11.3). The PAM brand attracts an older and more affluent audience. The challenge for the PAM brand is to generate a new base of users with a younger audience.

GENERATIONS AS AN AUDIENCE

We have discussed various demographic and brand usage approaches to identifying an audience. Another method is to find common ground among various generations of consumers. Generations are brief periods of time that are connected with popular culture. Consumers of the same generation are connected not only by age but by the

TABLE 11.4 List of generations in the Western world

Generation	Born	Notable occurences
G.I. Generation	1911–1924	• Fought WWII as adults • Called the "Greatest Generation" • Great Recession
Silent Generation	1925–1942	• Repressed childhoods due to WWII
Boomer Generation	1943–1965	• Civil Rights movement • Woodstock
Generation X	1965–1985	• Rise of mass media • End of Cold War • MTV
Generation Y	1986–2001	• Rise of Information Age • Internet
Generation Z	2002–2009	• 9/11 • Social Media
Generation Alpha	2010–	• Covid-19 Pandemic • Streaming media

various milestones they have reached together. Some unifying characteristics include music, fads, inventions, politics, and social movements. For example, the 1960s ushered in the British invasion of rock stars to the United States, led by the Beatles. World War II colored two generations: The first has been termed the G.I. Generation because its members fought in the war as adults; in the United States, this generation was later referred to as the "Greatest Generation" for defeating the Axis of Evil. The second generation impacted included those who were children during World War II; dubbed the Silent Generation, these Americans grew up in families that were preoccupied with the war. Table 11.4 offers a list of different generations in Western culture for the past 100 years. While the older generations in this table may be different in non-Western countries, the Internet has created a global culture where perceptions of Generations Y, Z, and Alpha are fairly consistent around the world.

Generations can be a very effective approach to developing an audience. Members of these groups are connected not only demographically but also emotionally and historically. Many times, an advertiser will choose music or images that stir emotions within a particular generation. From a media perspective, it is important to be sensitive to the demographic nuances of generations as well as to patterns of culture, either of which may be a good forum for delivering an advertising message.

BEHAVIORAL TARGETING

Another way to reach your market is by how its members behave. This type of targeting is very popular in the online world, where it is possible to track the websites someone visits in real time. For example, if you have just visited a website on border collies, you are likely to be a pet owner and receptive to a new dog food brand. That's how behavioral targeting works in the online world, and is very helpful for developing global reach of brands. But this type of targeting is not exclusive to cyberspace. Offline, you can try to reach people who drive electric cars. Or you can try to reach golf enthusiasts. The idea of behavioral targeting is to have a relevant message for someone at the time it is most relevant to them – that is, when they are actually demonstrating or behaving in a way that indicates your brand is important to them.

Assessing behaviors can be stretched to more than just activities. You might consider targeting bargain hunters, those people who clip coupons or visit websites that sell discounted goods. During the global pandemic, many people around the world changed purchasing behaviors: a study by McKinsey estimated that globally, 70% of people tried a new method of shopping (such as purchasing online or using a meal delivery service). However, the percentage of people who changed these behaviors (such as purchasing online or using new delivery systems) differed greatly by country. In India, for example, almost 96% of people tried a new method of shopping, while is Japan, only 30% did. Regardless of where they live, about 80% of people who purchased something in a different way will continue this behavior after the pandemic ends. In this way, you are discovering some behavior outside of the brand's purchase dynamics that might be a good fit for the audience.

PURCHASER VERSUS INFLUENCER

So far, we have talked about the brand in terms of who is buying a given product. For packaged goods, this is typically the mother in a household. But she is not always the one consuming the products. Although our secondary research tools do an excellent job of defining the purchaser, they do not necessarily define the actual consumer of the product.

To understand this dynamic, the brand needs to do primary research to see whether there are influences that tip the scale beyond the actual purchaser of the product. For many items, the child in the household exerts the brand influence. Many households purchase private-label cereal and put that cereal in an already used branded box so children will think it is from their favorite branded source.

The challenge for the brand manager and the media group is to determine how to balance these influences. In the case of cereal, do you advertise to mothers or do you try to reach only the children? Of course, you would like to do both, but if you lack sufficient funds, which one do you pick? Or should you blend the funds in a ratio of, say, 70% for mothers and 30% for children? These issues certainly need to be resolved before the media plan can be fully developed.

The issue of purchase influence is not confined to mothers and children. Many household purchases, from the family car to the house to vacations, are made with varying degrees of influence from both members of a two-headed household. Recent trends in healthcare show that adult children assert influence over their now-senior parents. So the issue of purchase influence is very far-reaching and can be the key decision in the media targeting process.

OTHER BRAND INFLUENCERS

The issue of brand influence is not just the domain of brand purchaser versus brand user. In the retail and service area, internal audiences such as employees may exert a huge influence on the delivery of a service and is the key to customer satisfaction. As a result, a retailer or service brand manager often makes sure that the employees are an audience for the advertising.

Sometimes retail or service advertising is based around a promise made to consumers – a promise that employees must fulfill. For example, a grocery chain ran this promotion: If you aren't checked out within five minutes, you'll receive a discount off your groceries. To ensure that the employees were up for the challenge, the marketing manager ran an advertising campaign saluting the great employees of the store. This campaign led to a big increase in store pride on the part of the employees, so when the promotion hit, they were more than ready to execute it.

The world of business-to-business marketing has a very complicated set of influences. Because the purchase of a business item for your company doesn't involve your own money, it comes with an entirely different dynamic. For instance, when a company buys a computer, the user of the computer wants something he or she can be comfortable with; the information technology (IT) group wants something that fits into their overall IT framework; the finance group wants to minimize costs; and the CEO wants the greatest productivity. All of these customers have influence over the purchase. In many cases, the actual purchaser (the person who writes the check) has the least amount of influence over the purchase.

So, as a business-to-business brand manager, it is important to walk the advertising agency and the media group through the sales process so that they understand its various components.

DEVELOPING A PERSONA FOR PLANNING PURPOSES

While targeting can become a numbers game, you should constantly work to humanize the audience you plan to reach. After all, you will be marketing to human beings regardless of what you are selling. One way to do this is by developing a persona to better understand the audience. A persona is a fictitious character that embodies the characteristics of the market. Rather than list a variety of demographic attributes, buying behavior, and/or motivations, the persona encompasses all this information in a nice, neat story.

Persona development is very common for use in messaging. It is much easier to write for a specific person than for a set of personal attributes. Persona development is also common in developing online experiences as well as in personal selling. The persona becomes a shorthand version of the market.

The media team can add a lot of value to creating a persona. Broad media habits can be integrated into a persona to round out what this person is all about. This helps the brand manager visualize how media play a role in a day in the life of the market.

Persona development can be done through a personal name or by a descriptive segment name. For example, imagine that you are trying to reach a married working mother with two children, an 8-year-old son and a 14-year-old daughter. They live in a middle-class suburb near Washington, DC. This segment could be called "Amanda" and/or "Pressure Cooker Mom." Here is a brief persona example.

> ### Pressure cooker mom (Amanda)
>
> *Amanda is always on the go. She is up at 5:00 A.M. preparing to get her third-grade son and teenage daughter off to school, with a local news station on in the background. Once she gets them on the school bus, she drives 40 minutes to her accounting job. While in the car, she listens to her favorite podcast, finding that the show keeps her company on her long commute. At work, she juggles her time between meetings and analysis. At noon, she takes a break and usually reads news (both national and local) online, checks her Instagram page, and looks at videos on YouTube. On her way home from work, she uses her DoorDash app to order dinner from the family's favorite restaurant. She demands that her family have a family meal together, so at 6:30 P.M. every night, it's family meal time. When the meal is over, she helps her son with his homework until 8:00 P.M. From 8:00 to 9:00, she joins her husband and son to watch a comedy show streaming on Netflix or Apple TV, or to watch a live sports event on ESPN. Then, it is the children's bedtime at 10:00 P.M. Amanda stays up until 11:00 or so, reading or streaming a favorite mystery program.*
>
> From this brief persona development, you can get a sense for what members of the audience are like as real people. You sense their busy lifestyles and can begin to think about how you can find ways to ensure that your brand message fits in. Once the audience is defined, personifying them is a great way to help bring it to life.

GROWING ETHNIC DIVERSITY

In the golden age of television, the media audience was fairly easy to discern. Take a look at *Leave It to Beaver* and you have your audience. It consisted of a white family with a working husband, a stay-at-home mom, and two kids. Of course, that was around 1960. The times have changed a lot since then. Many women are now working women, and the ethnic composition of the United States (and other countries around the world) has changed.

In the United States, more than 40% of the population identifies their race as something other than white. There are many large markets, such as those in Los Angeles and Miami, where whites are not the majority. The most rapid growth in the population is coming from Hispanic and Asian populations, followed by African Americans. While 80% of people in the United Kingdom identify as white, less than 60% of people living in London do.

These growth patterns have a lot of bearing on media planning and targeting. Ethnic audiences watch, listen to, and read general-market media, but each ethnic group also uses culture-specific media. The media planning dilemma is to determine when additional resources should be funneled into ethnic media.

There are two schools of thought on this issue. The first is to determine what percentage of the ethnic population is underdelivered by the general-market media and then to make up that difference in ethnic media. For example, if you were trying to reach men who drink beer, you might schedule a commercial on *Monday Night Football (MNF)*. If *MNF* delivers a 12 rating for all men but only an 8 rating for

Hispanic men, there is a 33% shortfall for Hispanic men. You can either accept this shortfall or look for programming that will balance the delivery for Hispanic men. Assessing underdelivery of various demographic groups is an excellent form of media analysis. This example suggests that the current buy of *MNF* might not be enough if Hispanic men are a key part of your audience.

This brings us to the second school of thought, which focuses on marketing versus media. If Hispanic men are a crucial audience, then you should market to them. Scheduling support in media that is directed specifically to the Hispanic market (such as the Univision cable station or Palabra, the website of the National Association of Hispanic Journalists) is as much a political statement as it is a method of reaching the right audience. It means that you recognize the importance of this group, and that such recognition has an impact that goes well beyond the impact of the standard media analysis.

It is important in ethnic markets to understand the media impact of the plan in terms of media delivery. If an ethnic segment is growing and is important, then develop a marketing program to cultivate that group. That is where the brand manager and the media team need to work together to ensure that all aspects of strategic thought are represented before proceeding.

ECONOMIC IMPACT OF TARGETING

We have looked at media targeting from the perspective of who makes up the best audience to reach in order to make your business grow. There are also economic implications of targeting. Each decision you make on defining your audience has an effect on the cost of media. Thus, assessing the cost impact of your decision is crucial to finalizing your audience.

The harder the group is to reach, the more it costs to reach them, which seems like a pretty basic maxim. The curveball here is that some media are designed to reach a very narrow audience rather than a broad one. This holds true for the regular television networks, but it does not necessarily apply to cable, where programming is very specific.

In general, the broader the audience, the lower the cost to reach them. The cost per thousand to reach women aged 25–54 tends to be less expensive than working women with kids under age 12. Of course, today many media vehicles are designed for specific audiences: radio formats are tailored for narrow age cells, magazines and web sites are created for niche audiences, and social media properties collect such a broad range of user information that pinpointing a very specific audience is necessary. Therefore, a thorough investigation of a range of media costs is important for every individual brand.

The other economic implications of targeting involve your media budget. If you are like most brand managers, you usually do not have enough resources to do what you want to do. Every brand is under pressure to deliver profits, and media support is one of the easiest budget cuts because it is considered a variable expense.

If you are faced with marketing a national cereal brand with only $3 million for advertising, and the competition spends $15 million, you have some tough challenges. Your $3 million will not go far against a broad "mothers" audience, but it is certainly enough to generate some noise in the children's market. Or you may want to tackle an ethnic market with your limited budget. Therefore, when working with the media-planning group, it is critical that you understand the cost/impact dynamics of an audience.

SUMMARY

The audience is the cornerstone of the media plan. Defining the proper audience is crucial for success. It begins with setting the right objectives and then using the tools at your disposal to better identify the audience. Once you have weighed your options from the perspectives of opportunity and economics, you are ready to finalize this aspect of the media plan.

Reaching the "Silver Tsunami"

So many media plans list the age demographic group as adults 18–49, given the perception that younger adults spend more as they have kids, buy homes, and need new cars. Some believe this age group is more likely to try new brands. Planners often ignore Baby Boomers as they're too set in their ways, not engaged with technology, and are more interested in downsizing than acquiring goods.

New research shows that this perception is just not true. The "silver tsunami" encompasses 70 million people aged 56–74 who are tech savvy, still employed, taking active vacations, and shopping online. For those who do retire, many see retirement as "the next chapter" and will discover and explore new passions. They tend to watch more cable than other groups as well.

So don't think about the Boomer target as appropriate only for medications and cheap cell phones. This group is ready and willing to spend, when reached with the right products.

Targeting color blind consumers (and the people who love them)

Did you know that globally, 1 in 12 men and 1 in 200 women suffer from color vision deficiency (CVD), also known as color blindness? That's more than 300 million people worldwide. CVD is the decreased ability to see color or differences in color. For most people, the condition is relatively minor, and these people can use different tools to adapt to the condition. As a result, many people with CVD don't talk about it.

A European brand called EnChroma makes one of these tools: Special glasses that help people differentiate between colors. The company's insight was that one very challenging place for people with CVD was subway stations, as many cities use different colors to identify different lines and stations. The map for the subway in London, known as the Tube, features eight different colors, for example.

To raise awareness of CVD and the brand's products to support people with the condition, the brand created posters for subway stations that featured some of the colors most challenging to people with CVD (such as red and green). The posters alerted people that five of their friends couldn't differentiate between the colors in the poster, and recommended they could give the "gift of color" to these friends.

In another innovative outdoor installation, EnChroma partnered with the Tennessee Department of Tourism Development to install EnChroma lenses in viewfinders at scenic outlooks in Tennessee – such as Ober Gatlinburg and Ruby Falls. Due to the lenses, people with CVD can enjoy the fall leaf colors. EnChroma is credited at the viewfinders and is also featured on the tourism website.

CHAPTER 12

Geography's role in planning

....

WHERE IS THE WORLD ARE YOUR CUSTOMERS?

Where your product is marketed is just as important as *who* makes up your target audience. Whether your brand is international or found only at the corner grocery store, when it comes to media planning, *geography* is an essential strategic issue. How you define where you want to advertise and how much weight you give to one market versus another are key questions in deciding resource allocation.

Geography ties into the target audience definition. As mentioned in Chapter 11, PRIZM or Spectra data can be mapped to provide a look at regional pockets of strength or weakness for a brand's target market. Then, as the brand manager, you can decide whether to support a geography that has a high concentration of customers, or to go fishing for new customers.

Before we get into geographic analysis and the impact of geography on media costs and media vehicle selection, we first need to define our geography. Nielsen, the company that measures television ratings, uses the concept of a designated market area (shortened as DMA) when analyzing television ratings. A DMA is a particular location where people get the same television and radio options. Other syndicated research services use different measurements for geography. This will be explained more in the next section.

HOW TO DEFINE GEOGRAPHY

Consider this scenario: You, the brand manager, tell the media planning group that you want to "heavy-up" (or apply more advertising weight to) for a client who is advertising in Birmingham, Alabama. The media planning group walks away thinking that you simply want to advertise in the Birmingham designated marketing area (DMA). You, on the other hand, are thinking that the media planning group is looking at

DOI: 10.4324/9781003258162-12

TABLE 12.1 Nielsen Designated Market Area compared to IRI (InfoScan) Market

DMA	Total TV Households (000)	% of InfoScan Market Coverage
Birmingham	730.4	36.5
Huntsville-Decatur, Florence	351.6	17.6
Montgomery	207.2	10.3
Mobile/Pensacola	518.7	25.9
Columbus, GA	183.6	9.2
	7.8	0.5
Total	1999.3	100.0

the Birmingham Infoscan Market. The Infoscan market is measured by Information Resources, Inc. (IRI's), and it consists of seven different DMAs (see Table 12.1).

Obviously, you have a problem. One of the most common problems a brand manager faces is matching up marketing areas to media planning geography. This may sound fundamental, but it is a crucial area that is often overlooked until it is too late, or until a critical mistake is made.

The media planner generally defines geography based on television DMA from Nielsen. A DMA is a group of counties that get the majority of their television viewing from the same home market. There are 210 DMAs in the Nielsen television system. DMAs are fairly static, but changes can occur. For example, at different times Sarasota, Florida, was both its own DMA and a part of the Tampa/St. Petersburg DMA, depending upon how strongly its local station performed in its home market. Although counties may shift from one DMA to another, DMAs are fairly consistent from year to year.

A second geography, or geographic unit, used by media planners is the metropolitan statistical area (MSA). An MSA is a central metropolitan area as designated by the US Census Bureau. Each MSA comprises a certain number of counties and is smaller than a DMA. Radio stations typically use the MSA as their geography for their signal strength. Some brands use the MSA as their trading area because the MSA contains a considerable amount of census data that can be used to analyze the area. There are approximately 280 MSAs in the United States.

Packaged-goods marketers use either Nielsen panel data or IRI data to analyze sales information. Each of these sources uses broader marketing areas than either a DMA or an MSA. To describe their geography, Nielsen and IRI use approximately 60 market areas, which incorporate the 210 DMAs.

Regardless of the source you are using, it is important to match up these market areas with DMAs before proceeding with media planning. Thus, when you say "Birmingham," you will get all the DMAs in the area and not just the 40% of the total marketing area that lies in the Birmingham DMA.

If you are a brand manager of a retail chain, then you define your market by the store's trading area. A trading area is a geographic area based on where your customers

TABLE 12.2 Georgia trading area analysis: Larry's chicken shack

ZIP Code	# Households	Sales	% Total	Sales per HH
30112	11,400	$350,000	7	$30.70
30134	21,600	$600,000	12	$27.77
30135	30,450	$750,000	16	$24.62
30187	4,070	$105,000	2	$25.80
30013	12,200	$275,000	6	$22.54
30016	27,500	$500,000	19	$18.18
30054	16,000	$290,000	6	$18.12
31064	1,500	$75,000	2	$50.00
30070	1,000	$30,000	1	$30.00
Top 10 Total	125,720			
All Others	140,000	$1,850,000	29	$13.21
Total	265,720	$4,825,000	100	$18.15

actually live or work. For example, most fast-food restaurants use a three-mile trading radius as their standard for defining their individual stores' trading areas. Other retail stores may draw from a wider area, but most retailers have a specific part of the market that makes up the majority of their customers. To market effectively to this group, a retail brand manager conducts a trade area analysis. This is usually done by evaluating the point-of-sale system used by retailers to capture customer names and addresses. Table 12.2 shows a ZIP code analysis for a fast-food chicken restaurant in Georgia.

As Table 12.2 shows, a concentration of sales comes from just a few ZIP codes. This provides the media planner with information to make an intelligent decision on a variety of media. Perhaps there is a billboard location that makes sense in this area. Or there may be a need to provide inserts or direct mail with coupon offers to area residents.

Geography can play a role in business-to-business marketing as well. The difference in business marketing as opposed to consumer marketing is that the decision process can involve more than one market. For example, a cellular phone company that markets to the offshore oil industry found that the users of their service lived in rural markets near the coasts of Louisiana and Texas; the decision makers, on the other hand, working on the oil rigs with the workers, lived in more urban markets such as Houston, New Orleans, and Baton Rouge. In addition, the headquarters for most of the oil companies were in a western suburban area of Houston, more than 100 miles from the coast. In this case, the brand manager had to develop a different strategy for rural-based users of the service versus the urban-oriented users at corporate headquarters.

So, any goods or services will have geographic influences, whether they are national, based on a local market, or even as micro as a city block. Regardless of your brand's situation, the same discipline and tools should be used to determine the appropriate geographic media approach.

HOW TO ANALYZE GEOGRAPHY

Now that everyone is working with the same definitions, it's time to analyze your sales by geography to determine strengths and weaknesses. The classic method is to develop a BDI/CDI analysis.

BDI stands for *brand development index,* which tells how strong a market's sales are in relation to its population size. This index is the percentage of your brand's sales compared to the percentage of the population in a certain market. Suppose you have 3.4% of your sales in Dallas, a city that represents 1.7% of the population of the United States. The BDI would be 200 for your brand (3.4 ÷ 1.7 × 100).

An index of 100 means the brand sales in that market mirror the population. If the index is less than 100, then the brand is not consumed up to the per capita level; if the BDI is more than 100, consumption is greater than the per capita level.

CDI stands for *category development index.* Just like a BDI, a CDI is the percentage of category sales compared to the percentage of the population. You use the CDI as a measure of potential, whereas the BDI is a measure of actual brand strength.

The best way to look at a BDI/CDI analysis is to graph it in a quadrant chart. Table 12.3 shows a quadrant chart with each grid reflecting a different relationship between the brand and the category. In quadrant I, both the brand and category are strong. This is a good area to defend. Quadrant II shows that the BDI is much stronger than the CDI, which means that the only brand growth here would be limited to growing the category. In quadrant III, the category is stronger than the brand. This is the area of opportunity. And quadrant IV shows that both the brand and category are weak. This is an area where you will avoid spending advertising dollars.

One last analysis involves creating your own *brand opportunity index* (BOI). This is done by dividing the CDI by the BDI. For example, you have a brand where Atlanta

TABLE 12.3 Brand opportunities analysis

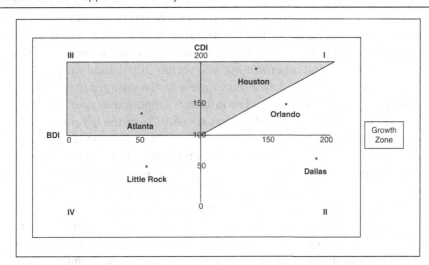

has a CDI of 120 but a BDI of 80, which corresponds to a BOI of 150 (120 ÷ 80 × 100). On the other hand, if Orlando has a CDI of 120 but a BDI of 150, then the BOI of 80 (120 ÷ 150 × 100) might make it less attractive as a growth market than Atlanta, even though both the BDI and CDI would put Orlando in the top quadrant (see Table 12.3). Both Nielsen and IRI research show that advertising has the best opportunity to "grow" a brand where it has a strong BOI. So, once you calculate your BDI and CDI and put them in a quadrant chart, calculate your BOI for the final opportunity analysis.

The same BDI/CDI analysis can be done in the retail as well as the business-to-business arena. In retail, you may want to look at BDI/CDI on a market level, not just on a trading area basis. Because the number of stores can determine the strength or weakness of a market, retailers use a sales-per-trading-area analysis to evaluate one store versus another. This can be done by simply calculating the sales of the store and dividing by the number of households within the store's trading area.

On a global basis, the BDI and CDI can be calculated by country to help identify what countries offer opportunities.

FACTORING IN DISTRIBUTION

The BDI/CDI analysis is a classic one, but before finalizing your market "heavy-up" decision, you should dig a bit deeper to understand the reason behind the numbers. Suppose that in the Atlanta example, where your BDI is only 80, your brand was in less than 50% of the available points of distribution. Now, the opportunity market that you thought you had may not be one after all until you gain full distribution.

For packaged-goods products, the term for distribution is *all commodity volume* (ACV). This is a fancy name for the percentage of the distribution channel in which the brand is available.

Distribution is an important element when looking at sales by market. Distribution, or the lack thereof, may be one of the reasons why a brand performs the way it does. One way to equalize the effects of spotty distribution is to do a sales-per-distribution-point analysis. This analysis looks at the sales-velocity-per-distribution percentage. It may uncover where a brand is performing well yet has distribution weaknesses. This can be a good tool for the brand manager to use with the sales group to shore up any weaknesses in the distribution area. For instance, suppose that your brand has 2% of its sales in Dallas/Fort Worth, which has roughly 2% of the US population. You would say that Dallas is an average market with a BDI of 100. But if you found that you had your brand in only half the available retail outlets in Dallas, then you would say that Dallas actually has a BDI of 200 in the outlets where your brand is available as outlined in Table 12.4. Based on this analysis, Dallas looks like a great market now that you've gained that crucial missing amount of distribution.

From a media planning perspective, understanding the distribution of the brand is critical in selecting markets to "heavy-up" or markets for testing. Before proceeding with the BDI/CDI analysis, it pays to step back and ask about the brand's distribution.

TABLE 12.4 Brand opportunity index

DMA	BDI	CDI	BOI
Dallas/Ft. Worth	200	80	40
Atlanta	80	120	150
Houston	150	200	133
Little Rock	90	50	55
Orlando	150	120	80

APPLYING MEDIA TO GEOGRAPHY

Now that you and your team understand what markets you want to target and are working from the same market definitions, you can begin to analyze which media to apply to various levels of geography.

Although most media can be purchased nationally, regionally, or locally, each medium has its geographic nuances. Let's review the major media and how they can be purchased at various geographic levels.

- Television airtime can be purchased on a DMA basis locally or on a network television basis nationally. The major networks – ABC, CBS, NBC, and Fox – can even offer broad regional coverage based typically on five large regions. The only distinction is that network television uses syndicated programming, which is "cleared" locally. For example, a syndicated program such as *Wheel of Fortune* is actually sold DMA by DMA to a series of unrelated local stations. In exchange for taking the program, the local station gets a certain amount of commercial inventory to sell, while the syndicator keeps its "national" inventory. Depending upon the syndicator's success, a program might "clear" all 100% of the country or just a portion of it.
- Cable television airtime can be purchased locally and nationally. Most cable networks do not offer regional opportunities; nevertheless, there are regional cable sports networks available to purchase.
- Radio airtime can be purchased locally, nationally, or on an MSA basis. Locally, radio is similar to television; the only difference is signal strength. Some stations are stronger than others, which can impact listening on the fringes of the MSA. Network radio is fairly similar to network television and syndication. You can purchase commercials that air on stations across the country, and you can purchase what is known as long-form programming, which is similar to syndication. *American Top 40*, a radio countdown of the week's most popular songs, is an example of a long-form program.
- Magazine space can be purchased locally, regionally, or nationally. It is possible to purchase space in a magazine such as *Good Housekeeping* on a national basis, or just in the Southeast, or just in the Chicago DMA. The smaller the publication's circulation, the less likely it is that you can purchase space in it on a

regional or local basis. Obviously, there are regional and local magazines of every shape, topic, and size available to purchase.

- Newspapers are primarily local media, with the exception of *USA Today*, the *Wall Street Journal*, and the national edition of the *New York Times*. Nevertheless, there are products that come within a newspaper that you can purchase. Free-standing inserts (FSIs) run in the Sunday newspaper and carry a wide variety of coupons. The largest purveyor of FSIs is a company called Valassis. You can create a national, regional, or local buy using these inserts. *Parade* magazine is another vehicle that is distributed in the Sunday newspaper, and space can be purchased as in any other magazine. Newspapers offer the opportunity to market on a micro level, targeting inserts by ZIP code; insert-only companies such as ADVO provide the same service.

- Online advertising can be purchased on all, including worldwide, geographic levels. A web portal like Yahoo! offers any level of banner or other program support to the widest or narrowest geography possible. Search engines such as Google also offer these opportunities. Social media sites – Facebook and Twitter among them – also offer an advertiser the ability to target on a micro level. Social media as well as online media are increasingly moving to mobile platforms. This offers advertisers the ability to target not only geographically but by time of day or by geographic behavior. For example, if you have used social media to "check in" at your favorite Starbucks, you could receive an ad that may promote a sale at a retailer down the block. Digital media is a tremendous opportunity for geographic targeting. In addition, there are numerous sites that attract huge audiences from specific countries that are not used by many people outside that country, or that are geared specifically to that country (such as google.fr). A few examples are presented in Table 12.5.

- Out-of-home media (OOH) – billboards and signs on subways and buses – are, for the most part, a local medium. Still, you can buy advertising space on a rolling

TABLE 12.5 Top websites by country (in terms of visits)

	#1	#2	#3
Australia	Google.com	Youtube.com	Facebook.com
Chile	Google.com	Youtube.com	Biobiochile.cl
China	Tmall.com	qq.com	Baidu.com
Egypt	Google.com	Youtube.com	Youm7.com
France	Google.com	Youtube.com	Google.fr
Ghana	Google.com	YouTube.com	Ghanaweb.com
Hong Kong	Google.com	YouTube.com	Google.com.hk
Japan	Google.com	YouTube.com	Yahoo.co.jp
Pakistan	Google.com	Youtube.com	Facebook.com
Saudi Arabia	Google.com	YouTube.com	Google.com.sa
Thailand	Google.com	YouTube.com	Google.co.th
United Kingdom	Google.com	YouTube.com	Reddit.com
United States	Google.com	YouTube.com	Amazon.com

Source: https://www.alexa.com/topsites/countries

basis – that is, on bus routes that cover much of the country. Beyond these standard OOH media, alternative media such as airplane banners, beach logos, telephone-booth advertisements, and bathroom ads are extremely local.

RELEVANT PLACES TO CONSIDER

Another way to approach geography is from a consumer brand connection perspective. Where does the consumer come into contact with the brand? What would be a relevant place where the consumer might need the brand? Where does the consumer hang out? By answering these types of questions, you can begin to connect your brand message to appropriate places where your target market goes.

For example, a brand campaign for Wisk laundry detergent targeted mothers who had active young children. Active young children translate to lots of clothes washing. To understand this target market, the media team followed moms with active children to better understand their lifestyle. When they were done, they developed a media strategy called the "point of dirt." This was where moms and their children were when the children were getting dirty. You can probably guess where that was: playgrounds, soccer fields, football fields, baseball fields, parks, and laundromats. Armed with this information, the media team put together a plan to place the Wisk brand message at these locations. This unique approach broke from the traditional media approaches in the category and helped Wisk grow its sales.

Finding relevant places where the brand and the consumer connect goes to the heart of the job of a media planner: to understand the consumer. This can be as simple as not overlooking where a brand may be sold (such as a grocery store or convenience store). Or it may be connecting to where the consumer spends a lot of time. If you are targeting locally mobile salespeople, you may find that they stop often at convenience stores. Or they may be doing business sipping on a latte in their favorite coffee shop. These places then can become media planning opportunities.

MEDIA EFFICIENCIES

With so many possible choices for geographic targeting, it may be confusing to understand whether a local or national plan (or something in between) is warranted. One thing to look at is efficiencies. Depending on the number of local markets that are targeted, the cost of the local markets combined may be more expensive than purchasing national media for some types of media channels. In particular, it is likely to be more efficient to buy national or network television if you are going to spend money in two-thirds of the United States. These efficiencies will differ by media, so investigating these costs relative to your geographic strategy is important.

SUMMARY

Geographic planning is a key element in media planning. The first step in the process is to understand your market-area definitions. From there, you can analyze your brand's strengths and weaknesses. Next, develop your BDI/CDI analysis.

Determine how you are going to treat different market groups. Then look for economies of scale as you roll out your brand nationally.

The final frontier?

Is outer space the "final frontier" for outdoor advertising? A number of companies are boldly going where no advertiser has gone before and creating opportunities for brands to take advantage of this new opportunity.

Breath mint brand Tic Tac was aware that UFO spotters had often mentioned that these unidentified flying objects were shaped like a Tic Tac. Using a UK-based company that specializes in launching things into space, Tic Tac launched a vessel containing 100 packs of Tic Tacs and a screen that featured tweets from fans. The vessel reached an altitude of over 121,000 feet (almost 23 miles) and the voyage lasted about three hours. After announcing the launch on its social channels, Tic Tac saw over a 1,000% increase in engagements with the content.

Another company, startup Geometric Energy Corp. plans to blast a satellite into space aboard a SpaceX Falcon 9 rocket with a pixelated screen that will air ad messages. The satellite is tiny – a cube that is four inches on each side – and will have an attached type of selfie-stick that will beam the messages back to earth.

While it is unclear whether the spaceships owned by Tesla's Elon Musk, Amazon's Jeff Bezos, and Virgin's Richard Branson will accept advertising on the outside of their rocket ships, we should expect to see more extraterrestrial opportunities in the years go come.

CHAPTER 13

Seasonality and timing

....

WHAT TIME IS IT? TIME TO TALK TIMING!

The time of year your advertising runs is a critical factor in your advertising campaign. Just like your target audience or your geographic selection, proper timing can make the difference between an effective campaign outcome and a marginal result. The time of year affects media costs, media effectiveness, and consumers' buying patterns. Nevertheless, there are lots of other advertising media scheduling factors that you must consider, including schedule flexibility, the pace or rate of advertising, the share of advertising, and possible scheduling remedies for competitive actions.

SEASONALITY AND TIMING STRATEGIES

Understanding when to apply communication pressure is one of the key components of your media plan. Grasping the timing component requires doing market and consumer research. From a market perspective, you want to understand when the brand is purchased. Is it purchased on a certain day, at a certain time, in a certain month? Or is there no distinctive sales pattern to its purchase? The first step in determining when you want to schedule support is to analyze when consumers are buying your brand and competitive brands. You should also review when the competitive brands historically schedule their communication efforts.

From a consumer perspective, you want to understand when the consumer uses the brand, how often they use it, and what steps they take in purchasing the brand. Is it an impulse purchase or a studied purchase? Is it something they consume often or only once in a while? By understanding the consumer's approach to buying the brand, you can better direct your communication timing.

DOI: 10.4324/9781003258162-13

To a large degree, your message is going to dictate your timing as well. There are three basic ways to view timing relative to the consumer's purchase of the brand.

- Pre-need: Timing your communication to lead into the typical time when a consumer buys the brand.
- At-need: Timing your communication to be at the time when the consumer needs the brand.
- Post-need: Timing your communication to be after the time a consumer buys the brand.

Let's take a look at each of these timing approaches. Have you ever noticed how you start seeing messages touting Mother's Day approximately two weeks before that specific holiday? That is an example of pre-need advertising. By creating awareness prior to an event, advertisers hope to increase the pool of people who may buy their product. This is a standard retail approach for just about any holiday or time when there is a natural buying event. An example of a natural buying event is in August/September, which is when most students go back to school.

Trying to time your communication to intercept consumers when they actually need the product is another strategic approach. For example, if you are driving in your car listening to the radio around noon, you are likely to hear a number of fast-food restaurants advertising. These restaurants assume you may be hungry. They want to seed their message while you may be considering where you are going to eat. Another example is an auto parts store scheduling advertising for wiper blades during days when it is likely to rain. They are putting their message at the time of need. This technique is exactly why search or pay-per-click advertising is so popular. There is no better time to place your ad than when someone is actually looking for the product.

Timing your communication to fall after the consumer buys the brand is in recognition of relieving post-purchase cognitive dissonance, a phenomenon typically associated with a consumer purchase of expensive products. Having made a large purchase, consumers are sometimes unsure if they made the right decision and often look for a support or rationale for why it is a good purchase. This type of advertising can help bolster overall customer satisfaction with the brand and assure consumers that they have made the right choice. Luxury goods such as jewelry, watches, computers, and certain automobiles make use of this type of timing.

The timing of communication can either capture demand or help create demand. By timing your communication to coincide with when consumers are in the market for your product, you are attempting to capture demand. This is why so much advertising is done in November and December. Companies are using communication to help capture demand for holiday spending. Another method of timing is to help create demand at times that are normally slow. For example, De Beers, the world's largest diamond trader and manufacturer, developed a spring/summer campaign to encourage women to "reward" themselves by purchasing a diamond. The goal of this campaign was to stimulate off-peak demand, since more than half of all diamonds are sold in November and December.

TABLE 13.1 Media effectiveness by quarters of the year

| Network television | Index of Average household rating by Quarter Index based on annual average household rating | | | |
	1st quarter (Q1)	2nd quarter (Q2)	3rd quarter (Q3)	4th quarter (Q4)
Daytime	97	91	126	95
Early news	108	96	94	102
Prime time	107	94	92	107
Late fringe	101	100	99	100

Seasons and quarters

Certainly, advertising makes use of the seasons of the year: winter, spring, summer, and fall. But advertising media seasonality refers to a bit more than the four seasons. It also refers to quarters of the year. The first quarter is January through March, the second quarter is April through June, the third quarter is July through September, and the fourth quarter is October through December. These four quarters do not line up exactly with the 12 months of the year; rather, because there are 52 weeks in the year, a quarter is 13 weeks long. Therefore, advertising flights, or waves, are often 13 weeks long as well.

The cost and effectiveness of media vary with the time of year, too. Because so much advertising appears during the Christmas shopping season, the fourth quarter has the most advertising – in all media, print as well as broadcast. That means higher levels of competitive advertising during the fourth quarter, which also means that each advertising placement may be less effective during the fourth quarter simply because there are so many competing messages (see Table 13.1). Because of the high demand for advertising during the fourth quarter, the media vehicles may raise their advertising rates then, too, which can make advertising in the fourth quarter not only less effective but also more expensive (see Table 13.2).

On the other hand, there is comparatively little advertising in the first quarter, not because it is the beginning of the year, but because it follows the highly used fourth quarter. Many advertisers expend the bulk of their advertising budgets during the fourth quarter, so they pull back during the first quarter of the following year. But it is during the first quarter that consumers' media usage goes up because bad weather

TABLE 13.2 Index of advertising costs by quarter of the year (per: 30 spot)

Network television	Q1	Q2	Q3	Q4
Daytime	81	94	128	93
Early news	100	110	74	116
Prime time	93	102	84	121
Late fringe	96	106	92	106

keeps many people at home. In broadcast, especially television, there may also be good programming during the February ratings sweeps, because high-quality programs build viewership. The first quarter may be a bargain for television advertisers. Choice of insertion times is broad because fewer advertisers are trying to buy television advertising time, there are fewer competitive advertisements on the air, and viewership is at one of the year's highest levels.

Other media have their own seasonal patterns. For example, newspaper readership is apt to drop during the summer when people go on vacation and suspend their subscriptions. Magazine readership may dwindle during the Christmas shopping season and then increase after the holidays, when the weather is poor for out-of-home activities. Radio usage increases in the summer when school is out. And because days are longer in the summer, people spend more time outside than they do in the winter, resulting in good opportunities to schedule out-of-house advertising.

Minimal seasonality is seen for digital advertising and overall usage of digital devices, mostly because of the ubiquitous nature of mobile phones, which allow access to all parts of the Internet whether an individual is at home or out and about.

Buying patterns affected by the weather

Consumer purchasing patterns vary during the year, depending on both the product category and the weather. If there is a heavy snowfall at the beginning of winter, consumers may look for snow blowers, thinking it will be a long, snowy winter. If snow falls in March, consumers are less likely to shop for snow tires, figuring they have already made it through the worst of the winter without them. Similarly, a heat wave in May will spur sales of air conditioners, but a heat wave in September may not, again, because consumers believe that they have already been through the worst that the hot summer season has to offer.

Packaged goods may benefit from weather changes at any time, though. Whether there is a heat wave in May or September, sales of soft drinks will jump. No one is going to refuse a cool drink in September just because most of the summer has already passed. The cold weather in winter typically causes canned soup sales to climb; during the warm summer months, though, hot soup is not nearly as popular. Barbeque sauce is popular during the summer, but in year-round warm climes, barbeque sauce is popular all year long.

Weather and weather forecasts can be used as an advertising strategy. For example, Quaker Oats ran a historic campaign based on the theme: "Below 50 degrees is oatmeal weather," and the company worked with the media to trigger the message when the local temperatures fell below 50 degrees. Similarly, allergy medications work with media channels to create heavy-ups during periods when allergens are rising.

By using Google Analytics, you can predict the seasonal impact of a given brand. Just by analyzing the keyword for the category, competitors, and the brand, you can establish a seasonal pattern on which weeks and months consumers most often search for those words. This is a handy tool to establish or confirm the seasonal consumption patterns for the brand.

Day of week and time of day

The season or quarter and the annual climate may affect your media selections and insertions. Similarly, the time of day and the day of the week may be important, too. Golf balls may be advertised on daytime television, but likely only on the weekend. Hair products and packaged food items may do well advertised on daytime television during the week. Lawn fertilizer and health items may do better during the early news or on prime time (roughly 8:00 to 11:00 in the evening).

OTHER SCHEDULING FACTORS

Season, quarter, day, and time are all important, but they may be largely intuitive, and they are among the least complex factors in timing. Several other kinds of timing considerations also come into play in advertising media scheduling, all of importance, yet perhaps not as intuitively obvious.

Susceptibility

Consumers may be more susceptible to a message at certain times. Sylvania has had success in focusing its advertising for light bulbs on the day when daylight saving time ends and it gets dark earlier. Consumers are more attuned to lights at that time. A classic campaign was conducted for Brinks Home Security, which ran a radio announcement during work hours that asked, "While you are at work, who is watching your home?" These are good examples of exploiting certain times of day, based on consumers' susceptibility.

Flexibility

You may need flexibility in your media buys so you can switch from one media placement to others. Quick tactical maneuvers or other media schedule changes may be needed to meet competitive assaults or to take advantage of such external shifts as economic changes, unusual weather, consumer fads, and real or perceived threats.

When the World Trade Center was brought down by an act of terrorism on September 11, 2001, sales opportunities increased for security products and decreased for vacation packages. When crime rose on one Caribbean island, that locale developed a serious marketing problem; at the same time, other Caribbean islands made gains in tourism as they promoted their safety and security. During the first weeks of the Covid-19 pandemic, brands that could promote their touchless deliveries capitalized on new consumer behaviors, and brands increased their budgets in the digital sphere as digital allowed a much higher level of message flexibility, which was important given the levels of uncertainty in the world. If the economy takes a dip, sales of packaged goods may remain steady, but consumers may switch to smaller packages that require less cash outlay. A longer-than-normal rainy season in spring may delay purchases of lawn weed killers, making it necessary to extend the advertising flights to match; the same can happen with automotive antifreeze when extended warm weather lasts into autumn.

Rate of advertising

Even your advertising budget may be a scheduling factor. Low levels of advertising are likely to bring low levels of customer response. High levels of advertising, on the other hand, are extremely and sometimes prohibitively expensive.

We have already seen how advertising expenditures can be ameliorated or leveled out by advertising in waves. High-expenditure flights can be offset by low-advertising hiatus periods. Waves of advertising permit you to gain high visibility when it is needed, followed by reminders during less intense time periods. At the same time, the advertising budget is stretched out so the campaign can cover more of the year.

Share of advertising

Another type of unanticipated challenge may come from your competitors. If you have more to spend on advertising than any of your competitors do, congratulations! You are in a rare position. But even then, you need to turn your dominant share of money into a dominant share of advertising, which is not always as easy as it might seem. It requires at least parity in advertising message strength and competitive efficiency in media selection and buying. Otherwise, the financial advantage will disappear and your firm will be just another part of the competitive pack.

More likely, you do not have as much money to spend on advertising as your largest competitor does. If your competition is spending at a level that you cannot possibly match, then you will probably choose to advertise in waves. Determining when the waves should run depends on a number of factors: the purchase cycle of your brand, the likelihood of brand-switching by your customers, the anticipated levels of competitive activities, and the life cycle of your brand and your product category.

You can also meet a larger competitor by not trying to match dollar-for-dollar and insertion-for-insertion across the board. Instead, you may be able to match the strongest competitor during parts of the year; if so, why waste money by spreading it thinly throughout the entire year? Another approach is to match your largest competitor in certain markets rather than throughout the entire country. Or you may be more selective in your choice of audiences; this strategy will give you matching advertising weight against the primary audience, even though you may have to sacrifice reaching audiences of lesser importance.

VARYING ADVERTISING SCHEDULING PATTERNS

There are several reasons why you may wish to vary your advertising placement schedule. Sometimes customers can be "unsold" by too much advertising. In broadcast, it is possible to induce an *irritation factor*, when potential customers become so tired of seeing your advertising that they not only flip channels but actually begin to have a negative reaction to the surplus of advertising. You may not advertise so much that you irritate your audience, but there is no reason to advertise past the optimum point of exposure; going past the optimum advertising level is wasteful, even when it isn't irritating.

If you are using the same advertising schedule from day to day, and you have more than one television commercial that you can run, you may want to alternate the commercials so the viewers do not tire of seeing the same message over and over. If you have only one or two similar commercials, then consider varying the times when they appear so you are not always exposing the same audience to the identical message.

As mentioned earlier, some products have life cycles. If your goods fall into this pattern, it may be advisable to reduce or quit advertising for a while, allowing for a "gestation period" when the advertising information can sink in and have an effect.

Sometimes, short bursts of advertising such as in a wave pattern can produce more sales than a steady amount of heavy advertising. Saving money while gaining greater impact would certainly be attractive and it would make sense to follow through.

These possibilities may be unique to your brand or to your product category. Because of the differences between products and brands, it is not possible to lay out rules or standards for every kind of advertising media operation. Good research, close observation, and insightful common sense will determine which, if any, of these situations applies to you and how you should proceed.

STARTING DATE

Many advertising campaigns are scheduled for a year at a time – typically a fiscal year or a sales year rather than a calendar year. But no matter what kind of year, the advertising starting date need not be the first day of the campaign.

Let's say that your advertising is planned for the calendar year. Should you start your advertising placements on January 1? If you have an item that fits appropriately into New Year's parades and football games, maybe you should start then. Most products and services, however, do not fit that mode. New Year's Day advertising is competitive and, thus, expensive, yet viewers do not always pay close attention; they are often gathered in groups, talking and eating while the television set is on, and some members of the audience are likely to be recovering from the night before. All these factors make New Year's Day a less attractive advertising opportunity – unless, of course, your item fits in well and you can afford it.

Similarly, if your advertising campaign year begins at any other time during the year, you do not need to begin advertising placements on the very first day. Look at the buying patterns, competitive advertising, your budget, and your preferred waves or other advertising patterns. Base your decisions on your objectives and your strategies, including your scheduling strategies.

DIFFERENT CALENDARS

When most people refer to a calendar, they are talking about a January-through-December calendar year. Many brands budget for a calendar year; others do not. As a media planner, it is crucial to understand your brand's budget year. That year will have a huge impact over how you schedule your communication.

Many brands work on a fiscal year that is not the same as a calendar year. A fiscal year is how the brand or company reports their financial performance. If the company is publicly traded, each quarter is a crucial milestone for the company with Wall Street and its shareholders. It is not uncommon for a company to delay advertising or to cut advertising to meet a short-term financial target. As you build a media plan for such a company, understanding the financial implications of your plan can help you optimize how you schedule the support.

Most retailers operate on a February-to-January fiscal year. Instead of the first quarter being January, February, and March, a retailer's first quarter would cover February, March, and April. The purpose of a fiscal year is to help the company mitigate its financial risk and to provide time for proper accounting of its revenue. Since most retailers generate a large amount of their income from sales in December, they use January to sort out their year's financial situation. Consumer packaged-goods food companies often operate on a July-to-June fiscal year, otherwise known as a crop year. Crops are planted in the spring and harvested during the fall. By having a July-to-June fiscal year, these companies understand the impact of commodity prices on their various brands. This allows them to make decisions regarding pricing.

Many brands, advertising agencies, and/or media buying companies schedule their media using a broadcast calendar. A broadcast calendar is a standard calendar used to purchase television and radio time. It always begins on a Monday and ends on a Sunday. Every month in a broadcast calendar has four or five weeks with up to 35 days in the month. The number of weeks in a broadcast month is based on the number of Sundays that fall in that month with the period ending on the last Sunday in the month. As a result, a January broadcast month could contain days from the previous December—in fact, it is not uncommon for broadcast months to cross calendar months. Broadcast calendars are important in the advertising industry since much of the media billing is based on this calendar and not a calendar year. This becomes important as a brand ends its fiscal year and must reconcile its budget.

Of course, many countries are on a different schedule altogether, particularly those who are in the southern hemisphere of the world. In these countries, summer occurs in December, January, and February, while winter occurs in June, July, and August. In these countries, the school year may begin in February, not September. In China, the New Year begins sometime in late January or early February, and is as festive as the New Year's Eve celebrated in other parts of the world.

ADVERTISING SCHEDULING

When you plan your campaign schedule, start with a good calendar that includes all the holidays and special events; note, for instance, that candy sales increase for Secretaries' Day, an event that is not included on all calendars. Then begin to put together your advertising schedule. Most of the time, the calendar is transferred to a flowchart, which shows the patterns of advertising along with the levels of advertising, all on a sheet or slide that incorporates the proposed advertising schedule, advertising weights, and respective target audiences for the entire campaign period.

In addition to your marketing and advertising objectives, your audience targets, your geographic targets, and your scheduling aims, you will want to consider the competition and the creative needs of your brand's message and their implications for your advertising media plan. That is the subject of Chapters 14 and 15.

POLITICAL CAMPAIGNS

By law in the United States, political candidates get the lowest media rates offered by a media outlet, along with first rights to that inventory. There are specific times, called political windows, when this law is evoked. In the United States, a political window is a six-week period that leads into primary elections (usually in the spring) or a specific election, held in November, for a local, state, or national position.

The impact of the political window is particularly relevant to advertisers who use broadcast media where only a limited number of commercial units are available. The risk that an advertiser runs by scheduling advertising during a political window is that the ad may not run as scheduled. For example, there have been times in recent history when more than 50% of all news commercials have been aired by various political parties. Meanwhile, advertisers who may have booked that time well in advance are left looking for alternative programs or media.

The second impact of the political window is on media costs. Since broadcast properties must sell political commercials at their lowest unit rate, they are less likely to negotiate low rates with their regular advertisers during these political time periods for fear of losing considerable dollars per unit sold. For these reasons, your role as a savvy advertising media planner becomes even more crucial – and complicated – during an election year.

CULTURAL CONSIDERATIONS

Media and brand planners must be aware of the variety of cultural events and celebrations that occur around the world, and understand how that may affect planning. For example, Ramadan is the ninth month of the Islamic calendar, and Muslims around the world observe this month as a time for fasting, reflection, prayer, and community. From a media perspective, people celebrating Ramadan are likely to spend more time online; in some communities, people work fewer hours and have a preference to stay at home. Media activitiy regularly increases after Iftar, the nightly feast that breaks the fast.

In Japan, a three-day festival happens during July and August. The Obon festival, part of the Japanese Buddhist tradition, encourages people to return to their ancestral family homes. During their visits, people often visit the graves of their ancestors, and gifts are often left on gravestones or altars. Life during this time focuses on the family, and mediated messages may be less important than during other times of the year.

These are just two examples of cultural considerations that brand planners should be aware of when planning on a global basis.

SUMMARY

Seasonality and timing play a crucial role in your media plan. The seasonality of the brand's consumption pattern will help dictate when you schedule media. Seasonality also plays a role in the cost efficiencies of different media. Tactically, the timing of advertising can be used to make a larger-than-life impact on the media schedule.

Brinks scares you straight to buying home security

When the creative work and the media plan come together seamlessly, advertising magic happens. One example is from Brinks Home Security.

Recently, a host of do-it-yourself security systems have entered the marketplace – things like the Ring video doorbell and the SimpliSafe system. These differ from Brinks in that they do not automatically provide professional monitoring – that is, someone who will come to your home quickly if there is a problem. Some of the systems provide professional monitoring for an additional price, but Brinks provides it automatically as part of the purchase of the system.

However, Brinks was losing share to the new competition, so they developed a breakthrough strategy to market their home security system. It began by asking the question, "When are homeowners most concerned about home security?" The answer: When they are not home! This led to a media blitz during the morning commute and ending at noon with the simple message, "You aren't home. Do you know who is?" Radio ads aired during morning drive-time radio followed by digital ads tailored to the workplace at noon. Together, it scared up lots of business for Brinks.

South Side succeeds

When the cable channel Comedy Central introduced a new show called "South Side," it used the show's premise to guide its media plans.

The show, set on the south side of Chicago, tells the story of two young entrepreneurs and their sometimes crazy business ideas (such as selling popcorn on street corners). Media placements to promote the premiere included a takeover of the "L" train station near Guaranteed Rate Field on the south side, home of the Chicago White Sox. The channel also set up screenings of the show at south-side barbershops. While traditional television and radio spots were also used, one innovative scheduling had a TV ad placed on the broadcast of the NBA draft, running right after the Chicago Bull's pick.

Such innovative placements helped make South Side the top comedy premier in 2019 and the top cable comedy watched by African Americans.

CHAPTER 14

Competitive analysis

....

YOUR COMPETITION CAN TEACH YOU A LOT

If all we had to do to succeed in advertising media planning was figure out the right message to send, the right audience to receive that message, and the right number of times to send it, advertising planning would be a breeze. But most brands don't live in isolation. Just as we are trying to persuade the consumer to try our brand, some other brand manager is looking to do the same thing.

Competitive analysis is crucial for establishing a point of difference for your brand as well as for developing the competitive attack plan. Using a competitive analysis in a strategic manner can lead to a number of media strategy decisions. For example, suppose you see a trend emerging where all the competitors in your category are moving their money from television to magazines; that might indicate an opportunity to stand out from the pack by increasing your television exposure. Perhaps your spending is not keeping up with the other brands in the category; this may force you to rethink your national strategy and place greater emphasis on key spot markets where you have the greatest volume.

In today's environment, you must be able to react quickly to competitive threats. Most brands have contingency plans that are based on competitive scenarios. Fortunately, there are a number of competitive information tools on the market today that offer a wealth of data about your brand and the brands against which you compete.

COMPETITIVE TOOLS

For brands with hefty budgets, purchasing data from a syndicated source can quickly identify competitive activity. The largest of these sources is Kantar Media, a company that tracks brand media activities around the globe. Their service monitors

DOI: 10.4324/9781003258162-14

EXHIBIT 14.1 SWOT ANALYSIS

	Opportunities tomorrow	Threats tomorrow
Strengths today	You are poised to take advantage	You are strong to defend against threats
Weaknesses today	You are not positioned well to seize opportunities	Your survivability is threatened

hundreds of millions of ads each year across more than 20 traditional and digital media channels. Then, the ads are classified by product, brand, and category, and Kantar reports on daypart, ad network, format, length, and more. This allows brands to have a good snapshot of the media mix and expenditures of their competitors. They also can track whether TV and radio ads ran across 210 US and Canadian markets, helping brands understand their return on investment (ROI) from specific executions and placements.

Although the usual lag time between gathering data and actually reporting on it is approximately six weeks, quick "topline" reports allow brands to see information on a competitor's broadcast commercial within a week, so the data can be very current.

Let's take a look at how we can use some of this competitive intelligence.

SWOT

As discussed in Chapter 10, a common approach to analyzing an advertising and marketing competitive situation is the SWOT method, which stands for strengths, weaknesses, opportunities, and threats. The strengths and weaknesses analyze the internal situation as it is now; the opportunities and threats analyze the external situation as it will be in the future, usually three to five years from now. Exhibit 14.1 shows how these analyses work together to cover good and bad situations, both now and in the future.

The SWOT process is widely used because it is relatively simple and quick to administer. It provides useful information about a firm, a brand, an advertising agency, or any other similar organization. Many advertising managers make use of SWOT or similar techniques because of these advantages.

The outcomes of a SWOT analysis are simply assessed in a combination of visual and written analyses, as Exhibit 14.2 shows.

SHARE OF SPENDING VERSUS SHARE OF VOICE

The classic way to use competitive information is to understand how much your brand spends in relation to your competitors. Sometimes *share of spending* (SOS) is called *share of voice* (SOV) analysis. Although many media people use these two terms interchangeably, they are different. SOS is just that – the percentage of total

EXHIBIT 14.2 SAMPLE ADVERTISING SWOT

	Opportunities	**Threats**
	Targeted ads	Local economy downturn
	Partnerships	Aging population
	Growing audience	Operating expense inflation
	High demand for research database	Competition for employees Audience expectations changing
	Need for information	Stagnation
Strengths	You are poised to take advantage	You are strong to defend against threats
Financial strength		
Strong local franchise		
Ad content		
Local relationships		
Autonomy		
Ads get results		
Weaknesses	You are not positioned well to seize opportunity	Your survivability is threatened
Lack of diverse workforce		
Only two revenue streams		
Low understanding of customers		
Nonresponsive to audience		
Not tech savvy		
Cost structure		

dollars you spend in the category. So SOS uses absolute dollars as the measuring stick regardless of the medium. In SOS, a dollar is a dollar whether it is spent on television, print, or outdoor advertising. For example, in 2010, Subway was spending at an $80 million level in the fast-food category, which was 6% of the total spending for its category. SOV, on the other hand, involves the actual impressions delivered as a percentage of the total category impressions. SOV then takes into account the delivery for each medium, so it draws a distinction between television and print. Whereas Subway represented 6% of the total spending, the firm may represent 10% of the total impressions in the category because Subway had a more efficient mix of media than did the category as a whole. Because these two measures of competitive spending may yield different results, it is extremely important to clarify which analysis is being performed.

SOS/SOM OR SOV/SOM ANALYSIS

Once you get a grip on your brand's SOS or SOV, you will want to compare those figures to the market share (*share of market*, or SOM) levels you and your competitors have. This comparison is called either SOS/SOM or SOV/SOM analysis. For example, if your

TABLE 14.1 Share of voice and share of market comparison

	SOV	SOM	Index
Allworld	38	50	76
Big Bell	38	37.5	101
The Admiral	13	7.5	173
Cross Country	11	5	220
Total Category Spending (000)	$1140	$40	

Note: Fictitious insurance agencies.

brand has a 30% market share with a 15% share of category spending, then you would have a ratio of 50; to find this figure, divide the 15% share of spending by the 30% market share (15 ÷ 30 × 100). If you are aggressively trying to gain market share, you may want to spend at a level above your current share. If you are the leader in the market, you may want to maintain a spending level equal to your share so that competitors won't erode your market share. Regardless of your strategy, the SOS/SOM analysis is a good building block to guide you to the proper amount you should invest in your brand.

Many studies correlate these two variables. That is why many brand management teams review these calculations. Table 14.1 shows a hypothetical example in the insurance category. Notice that Allworld, the category leader, has advertising spending that is less than we might expect given its market share. The other competitors are spending disproportionately in an effort to take market share from Allworld.

NEW BRAND INTRODUCTIONS

Suppose you were tasked with introducing a new line of pasta sauce into a very crowded category. How much would you spend to introduce them? Without a market share, it is tough to do the SOV/SOM calculation. But competitive spending is still crucial to your budget plans. Most brands estimate the market share they want to garner in their second year, after the brand is introduced. Then they analyze the competition's spending. New brands typically peg an introductory rate at one-and-a-half to two times that of their Year 2 market share goals. For example, if your goal is to get 5% of the pasta sauce market, then you would spend up to 10% of the current category spending. Any marketer who is planning to introduce a new product relies on a competitive spending analysis to help determine how much money should be allocated to advertising.

MEDIA STRATEGY

Competitive spending is a good strategic tool for making media decisions. The Heath candy bar was a small brand that faced strong competition in its category. The majority of spending was done leading into Halloween. Heath's sales spiked in October. It had another spike in the spring, around Easter, when category spending was less pronounced. Heath shifted its spending to emphasize Easter and other key times of the year when the brand could make an impact.

TABLE 14.2 Total media spending (millions)

Brand	TV	Print	Social Media marketing	Digital display	Search (PPC)
Allworld	87	22	87	57	52
Big Bell	108	0	22	87	44
The Admiral	23	0	15	35	11
Cross Country	17.5	12	17.5	50	6

Another strategy decision might be in the media choice itself. If the majority of the category dollars are going to television and you have the opportunity to stand out in radio, then shifting your advertising to radio might be worth considering.

Competitive spending can also be used to determine tactical decisions: In what specific part of the day could your brand make an impact? Is there a creative unit that you might want to use to tell your story? Is there a specific day or days of the week when it may be more beneficial for your brand to run its spot?

All of these questions point to competitive gaps that can be exploited. So, when approaching media strategy, ask yourself if there is something that you can do to stand out from your competitors.

This is certainly the case in the insurance category shown in Table 14.2. Because Allworld and Big Bell dominate the spending, other brands are forced to look at alternative media in order to stand out. The Admiral and Cross Country both allocate a large amount of its budget into social media marketing and keep television spending to a minimum.

ADVERTISING-TO-SALES RATIOS

Another use of a competitive spending analysis is to determine the advertising-to-sales ratios for your competitors to see what percentage of their revenue they are spending on media advertising. The advertising-to-sales ratio is calculated by dividing the total advertising expenditures by the total amount of brand sales, or revenue. In our hypothetical example, Allworld is a $20 billion brand spending $437 million on advertising. Allworld's advertising-to-sales ratio was 2.1%. Contrast those figures with The Admiral, a $3 billion brand spending at a $151 million level, or an advertising-to-sales ratio of 5%. Allworld was spending almost three times the amount that The Admiral was spending on an absolute basis, but only about half of the ad to sales ratio (see Table 14.3).

TABLE 14.3 Advertising-to-sales ratio

	Allworld	The Admiral
Sales	$20 billion	$3 billion
Advertising expenditures	$437 million	$151 million
Advertising-to-sales ratio	2.1%	5%

The advertising-to-sales percentage is a senior management tool for determining overall budget allocation. Management can use this analysis to determine if the company is being too aggressive or not aggressive enough in its allocation of overall marketing and communication resources. When an overall discussion of how a company should allocate its money comes up, analysis such as advertising-to-sales competitive benchmarks become a crucial factor in overall brand marketing communication funding.

DETERMINING TRENDS IN SPENDING

Another great use of competitive spending information is to calculate a trend line analysis. The media planner should update such an analysis every year. You want to see whether spending in the category increases or decreases over time and at what rate. You can compare this result to the sales growth in the category to determine the vitality of the category. If the category is growing at only 2% per year in sales, yet advertising is growing at a 10% rate, it tells you that a healthy return is going to be tougher to attain. Conversely, if you have a fast-growing category with slower advertising growth, it might suggest that you step up your own support of the brand.

Trends can be helpful to identify a change in spending patterns over time. Perhaps the category is gradually moving money from television into print, or maybe dollars once funneled into the fourth quarter are now in the third quarter. Over time, you can see how the category behaves and use this information to help chart your media course.

MARKETING-MIX MODELS

Many brands today conduct sophisticated marketing-mix modeling. This research is made possible by the availability of a tremendous amount of consumer data. With so many grocery chains using loyalty programs that capture individual purchase behavior, the ability to track purchases and relate them to various marketing elements is a ready-made laboratory. Both Nielsen and IRI use these to purchase data and work with manufacturers on developing marketing-mix models. They combine this robust information with powerful multivariate statistical analysis to determine what aspects of the marketing mix are most effective. One element of designing a marketing-mix model is the brand's media spending and the competitors' spending. Marketing-mix models can help brand managers understand the impact of all their marketing elements as well as how individual media perform.

For example, in Table 14.4 we see that our fictitious brand, Bob's Beans, is extremely sensitive to advertising. For every dollar that Bob's Beans spends on media advertising, the brand receives a return of $1.50. This return is much higher than the return from using an FSI with a coupon or using trade promotions. So, based on this analysis, Bob's Beans should be an aggressive advertiser.

Each brand is going to have its own set of dynamics. One brand may be especially sensitive to advertising, whereas another may respond well only to trade promotion

TABLE 14.4 Marketing-Mix model: Bob's Beans

Item	Incremental profit per $1 spent
Media advertising	$1.50
FSI coupons	$1.00
Trade promotions	$0.85

or couponing. With the power of these customer databases, much of what works and what doesn't work can be explained. Competitive media spending plays a crucial role in this sophisticated analysis.

Competitive spending information is a powerful tool for media planning. It can lead to breakout strategies, help determine specific spending levels, and be trended and analyzed within sophisticated marketing models. Competitive spending can be significant in setting communication goals.

SUMMARY

Competitive media analysis provides a framework for making a variety of strategic decisions. It begins at the top by providing senior management with a method to gauge how much they should allocate to a brand's marketing communication budget; it then becomes a strategic tool for how the brand actually allocates this budget. This type of analysis can be used tactically to adjust the media mix to gain a competitive advantage.

CHAPTER 15

Working with creative

Implications in planning

···

IS THE MEDIUM REALLY THE MESSAGE?

In most advertising agencies, the term *creative* is used to describe the function whereby the actual advertising campaigns and specific advertisements are thought up and developed. Sometimes the term *creative* applies only to the copywriter and art director teams that work on an account; other times, it may involve production or digital development as well. Even though we are talking about the creative implications for the media portion of the advertising campaign, don't think that creative work occurs only when dealing with those who produce the message. Creative elements are vital to media selection and planning, in research, and in other phases of the advertising effort, too; creativity is not limited just to those who develop and produce the actual advertisements. Perhaps a better term would be *message functions*, like media functions, research functions, production functions, and management functions.

In this chapter, we use the terms *creative* and *message* interchangeably to reflect their use in the advertising industry while recognizing that there can still be creativity in other advertising functions.

CREATIVE WANTS

"We've got to use a :60 TV ad. It's the only thing that is able to handle our message, and we can run it on both network television and on digital," says the creative team. The media team looks at the advertising budget and replies, "Network television is completely out of the question. We can't afford it."

Many times, the creative people working on an advertising account will have definite needs that influence the media selection; other times, they will have preferences that may not be absolute requirements but that match their initial campaign approaches. For example, if a new shaving cream lends itself well to demonstration, there may be a concomitant need for such media as television, cinema, and digital, all of which offer forms of

DOI: 10.4324/9781003258162-15

demonstration. Similarly, if vivid color is needed, that requirement may preclude the use of newspapers and nonvisual media such as radio, whereas television and the Internet may remain under consideration, and other print media with good color capabilities (such as outdoor billboards and magazines) would be strong candidates for the media campaign.

At other times, though, the creative department may have a preconception about the creative approach that may or may not deserve control over media choices. A copywriter may say, "I envision a video commercial with a woman in a flowing gown, walking through a series of video montages." That may be a nice image, but it is essential to determine whether there is a real marketing-, product-, or service-related circumstance that actually requires the use of television or other visual media. It is simply an idea, one that may be accommodated by the media plan if it can be afforded.

In still other instances, the creative department may want to use certain media that are simply not good media choices because they do not reach the audience. If a creative person indicates that newspapers should be used to distribute coupons for an acne cream, it may be a poor media choice because the likely audience – teenagers – do not usually read newspapers, either regularly or closely. If you need to reach teens and teens are always on their phones and other digital devices, then digital media should be considered for the media buys. Don't get locked into preconceptions of how certain media work; for example, coupons and similar offers can be distributed through many kinds of media, not just traditional print.

Remember the persona that was discussed in Chapter 11? Whenever different creative opportunities are being discussed, be sure to refer to the persona to see how that media channel fits into their life. Think about the type of experience and interaction that person will have with the different media choices that are being considered. Putting the audience first is always a good strategy.

Good communication among media and strategic planners and the creative department is essential. Exhibits 15.1 and 15.2 provide some interesting perspectives from people currently in the field.

EXHIBIT 15.1 SOME THOUGHTS FROM AN EXPERIENCED MEDIA PLANNER

Maybe the point to be made upfront is that the overall media selection is an advertising decision. It requires that media and creative work together on the best approach to get the job done. There may be compromise on either side.

For example, when Motel 6 first broke its Tom Bodett radio campaign on network radio, the media group argued for a :30 spot because it is half the cost of a :60 spot. Stan Richards, the principal of the Richards Group, didn't feel that Tom could pull it off in a :30, so they went to a :60. It has been one of the most successful campaigns in radio.

On the efficiency side, nearly 50% of all network television commercials are :15, so media planners have had a real impact there.

What we do is a series of trade-off exercises with the creatives to see what is possible. That brings me to the other point, which is the actual creative unit used – the other major trade-off on creative. Do we use a magazine full page or can a two-thirds of a page do the job? How about 30 seconds versus the cost savings and time for the message in 15 seconds on television?

EXHIBIT 15.2 SOME THOUGHTS FROM EXPERIENCED CREATIVES

Essentially, there are no real trade-offs (between media and creative) anymore. The sheer complexity and breadth of media coupled with an increasingly diverse competitive landscape means that media and creative must be in sync. One without the other is a losing hand.

We worked on an auto parts chain where we did periodic window wiper promotions. Nothing special. Then a media planner obtained an analysis that indicated that the wiper buying decision spiked when the forecast called for a 50% or greater chance of rain. So, we tailored radio creative to that moment and worked with media to trigger ads at that forecasted level. The result: sales surged by 25%.

Anything that requires more work outside the norm has obstacles. We had a concept for a Burma Shave outdoor style campaign around the holidays with the first board reading "Naughty," The second "Nice," and the pay-off board of "Great for whatever list you are on." Simple idea. It required three consecutive billboards, which is a problem. We secured two, but the third was taken. So, we offered to buy that board from the client in exchange for three additional boards. Problem solved. Campaign noticed.

CREATIVE NECESSITIES

As we just saw, there are some instances when there are creative necessities, as opposed to creative wants, that should or even must be accommodated by the media selection process.

- Motion and demonstration: If demonstration is needed to communicate the selling idea, visual media are a must, most likely via television, cinema, and digital. Similarly, if other kinds of motion are needed, visual media are again indicated.

  Do not limit yourself to the most obvious choices. The human mind has a tremendous capacity for imagination and visualization, even when the visual is not actually present. Tell people to imagine driving a car in the Indianapolis 500, and they may do well by providing their own motion pictures in their minds. That approach will save media money and greatly reduce the cost of production.
- Visuals: If other types of visuals are needed, the media choices can expand to include print media, such as newspapers, magazines, and outdoor advertising. Don't think only of television when visuals are required.

  Again, do not limit yourself to even those most obvious choices. Imagine yourself on the first tee at Pebble Beach golf resort, or lounging in a hot tub while gazing at the Caribbean and sipping a cool drink. You can see the image in your mind, even though you may never have actually experienced it. In the same way, you can suggest visual images to the audience through radio, sometimes at lower cost and with the resultant higher reach and frequency that the budget will provide.
- Coupon distribution: Mention coupons and people automatically think of print media such as newspapers and magazines or online couponing websites. Outdoor

advertising is not typically considered: Yet by adding a QR code or an option to send a text and receive a coupon, an outdoor billboard can be transformed into a coupon delivery vehicle. A podcast can also include a brand sponsorship message with a discount code that can be used at the brand's website. Internet users can print out their own coupons. And coupons can be attached to posters, flyers, or an in-store display.

Another way to look at couponing is as a way to provide an incentive. There are companies such as Groupon that brands can tap into to provide short-term sales incentives. An increasing number of mobile coupon companies also provide a variety of sales incentive opportunities for brands.

Coupons do not have to be actual items provided by the advertisers. They can take almost any form. Ask consumers to get your product and use it as the coupon: "Bring any Pepsi item to the water park this week and get $4 off a regular admission." You may get both sales *and* the coupon incentive. Even better, get consumers to make their own coupons. When they write out the name of your product, their memories have an even stronger impression of your brand name than when they simply hear or see it. Ask them to print your product name, service logo, or advertising theme on a piece of paper and bring it along in order to save on their purchases. By couponing in this way, you can use almost any advertising medium, including cinema, radio, transit, and outdoor.

- Information: When you want to impart specific information to the audience, there may be legitimate media implications. Long passages of detailed wording may not lend themselves to broadcast media but may be handled quite well with some print media and with the Internet.

  When providing information in your advertising, your media choices will depend on a number of other factors, such as audience familiarity, message complexity, and legal requirements.

- Audience familiarity: How familiar is the audience with your service or product, or with your advertising theme? They already know what facial tissues do (so you do not need to demonstrate them), but they may not understand what a new car wax wipe does and how it is used, so they may need to see it in action. You need not explain what Dr Pepper is; most consumers already know. But if you have a brand-new soft drink entry, you may need to tell them about it and even show the can or bottle so they recognize it next time they shop.

- Message complexity: A very long or complex message requires adequate space. Sometimes it is possible to read those explanations very rapidly over broadcast media, although nobody will really hear them, or to superimpose passages in small type at the bottom of the screen, although the audience probably will not read them or understand them. Billboards do not lend themselves to long passages of body copy, either.

But traditional print media do, as do a brand's owned media, particularly the brand's website. A brand's social media posts can direct people to that website for the information. Your media choices may be influenced greatly by the complexity and length of the intended message.

- Legal requirements: If you conduct a contest, you must provide certain information about the prizes, odds, entry methods, and purchase requirements and their alternatives. Not all of this information needs to be in the body copy; often, it is presented in small type as a footnote. Still, it must be there, and including it affects your media choices. You may be able to include such footnotes on a television screen, but they will be read and understood by very few and may only marginally meet the legal standards, and radio may not be conducive at all to including lengthy legal language.

    The same considerations apply for including loan requirements, prescription medication caveats, and other messages under similar circumstances.
- In-depth information: Sometimes you want to include information not because you are required to, but because it enhances your selling message.

    For example, you want consumers to understand how they might make use of a new product; for either a new or an existing product, you need to convey the benefits of your brand. If you are selling a food product, you may want to induce usage by providing recipes that include the product. These message requirements will certainly affect your media choices.
- Political advertising: Selling political ideas, whether lobbying for charitable support or running political advertising, may lend itself to certain media. Research shows that audience members are most likely to read and listen to media that seem to agree with their own views: Republicans follow Republican media outlets, both on television and online, and Democrats follow the Democratic versions. To promote a candidate of a certain political party, advertising in the media vehicles that are read primarily by the opposition may not be productive, whereas promoting an independent candidate through those same media vehicles may prove fruitful. However, you must take into account the ideas and parties that you are selling, as well as the competing ideas and parties, and make sure that the message is a good match for the content.

IMPLICATIONS FOR MULTIPLE AGENCIES

Brands may use a creative agency, a media agency, a public relations agency, and perhaps even specialty agencies ranging from events to digital and social media. Each different agency will likely have its own perspective on the brand's message, and this can cause a dilution of messages. For example, a *creative* solution from a public relations point of view may be very different from that of a creative agency. Digital agencies come at the problem from a digital viewpoint, and so on. In this case, a media agency may be asked to be the communication planner. Or that may fall to the brand manager. Regardless of who ultimately makes the call, it is important to provide a structure so that the brand can elicit creative problem-solving feedback from all types of communication specialists.

Coordinating media in today's multifaceted media environment is no easy task. The way a brand may structure its agency communication relationships can play a big role in the outcome.

EFFICIENCY VERSUS IMPACT

Advertising media can be used in varying weights and patterns. Spending a lot of money on reach may limit how many advertisements can be included for each medium, as well as the impact that each ad carries. Spending money on large print ads or long broadcast commercials will limit the size of audience that can be reached. This situation is the classic "efficiency versus impact" dilemma encountered in almost every media plan.

Whether emphasizing impact or efficiency, the advertising can be directed at wholesalers and retailers. This method uses a "push" strategy – to force the product or service through the distribution channel. The advertising also can focus on the eventual consumers, trying to "pull" services and products through the channel.

Only one brand can have the largest budget within any product or service category. Thus, all the remaining competitors must work with budgets that do not match that of the leader. It may be possible to have better advertisements, although there is always the danger that a highly entertaining ad will draw the audience's attention to the wrong elements. Many campaigns that have been recognized for their originality, creativity, or entertainment have failed to impress the brand name in the audiences' minds.

Those trailing brands may be able to match the budget leader in certain areas of the country, or in certain media, or for certain periods during the year, even if they cannot match up in all media for the entire campaign.

SUMMARY

Creating the best media plan possible requires the media team to work hand-in-glove with other agencies and sometimes outside company disciplines. Each discipline has its distinctive point of view. It is up to the media team to help manage this process and vet different creative ideas. Ultimately, it is through creative problem solving that the best communication and media plans are developed.

Sign spinners drive retail traffic

Picture this: you're driving down the street or walking to get coffee when you encounter someone spinning a giant arrow pointing to a mattress store or a tax preparation office. Perhaps they're dressed in costume, or standing on a corner near the mall, spinning that sign like their life depended on it. Have you ever thought "what's going on there? Is that a viable media strategy?"

Sometimes in our global and digital age, the oldest and simplest ideas can still have impact. Take the case of Arrow Signs. Arrow Signs is a franchise that provides turnkey products for sign spinning. They hire people to twirl a sign promoting a nearby retail location.

Sounds silly, doesn't it? Yet it works. Arrow Signs has a series of clients from apartments to restaurants to small retailers who swear by sign spinners. Sign spinners are effective because they can be used strategically, such as when shoppers are out doing errands on a Saturday morning. Sign spinners often perform tricks and they often smile and make a human connection while they're doing their thing.

Case studies from Arrow Signs show that the use of a sign spinner can increase traffic (that is, visits to stores on the sign) of upwards of 30% when stores hire someone to work the giant arrow. Now that is some serious spinning.

Comcast uses addressable ads to micro target in broadcast

Digital advertising is very attractive because of its ability to discreetly target a message. You are likely to see a different ad on Instagram than the person sitting next to you, all because digital platforms can track what you look at and what content you create and find messages that they think you will be likely to engage with. This ability has made digital advertising a marketing channel of choice for many advertisers.

So, why not apply those same principles to broadcast? Enter Comcast, a large US-based media company. Comcast pioneered what they refer to as addressable advertising in its cable system. This innovation means that different households watching the same program may see different commercial messages tailored to their specific lifestyles. Now advertisers can broadcast and micro cast at the same time.

One key benefit is that it allows advertisers to focus on reaching consumers, not worrying about matching the content of the program to possible viewers of the program.

For example, by using first- and third-party data, an automobile company like Honda could advertise its Odyssey minivan to a household consisting of two adults and young children, and the Honda Fit (their small electric car) to a household with a younger single adult. Both of these messages would appear in the same program, where before advertisers might select separate programming to reach these two audiences.

CHAPTER 16

Working with a budget

....

SHOW ME THE MONEY!

All brand plans begin and end with an accounting of the budget. The amount of dollars allocated to brand efforts will largely dictate the type of communication channels and tactics that are possible. For example, if your communication budget is $3 million, you won't be scheduling a national Super Bowl commercial for $6 million. The budget puts a parameter around what can be done. At the same time, though, it is up to the media planning team to develop the best recommendation given the parameter. There's a big difference between saying "the budget is $3 million" and "the budget is $3 million, so only look at digital media since it is inexpensive." As discussed in previous chapters, a number of analyses will help identify seasonality and geographic opportunities, and these opportunities may broaden the types of media that a brand utilize.

Companies develop their communication budgets in a variety of ways. Some develop the budget based on the task or objective. Others update their budget based on the previous year's efforts. Still others develop their budget based on the competition. There is no right or wrong way to develop the communication budget. It is up to the company and the precision with which they can tie communication dollars to a specific marketing and business outcome.

COMMUNICATION BUDGET AS A PERCENTAGE OF SALES

Regardless of the method of developing the communication budget, it will undergo scrutiny from senior management. Every budget is put into the context of the total sales or revenue of the company. The marketing or advertising manager will be asking senior management for money, but so will other departments such as information technology, human resources, and operations. No company has unlimited resources, so the CEO must ultimately decide what percentage of his or her company's sales will be devoted to marketing and to communications.

DOI: 10.4324/9781003258162-16

TABLE 16.1 Communication budget as a percentage of sales

Brand	Communication budget (million)	Total sales (billion)	%
Allworld	$437	$20	2
Big Bell	$435	$15	3
The Admiral	$151	$3	4
Cross Country	$117	$2	6
Total	$1140	$40	3

Note: Fictitious insurance agencies.

Table 16.1 is a hypothetical example of four companies who compete in the insurance category. Each brand is detailed in terms of total sales and in terms of how many dollars and what percentage of their budget they allocate to communications.

For example, Allworld allocates $437 million to communications. They have total annual revenue or sales of $20 billion. The percentage they allocate to communications is about 2% of their total sales. This is calculated using this equation: $437,000,000 \div 20,000,000 \times 100 = 2.185\%$).

From this simple analysis, you can see that the average percentage spent on communication among the four brands is approximately 3% of total revenue. The range is from a low of 2% for Allworld to a high of 6% for Cross Country.

A CEO would request this type of analysis to understand the context in which her competition is allocating their resources compared to her brand. Based on such an analysis, she may adjust the overall amount of dollars allocated to communications up or down.

CATEGORIES OF COMMUNICATION DOLLARS

Once an overall communication budget has been determined, there are four broad categories that the marketing director or advertising manager reviews. The four categories are as follows:

Working dollars

These are dollars that are allocated to programs that will have an impact on the market. They can be spent on all types of paid, earned, and owned media, including public relations and digital initiatives. Any activity that is directed outward or is influencing the marketplace is a working dollars activity.

Nonworking dollars

These are dollars that are allocated to the creation of the programs. They can be spent on the production of the creative unit or message, the talent cost for a spokesperson or celebrity, any digital hosting costs, or other items that facilitate the creation of the messages. The nonworking costs are necessary to activate programs, but without a program, they will not have an impact on the marketplace.

Contingency dollars

These are dollars that are set aside for a variety of situations. They may provide a cushion for potential cost overruns or serve as a fund to purchase opportunistic media properties or programs that might arise during the course of the year. For example, if an advertiser cancels its ad in the very expensive Super Bowl, the ad space could be resold at a "fire sale" price that could attract a new advertiser to the Super Bowl.

Agency compensation

These are the dollars that are allocated to compensate the agency or agencies for their work. This can be done on a fee or a commission basis, or by a hybrid of methods. The budget item is how much the advertiser will compensate their agency partners for their work in devising and activating the programs.

The goal of the marketing director or advertising manager is to optimize the working percentage of the communication budget. More working dollars lead to greater market success. These four areas become discussion items in management meetings regarding the overall use of the communication dollars.

COMMUNICATION ALLOCATION

The challenge of the communication planner is to allocate the working dollars to the appropriate channels. The communication budget may include agency compensation and contingency, or it may exclude those items. Regardless, the task is to allocate the dollars across the channels.

At this stage of the process, the communication budget is allocated in broad terms to working areas such as paid media or advertising, promotions, public relations, and digital areas. It is also allocated to nonworking areas such as production. Once this is established, each respective area is responsible for developing the strategies and tactics from their specific budget.

Table 16.2 is an example of the communication budget allocation for each of the four hypothetical insurance companies introduced in Table 16.1. As you can see, each

TABLE 16.2 Media communication budget allocation percentage – A media mix example

Brand	Paid media[a]	Email marketing	Content marketing	SEO[b]	Search (PPC)	Landing page/ Website	Social media marketing	Digital display	Production
Allworld	28	5	2	5	12	5	20	13	10
Big Bell	25	2	3	15	10	10	5	20	10
The Admiral	15	10	10	7.5	7.5	10	10	25	5
Cross Country	15	10	5	5	5	5	15	30	15

Note: Fictitious insurance agencies.

a Print, TV, radio ads
b Search engine optimization

brand has a slightly different weighting of the communication channels. For example, Allworld allocates 28% of their budget to paid media, whereas Cross County allocates just 15%. Big Bell focuses much more on search engine optimization and pay-per-click search.

There is no overall right or wrong way to allocate communication dollars. The allocation is driven by each brand's marketing and communication objectives. As we have seen in Chapter 14 communication planners do review how budgets are allocated in a competitive context, just as the CEO reviews overall budgets within a competitive context.

SUMMARY

In summary, allocating the communication budget is the key strategic item in meeting the larger communication objective. The overall budget is reviewed by the CEO and the specific allocation of resources is then reviewed by the marketing or advertising manager. The communication planner is responsible for the complete strategy of the budget and works with the marketing and/or advertising director to determine the overall budget.

CHAPTER 17

Setting communication and media objectives

....

YOU HAVE TO KNOW WHERE YOU ARE GOING BEFORE YOU PLAN HOW TO GET THERE

As discussed in Chapter 8, setting objectives is the first action item prior to starting campaign planning. It is critical that you know where you are going before you begin idling on any aspects of the campaign. A good analogy is that you would never get behind the wheel of a car and begin a road trip, or discuss stopping points or side trips, without determining where you are headed in the first place. A campaign is only as good as its objectives, which help both guide decisions to be made along the way, but also ultimately determine if success was achieved.

This is also the appropriate time to make note of the evolution of media planning from a function of simply getting the brand message to the right people at the right time, to being the builders and keepers of one of every brand's most valuable asset – their community. Well-written objectives help tie the brand's business needs to the needs of the people who make up the brand's community.

Because of their importance, let's dig deeper into the terminology and processes of setting objectives.

OBJECTIVES, GOALS, STRATEGIES, AND TACTICS

For our purposes, the terms *objectives* and *goals* can be used interchangeably. These words both represent the destination, or specific measurable desired outcomes. By comparison, strategies represent the methods your brand will employ to meet the objectives or goals that have been set. Finally, the term *tactics* represents the detailed action plan filled with logistics as to how the strategies will be crafted and acted on. For example, a media strategy for a non-profit fundraising drive might

DOI: 10.4324/9781003258162-17

be to use emotional localized search engine marketing messaging opportunities to showcase the impact donating locally can make at the individual level, where the tactic would be to buy locally geofenced search engine marketing (SEM) ads based on keywords such as "making a difference" or "helping my community." The corresponding creative strategy might be to feature stories by recipients of support from previous campaign drives, while the tactic would be the physical ad created for the campaign including the talent choices, visuals, and copy all to final size and specification.

When a brand prepares to enter the marketplace with strategies and tactics, it is critical to first set objectives that are appropriate to the level in the consumer journey on which the campaign will focus. To do this, a brand must first understand the marketing communication funnel.

UNDERSTANDING THE MARKETING COMMUNICATION FUNNEL

As a consumer moves down the path of first hearing about your brand to ultimately buying it and perhaps becoming a loyal advocate, they follow stages along what is called a marketing communication funnel. It is important to note that although brands can choose to focus certain campaign goals on deeper levels within the funnel, they are never fully done with or beyond additional campaigns at the upper level as new consumers are always potentially moving into their community. Brands must continue to establish new relationships in order to sustain their business.

Although there are a number of variations on the idea of a marketing communication funnel, and depending on the circumstances, each stage may be experienced in different ways, the typical funnel used to describe how consumer journeys play out includes the following levels.

Upper funnel communication goals: Awareness and knowledge

This is the point at which your consumer first comes into contact with and develops a conscious understanding of your brand or of a particular offering you have in the market. For example, it can be a consumer being exposed to and mentally noting your natural soda brand name and logo for the first time, or can be more complex such as them comprehending your new natural soda flavor or even a special sale going on for your soda over the next few days. Regardless, setting an awareness goal means that you have gone beyond simple exposure to creating an understanding. Depending on the level of detail you want the consumer to have, this might be written as a knowledge goal. An example would be for 40% of the market to be knowledgeable of the new summer berry flavor being offered this year.

Awareness and knowledge goals are considered top or upper funnel goals. Many new brands, those with the need to reinvigorate, and those with new offerings often set goals for this stage. However, although critical to brand success, most campaigns do not stop at this level.

Middle funnel communication goals: Perception, consideration, and purchase intent

Once consumers have a certain understanding, an outreach campaign may be used to change or enhance their perception of the brand, to inspire consideration of the brand (which may or may not include them conducting additional research), or potentially develop into actual intent to purchase the brand within a reasonable time period. Goals set for the middle of the funnel are very common, particularly for highly competitive categories.

Lower funnel communication goals: Conversion or transaction

The act of purchasing – the transaction – marks this stage in the funnel. This is the point at which the consumer's thoughts and beliefs translate into a realized sale or other financial commitment such as a donation. Ultimately, brands hope to get consumers to this point in order to generate the return on investment or market share they are aiming for, or the fundraising level they have set if a non-profit. Even though this funnel level determines whether a brand has reached its sales goals, it cannot be the sole focus of campaigns. More than ever, consumers want to have relationships with the brands they support. It is critical that we keep them informed and engaged at all levels, including beyond their purchase to sustain the brand moving forward.

Beyond the funnel communication goals: Loyalty and advocacy

In today's marketplace where word of mouth via social media and other platforms has such substantial impact, it is critical that brands live beyond the transaction of the lower funnel. Campaigns for this level of performance aim for interaction, engagement, loyalty, and even advocacy from customers so that not only they, but also those they influence might become long-term supporters of the brand beyond the current campaign or the most recent purchase.

It is important to consider all levels of the funnel when constructing communication goals. Brands who focus in just one area without a full funnel approach can stagnate and lose touch with their consumers who continue to evolve and have changes in their lives and needs.

Setting communication objectives is a complex task that takes significant strategic thought. Once these are in place, brands can move on to setting their media outreach objectives. As media has evolved so too has this process. In today's market, there are now two big types of media outreach objectives to consider and set.

Traditional audience delivery objectives are still critical to ensuring a brand is talking to the right number of people at scale and the optimal number of times within the appropriate time window. However, the function of media no longer stops here. Rather than just measuring audience delivery, media planners are now held responsible for making sure the campaign created the impact that was intended. Let's look at media delivery goals and campaign impact goals individually.

MEDIA DELIVERY GOALS

Because budgets are always a factor, as with most brand decisions when it comes to setting delivery goals, there is no exception to the rule of having to consider trade-offs, create priorities, and make choices.

Media delivery goals or objectives are about the *audience delivery* needs of a campaign. Often these goals are categorized into four dimensions. The first dimension is *reach*: How many potential customers do you need to contact? The second dimension is *frequency*: How often do you need to contact them? The third dimension is *weight*: What are the total combined conversations or combined reach and frequency volume that is needed to accomplish the task of the campaign? Finally, *continuity*: How many days, weeks, months, and patterns of advertising do you need at the appropriate reach and frequency levels?

It is important to note that delivery goals will need to be set for each active period in a campaign as determined by scheduling needs as discussed in Chapter 13, as well as for each individual target, and for each media platform that will be used in a campaign.

Setting delivery goals: Reach

Looking at your brands purchase cycle and seasonality, you are ready to establish reach and frequency goals. Suppose that you are marketing an established line of frozen dinners. The brand's product purchase cycle is four weeks. You want to set your reach and frequency levels to that four-week period.

First, let's tackle the reach dimension. To continue to grow the brand, you want to reach the majority of your consumers with some sort of message within that four-week time frame. Let's set a goal of 80% target reach.

How did you get to 80%? Media planners can run an analysis of how much it costs to reach an audience. There is a threshold or plateau point at which it is difficult to get incremental reach. Typically, that point begins at around 80%. So that is why you might not set your goal at 90%.

Why not less than 80%? Assuming that the brand needs to reach the majority of its consumers, you pick the point at which it is most economical to do just that. Reaching less than 80% seems like you would be leaving revenue on the table.

This does not mean that you should always set 80% as the reach level. There are reasons to set it lower and reasons to set it higher. Most brands rarely set their reach goals at less than 50% for the purchase cycle; rather, they stay in the 66–80% percent range.

Setting delivery goals: Frequency

Now that you have the reach level established, how many times should you reach your potential customers? In the above example, you set your goals based on a four-week purchase cycle. It seems like common sense that you would want to reach potential customers at least one time per week, an average of four times per month.

Most reach and frequency objectives use the average-frequency concept. Whether it is three, four, five, or even 20, that is the average number of times a consumer would see or hear your brand's commercial message in a given timeframe.

In this example, we have a reach goal of 80% and now have added an average frequency goal of 4.0 within the four-week time frame. But 80% of the consumers are not exposed to your message four times each. Some may see it only once; others may see it eight times or more. Because it is an average, about half will likely see it fewer than four times, whereas the other half will see it more than four times.

This dynamic of frequency of exposure has led media planners to set certain levels of effective frequency.

Setting delivery goals: Effective frequency

Research studies indicate that consumers typically do not retain an advertising message until they have seen it at least three times (3.0+). This figure is the basis for *effective frequency* – that point at which the advertising frequency becomes effective or motivating. Media planners then translate effective frequency into effective reach level – the percentage of the audience reached more than three times.

Many media planners use 3.0 as the sacred rule of thumb because this body of research is so compelling, yet somewhat dated. In addition, with the advent of digital media and personalized communication now possible, others use their own effective frequency level to determine at what point to pause outreach to individuals who are not responding once the effective level has been achieved. These savings can then be reinvested into outreach targeting those who might not yet be at the effective frequency level.

Developing the appropriate effective frequency level is as much an art as a science. There are factors that might suggest the need for more frequency or less frequency. Weights can be applied to the first and second impressions ranging from 100% effective to 25% effective, depending upon message strength and creative approach.

Some advertisers want even higher frequency levels. Some research indicates that with the complexity of the marketplace, it may require ten or more messages to result in effective recall of a sales message, so sometimes the 3+ effective frequency is expanded to a 3–10 effective frequency. And again, because we have so much more accuracy with digital campaigns, this number might be more specialized to a brand's own learnings.

Keep in mind that even though this concept is referred to as effective frequency, it is actually a reach level: The percentage of the audience that will be reached at the pre-determined number of times to be effective during the campaign period. Setting the effective frequency level can be a complex process. Let's look at some of the factors that might affect your decision.

Beyond the obvious of having to reach your target a minimum of once with the campaign offer you are placing into the market, the real question is how many more times do you need to reach them with your message before it actually motivates them to act? This is one of the million-dollar questions of media with no set answer, but there are some best practices to help narrow it down.

For example, if you were introducing a new brand, you would need to have more frequency than you would need for an established brand. The same would be true if your brand had very low awareness.

Perhaps you are in a category that has had a number of new entries, and the marketplace is becoming a real dogfight. That may warrant more frequency just to maintain your current position in the category.

The advertising message can also affect the amount of frequency you assign. If, for instance, you have new copy that would warrant more frequency to seed the message, or if you have a limited-time offer that expires in a week, then you would want more frequency to ensure that it is noticed and remembered.

Table 17.1 shows a frequency planning matrix that considers brand maturity, awareness, competition, the newness of the copy, and the type of message that is to be advertised.

Depending upon where your brand falls in relation to these elements, you simply add the outcome to the base level of 1. If your brand is more than five years old, totally dominates the category, has more than 90% awareness with every audience available, faces no competition, and has a brand campaign that is more than two years old, then we applaud you. Based on this matrix, you don't need to advertise. We have yet to meet a brand manager who doesn't need to advertise, so until we do, the matrix stands as an example of how to assign values to get effective frequency – that is, the appropriate frequency level.

Just to put the matrix to the test, let's suppose that you are introducing a new product into a heavily advertised category. Because your brand is new and has no awareness, you would add frequency to the base of 1. Also, you have a new campaign and a very competitive category, so you add frequency there as well. Although you are using short-term promotional tactics such as coupons and price promotions in-store to gain immediate consumer trial, you have decided that your advertising message will be a brand-differentiation message that is in it for the long haul. Using the matrix, you come to the effective frequency level of 4.0+, so you would peg your objectives to reaching so many of your target consumers four or more times within a given product purchase cycle.

TABLE 17.1 Frequency planning matrix

Factor	Add to base level of 1		
High (1)	**Average (0)**	**Low (-1)**	
Brand maturity	New	Brand in market 2–5 years	Brand in market 5+ years
Brand awareness	New or low awareness	Average awareness	Strongly established leader
Competitive category	Very aggressive	Some spending but your brand is on par	Little spending. Your brand has more than 50% share
Advertising campaign	New campaign/ message	In second year	Has run for 2+ years
Type of response	Short-term promotion	Mix of promo/brand	Long-term brand

Setting delivery goals: Weight and continuity

In finalizing reach and frequency levels, it is critical to realize that reach and frequency exist in an opposing relationship. This means given a fixed budget, once can choose to reach more people fewer times, or to reach fewer people more times. In the end, the fixed budget will determine what the total weight of a campaign can be. It is up to the planner to determine the optimal combination of both reach and frequency within this context while also considering how these delivery goals come together within the calendar that they are planning. Remember, there is no one size that fits all. As we have discussed in multiple chapters already, it all depends on your brand's situation and relationship to the category in which it competes.

If you have a new brand or are restaging an old brand, then you are more likely to consolidate your reach and frequency in fewer but heavier periods of time to create a more concentrated weight for your communication goals. If you oversee a mature brand that is consistently purchased and you need more of a constant contact with a broad target group, then you are more likely to spread out your reach and frequency into more, less weighty periods of time. As with most strategies, there are hybrid strategies that come from either side. The real trade-off is the amount of media weight in a given purchase cycle versus the number of purchase cycles with media weight.

Looking at an example, let's say that your brand is canned green beans and that you can afford 1,800 target rating points (TRP) a year. Knowing that canned green beans have a relatively flat seasonal purchase skew and are purchased every four weeks for the same budget dollars, you could schedule 60 TRP for 30 weeks and cover nearly 60% of the year with your advertising, or you could schedule 120 TRP a week and cover 15 weeks of the year. Both approaches total 1,800 TRPs. However, one schedule offers more continuity and the other more concentrated delivery. As the strategist, it would be your decision to choose more weeks at lower weight levels or fewer weeks at higher weight levels.

In this case, scheduling more active weeks than not seems like the best course of action. This is particularly true if each week basically represents approximately 2% of sales. One schedule covers around 60% of sales, while the other covers only 30% of sales. So, the delivery of the second schedule must be worth two times that of the first schedule for it to pay out.

The other aspect of weight is the need to break through competitive clutter. This can refer to the amount of media weight or pressure necessary, or it can refer to creative implications. From a pure media communication perspective, a retailer setting a goal of reaching 90% of the audience 3.0+ times in the four weeks from Thanksgiving to Christmas could, theoretically, be effective. There is a research basis to make this decision. But suppose that the retailer's competitors have historically spent at twice this level during the same time frame. Now that decision seems less likely to work. The need for more delivery should adjust the other media communication objectives. In this case, those effective frequency objectives may need to be weighted for competitive clutter. This tactic can be used when approaching creative units. For example, if you are a fashion advertiser, then you may elect to schedule a paid social media post campaign featuring your new spring line. If your competitors are all scheduling display ads in these same platforms, then you should find a way to stand out. That may mean not only running a heavier paid social campaign, but also supporting video-based paid social posts to compete more aggressively. Whatever the tactic, your overall goal is to garner more attention in an important yet cluttered environment.

IMPACT GOALS – KEY PERFORMANCE INDICATORS [KPIS]

From the beginning, media has been about audience delivery and thus delivery goals have been a part of the conversation. However, as data has infused our decision-making process and media has become a tool that can be more directly connected to outcomes, the rise of considering impact goals when planning media has become the norm. Although audience delivery goals are still vital components to the media planning function, they have become more of a steppingstone to the real measures of brand success – also known as campaign impact. In other words, it is not enough today for media planners to be content with meeting audience delivery goals, but rather to know what the resulting outcome was from those goals being achieved. That end can range from an awareness gain to a change in attitude to generating more traffic to a store.

Impact goals directly tie media back to the communication objectives that were set earlier. Regardless of your situation, you are looking for some form of response from your advertising dollars. This has given rise to the use of key performance indicators. Otherwise known as KPIs, these impact goals go beyond delivery to include answers to the question what happened after we reached the right number of people the correct number of times.

Using impact goals: KPIs

It is important to note that advertising campaigns today are placing increased emphasis on engagement, which is a type of KPI. Setting, planning for, and measuring KPIs is an integral part of the job media planners today. It is no longer enough simply to inform the audience. Instead, it is essential to engage the audience with interaction, involvement, searches for additional information, and other methods in conjunction with the product or service.

Most consumers today have a more skeptical view of advertising and brands as whole, so engagement can help build emotional relationships between audiences and products or services. An impact goal of establishing an emotional link, such as trust, helps overcome the lack of connection, which will hopefully lead to more interest in the brand and eventually to greater involvement, engagement, and trust.

Let's look at an example of using the KPI of sales response that you are trying to achieve with media dollars and working backward. For example, if you have an advertising budget of $1,000 and you know that you have the KPI of generating $10,000 in incremental sales within a campaign to be successful, you now have an impact goal. If you also know that the average customer spends $50 in your store, then your advertising must generate 200 additional customers for you to be successful. Armed with these facts, you now know that you have a ceiling of $5 per new customer, or your advertising will not pay out. (This rate was calculated by dividing the $1,000 ad budget by 200 new customers.)

So, if your media plan has a mix of media that costs 10 cents per person, it would generate 10,000 impressions. If 2% of these people respond to your offer, you are home free. You can connect your impact goal of incremental sales to determine the audience delivery that will be needed.

The point of this exercise is to show that sales response as well as other KPIs are a crucial component to setting communication goals. Whether it is through sophisti-cated marketing-mix models or just looking at next-day sales, the response to adver-tising is the barometer for how much advertising you are likely to do. This type of information is vital to media planners as they begin to construct a plan. There is no sense in coming up with a plan that will not deliver the expected results. Over time, most brands have a track record of what works and what does not. Using response information in conjunction with reach and frequency analysis is an excellent method of determining how many resources you should allocate toward a campaign.

Response analysis is the core of setting communication goals for online media. Online media have built-in response analysis tools, so online plans are highly measur-able. Most online campaigns have specific response goals established as benchmarks prior to the campaign. As the campaign unfolds, the online media professional begins to adjust creative or media strategies to meet these goals.

SUMMARY

Setting communication and media objectives is a complex task, often started with industry best practices and modified with brand specific information garnered through trial and error. It is critical to really understand the process of your brand's purchase dynamics and the marketplace variables that impact both the levels and the scheduling of audience delivery. From there you can assess the appropriate levels of reach and frequency necessary to achieve the specific advertising response. It is important to meld delivery goals such as reach, frequency, and weight with other impact goals such as any sales or other response metrics to build the overall most appropriate goals for your brand.

Ultimately, objectives in media have moved beyond simply informing, to engaging consumers, building loyalty, and directly increasing sales response. Media planners have evolved from simply using reach and frequency to talk to consumers to being in the business of fully developing the relationship with a brand's community. Setting objectives and managing media weight in campaigns toward specific KPIs allows media planners to build and keep robust and thriving brand communities.

CHAPTER 18

Communication platforms and campaign briefs

···

WE'RE ALL ON THE SAME TEAM

To maximize a brand's investments in the marketplace, while minimizing market confusion, every communication plan must be crafted and executed from start to finish around a single origin point. This concept is one that has traditionally been referred to as the brand's Big Idea.

If you ask communication and marketing professionals for an example of a Big Idea, you are likely to get a variety of responses. Most will cite some form of creative execution or advertising campaign. Some may cite a specific tagline. Others may cite a particular moment in the advertising or even a jingle. You will notice that these examples all focus on the creative execution of the brand in one way or another. This is because creative executions used to be the starting part for most campaigns and creative executions also tend to be the most tangible manifestation within campaigns. However, as the marketplace and capabilities have both drastically shifted, over-arching data-informed, creatively inspired strategic planning has taken the lead in brand campaign development. With other functions such as media and public relations (PR) now elevated as critical competitive differentiation, the scope and intent behind the Big Idea and its creative-only implications simply are no longer, well, big enough. For most brands today, the construct of a Big Idea within integrated campaigns has been modified to include all functions involved in outreach and, thus, given rise to the much broader concept of a *communication platform*.

By its nature, a communication platform is created to be all-inclusive of everything a brand does in outreach planning. It is not limited to one campaign or one function area but rather drives every decision made in communication planning. Let's look closer at communication platforms, otherwise known as *comms platforms*, and the process of crafting one.

DOI: 10.4324/9781003258162-18

THE COMMUNICATION PLATFORM

A communication platform should be thought of as the brand's outreach home base, origin point, center, or core. It is unique to each brand, transcending beyond any single target, set time or season, or channel. It is something that the brand can own indefinitely and literally sustain in all activities regardless of the call to action.

A solid communication platform can be derived only after extensive research of all types have been conducted. Because it is so pivotal to everything the brand does, it takes a significant amount of time and quality thinking to identify and verbalize. Shifting through key insights found in discovery and confirmation research from primary and secondary sources that is both qualitative and quantitative is the seed for any good communication platform. If well-conceived, the communication platform will be able to be expressed in no more than a few words. If more is needed, the platform has not been honed enough and will need to be revisited and refined.

Once firm and approved, the communication platform informs all decisions. It is the litmus test to confirm whether a future strategy or tactic is not only a good one but also on point from a strategic standpoint. It is the glue that binds the message and media together. Remember the MasterCard "Priceless" campaign? While this campaign was one of the classics of our time, "Priceless" is not the brand's comms platform. The comms platform is "MasterCard empowers the things that matter most." With this in mind, all communication then focuses on dramatizing things that matter. The creative *expression* of that idea is "Priceless." You can also begin to imagine what types of media and public relations implications are based on delivering "things that matter." The creative media possibilities are endless.

Dove is another example of a brand with an award-winning campaign. The inspiration behind the Dove campaign was to change the personal care conversation from selling soap to selling "self-esteem." The Communication Platform is that "Beauty is so much more than skin deep." This set the platform for the "Campaign for Real Beauty," which created a debate about how beauty should be defined as well as transformed the role that brands play in the space. This Comms Platform shaped the media plan to focus on engaging with women so that they could share their stories and join in the conversation. Without a unifying and inspiring Communication Platform, the Dove campaign could have been just another media plan within the cosmetics category.

The formation of the comms platform can be thought of as the bridge between the research insights stage of planning, and the recommendations and tactics stages. It sets the foundation for all objectives, strategies, and logistics that follow. Once determined, campaign development from media and PR tactics to creative messaging and assets can begin, but before things get into full swing, the research and resulting communication platform must be concisely shared with the teams. In order to achieve this, a campaign brief will be needed.

THE CAMPAIGN BRIEF

Just as the communication platform is a contemporary and more inclusive adaptation of the Big Idea, the campaign brief is a tool that morphed out of what was historically really a creative brief that focused solely on message development. Again, with

---

EXHIBIT 18.1 CONTEMPORARY CAMPAIGN BRIEF

1. What are the background and key research insights?
2. What are the campaign needs, the desired outcomes, and quantifiable objectives?
3. What is most relevant about the company and product attributes, including the brand's truth to be communicated?
4. Who are the people this outreach is intended to inspire? What are some of their key behaviors and shared characteristics? Are there multiple groups or dynamic personas involved?
5. What do they currently think, feel, say, and do?
6. What would we like them to think, feel, say, and do?
7. What is the communication platform that will resonate and motivate them?
8. What are the best ways to consider connecting the idea to the consumer?
9. What is the geographic footprint of this campaign?
10. What is the seasonality of this product and potential campaign timing?
11. What is the budget for this campaign?
12. How will we measure success both during and after the campaign?
13. What are the mandatories including legal requirements, existing relationships, or other set expectations that are not negotiables?

---

the increasingly complex world of communication and a need to fuel execution ideas for all teams such as media and PR, creative briefs were expanded to become the campaign brief of today. With this evolution the creative team, media team, digital team, public relations team, and perhaps a marketing services company can all work in tandem toward the same vision.

Exhibit 18.1 is an example of a contemporary campaign brief that illustrates the information necessary to set the scope of work for a project as well as provide pertinent details needed by all for campaign development.

Many companies and agencies have their own proprietary briefs, yet in general, they all deliver the same types of information. Let's break each of these sections down a bit further.

Background research and insights

What are the biggest findings that pre-campaign research brought to light? What do we know now that we might not have before about the many variables that can impact this campaign? For example, have there been additions to the competitive set that have changed the playing field? Is there a pop-culture trend or new technology that has shifted consumer expectations or the way we do business? Bigger and smaller details that will set the context for planning should be shared here.

Campaign needs, desired outcomes, and objectives

A clearly stated campaign need is essential. This is the concise problem that communication must solve. Stating that sales are soft is not a communication problem.

We need to know the underlying consumer-centric reason why sales are soft. The problem stated should be a consumer or target market problem. That is what communication solves. Properly stating the need will get you halfway toward a solution. A good way to frame this discussion is to ask *what is the purpose of this outreach?* An example of a simple problem that communication can solve is, "Young adults are not buying our brand because they are not aware of it." Another is, "Young adults are not buying our brand because they perceive it to be old and stodgy." The need will next be translated into specific, quantifiable outcomes and objectives. This will include business outcomes, communication objectives, and any other measurements that have been successfully tested and previously benchmarked by the brand such as media delivery and impact goals.

Relevant company, brand, and product attributes

What facts, features, or benefits of our brand both resonate with the target as well as prove the position we will take is valid? How does our consumer use our category and our brand? It is important in this section to set boundaries and distinguish our brand beyond just physical characteristics to include emotional differentiation we already have or want to achieve within the consumer mind space. This can be boiled down to what is considered the *brand's truth*. For example, if selling bottled water, are we not just another version of H_2O in an already highly cluttered category? What is it about our water that sets us apart? Another good example is the automobile company Subaru. Although the company physically sells cars of various sizes, performance levels, and price ranges, they all live under the brand's truth which is that Subaru does not just get you from point A to point B. This is a brand that empowers you to explore the things you love with the ones you love, which gave rise to the company's highly successful and long-running "Share the Love" campaign. Notice that very little of any of Subaru's focus within their campaigns is on car specifications, but rather on the brand's truth, which is then crafted into a future comms platform and manifested in all aspects of the campaign, from media, to PR, as well as the creative messaging.

Outreach target community

This section of the brief describes the target – the audience, the consumers, the people you want to reach. Painting a vivid picture of the target market in human terms is crucial for communication. Attaching a target persona to the brief can be helpful. The media team may need more detail than just a persona. To analyze media habits, the media team will want to understand the behavior and demographics of the target market. For example, is the target market a heavy or light user of the brand? The answer to this question could have an impact on future media analysis. The same holds true for demographics. Since some media tie their rates to demographics, the media team needs a clear understanding of the demographic makeup of the audience. Because the target market is such a crucial part of any campaign, it is important to ask all parties working on the brief to provide input on what they would like to see in a target description.

What do they *currently* think, feel, say, and do?

Here is where we can add significant depth to the ask. This is a perfect opportunity to include the customer empathy map if one has been conducted. For example, if consumers think that all auto insurance is the same, then their behavior is to shop for the one with the lowest price. The media team would want to understand the diagnostics behind this section. In assigning a media objective, the team may want to set specific goals in terms of awareness or brand preference and behavior. Clearly stating how the consumer thinks and behaves toward the brand is the first step. Providing the underlying research is the second step in this section of the brief.

What do we want them to think, feel, say, and do?

Knowing where we want the consumer to land after the campaign is key. It is important to look at the impact our campaign will have at this human, empathetic level just as we did before the campaign. Looking at the impact of the campaign from this perspective will keep the team focused on outreach that is both relevant and well received.

Communication platform

Straight forward and simple, this section is where you state the communication platform or overarching idea that everyone must follow. It should be stated in a one-sentence format. To follow, you may want to provide a reason why this idea is compelling so that everyone understands the thought process and research foundation behind the idea from where they are building.

Best ways to connect

It is always preferrable to have a starting point other than zero. New thinking and experimenting with different media channels are always expected, but it is even better if will build on prior experiences rather than with a blank slate. After all, if our brand has prior in-market experience, using that knowledge and investment equity moving forward is key. Are there any findings to be shared in this section from previous activities, plans, or outreach including any test-and-learn roll outs that can let strategists know more about the impact potential, message receptivity, or anticipated response?

Geographic footprint

This section answers the "where" of the campaign. What coverage is needed for this message? Is it a national, regional, or local campaign? Are there different levels of activations working in tandem with each other? What market variables might also be influencing a brand's decision-making. A full geographic analysis should be done with the important variables and highlights shared here.

Scheduling

This section addresses the "when" of the campaign. What is the timing of this outreach? Are there multiple stages or phases? Is this an annual campaign, or is it a short, immediate call to action? Is there an evergreen component with seasonal modifications needed? Are there critical tent-pole calendar moments already identified for outreach to be built around?

Budget

It is important to not only know how much money the brand has budgeted for this campaign, but any other parameters that are in place. For example, is this a gross or a net budget? Are their guidelines such as no more than 20% of dollars to be spent in non-working areas? Are there any other limitations in spending such as per quarter or by geography? It is critical that each team contributing to the outreach plan fully understand the resources they are working with in order to make sure that time in planning is spent appropriately and realistically.

Measuring success

Because everyone's job is based on achieving success, and all are working toward the same outcomes and impact, a detailed benchmark and measurement plan must be subscribed to in the brief. How success is measured is one of the keys to its delivery. For a communication campaign, it is important to understand where on the objectives funnel the campaign is aiming. This must be detailed in the brief. For example, it is possible to change a perception about the brand but not any behaviors. On the other hand, a short-term sales incentive may change behavior but not significantly alter the brand's perception. Understanding these dynamics and the impact the plan is having is a crucial component to the program.

Success measures will factor into the media planning objectives when planning begins. The media objectives should be aligned with the ultimate brand-success metrics. In addition, measurements of success will need to be built into the outreach plan so that activations can be monitored and optimized during the campaign, and not just analyzed at the end.

Mandatories

Mandatories are items that are required in the campaign. For example, a creative mandatory may be to use the brand's slogan, an icon, a certain color, or a piece of music in a campaign. Important media items in this section should include any media purchases or sponsorships to which the brand may have agreed. For example, the brand may sponsor a PGA golf tournament every year. Or the brand may have already purchased space or time in a platform so they can tie into that publication's promotional support.

Any legal disclaimers or restraints should be outlined in this section as well. This is especially true in the case of a pharmaceutical product, where you may have to run a full-page ad of legal disclaimers or have: 15 seconds of audio for every ad you schedule.

The other part of the mandatory section is the timeline for developing the plan. Every plan must have due dates. In a communication plan, it is important to establish a few check-in points where you bring all parties together to discuss their progress on the plan. A media idea could spark something in the creative area or vice versa.

SUMMARY

Having a unified, inclusive, highly researched, and creatively inspired communication platform is the key to success for all involved in outreach planning process. This is the single biggest thing that all are working toward to be used as fuel and energy in the planning process. A well-conceived communications platform can be a game-changing competitive advantage for a brand because it can be used to tie critical research insights together into a single, focused trajectory.

In addition, once all research and strategic set up has been completed, a comprehensive campaign brief will be required at the kick-off stage of planning to ensure that all parties and functions are operating toward the most viable integrated campaign. The development of these important grounding pieces can be intense and time-consuming, but when done right, they greatly increase collaboration, productivity, and potential success.

CHAPTER 19

Media strategy and tactics

....

OFF TO THE MARKET WE GO!

If media objectives are the "what," then media strategies are the "how." Media strategies must be inextricably linked to and fall out of the media delivery and impact objectives that have previously been discussed. Media strategies are the answer to what you will specifically do to achieve these objectives. Put simply, media objectives outline where you want to go. Media strategies outline how to get there. Media tactics provide the specific details of how to get there. For example, if your objective is to get to New York and your strategy is to fly there, the tactic is to take Southwest Flight #9 that departs Tuesday at 2:00 P.M., arrives at your destination at 6:00 P.M., with a two-hour layover in Baltimore, and costs $350 one-way.

One simple way to frame objectives is through action words such as "to do something." By comparison, strategies are best talked about using words such as "by doing something." Media strategies, then, are the overall use of media to achieve the media objectives, and they take two basic forms. The first part of a media strategy is the *media mix*. This is the specific media you recommend to achieve the outlined objectives and in what proportion. For example, the digital portion of a media plan may have a media mix or budget made up of 50% expenditures in search engine marketing (SEM), 30% expenditures in social, and 20% in online display networks. The second detailed section of a media strategy is *scheduling*, which includes the planner's recommendations for deploying the various media types to meet the objectives.

Media strategy is often confused with media tactics. Media strategy is the broad strategy of using media, whereas tactics are the specific media vehicles. For example, a media objective may be to reach and engage with 80% of women who are small craft business owners. The strategy to accomplish this objective is to use a combination of

DOI: 10.4324/9781003258162-19

Objective	Strategy
To reach 90% of teenage boys an average of 1 × per week	By using a broad mix of television, online display, paid social, and dynamic in-game messaging
To provide support for all four-week product purchase cycles	By providing continual SEM support and four-week flights of paid social
To provide national support with emphasis in the top 10 DMAs	By using national cable and for national support and by using out of home and in-store media within the top 10 DMAs

FIGURE 19.1 Objectives and strategies

cable television, social media, and online display. The tactics would be to place messaging in the Magnolia Cable Network, Pinterest, and the Google Online Display Network.

So, media strategies refer to categories of media, while media tactics are the specific media vehicles. The only time that this is not the case is when there is no broader umbrella for the category. A sponsorship of the Super Bowl would be an example of this.

MEDIA STRATEGY EXAMPLES

Media strategies should match specifically to media objectives. You should never devise a media strategy in a vacuum, nor should you put any thought into strategies or tactics prior to fully finalizing all objectives. The best way to organize media strategies is to match them to the four overall media objectives: *target, reach/frequency, geography,* and *seasonality/timing.* Figure 19.1 has examples of media strategies for each of these objectives.

Again, because of the importance, let us underscore that media strategies follow media objectives, and media tactics follow media strategies. Always! Each and every dollar a media planner recommends on a tactic must be traceable through the upstream guiding strategy all the way back to the objective or objectives it is working toward. Strategies and tactics are the action plan for how you are recommending the budget be allocated.

STRATEGY SCENARIOS

There are always multiple ways to craft media plans to meet the objectives outlined. This is where the informed but highly creative ideation part of media really comes into play. Media strategy involves the allocation of resources. Basically, where are you going to place your bet? Do you put all your money on a single media channel or do you spread it around? Do you focus all of your activity at a specific time or do you parse it out across the year? Those are the strategic decisions that media planners make on a daily basis. Because of the trade-offs involved and options available, media planners are really good at asking and answering the question "what if?"

One method that many media planners use when developing a media plan is to cultivate a variety of scenarios or options for the same campaign and weigh out the pros and cons of each option prior to choosing a final recommendation. Scenario planning allows the media team and client to understand the trade-offs of different media channel alternatives. For example, if the overall goal of the plan is to reach 90% of the target an average of four times per month, the media planner may develop three or more alternative plans for review. These plans would have different combinations of media or different weighting of the same media. Each alternative strategy would be analyzed in terms of how it meets the overall media objectives and carries the message to the consumer in the way intended to in the campaign. This is a routine method that media planners use to justify their specific recommendation.

Where scenario planning gets more interesting is when you approach it from very different angles. What if we just used social media and publicity to build our brand? Now compare that approach to a program where we focused on only digital media. Or could we develop a plan that is built on the media that the brand owns? Scenario planning helps media planners challenge conventional category wisdom. It is a systematic way of applying creative thinking to solve the problem.

CHANNEL PLANNING THROUGH THE PURCHASE FUNNEL

One of the main questions to ask when developing media strategy is what stage of the purchase funnel are we trying to impact? You will remember from the previous chapter on objectives that creating campaigns that focus on different stages of the funnel means the campaign will have different needs and desired outcomes.

Because various media have differing strengths and weaknesses, they each play a different role in each stage of the purchase funnel. For example, if the goal is to gain immediate awareness, broad-based media such as linear and streaming video or out-of-home may be appropriate. If the problem is to affect a shift in brand perception, then perhaps a digital display campaign schedule that directs consumers to the brand's website may be in order. On the other hand, if the goal is to enhance brand purchase intent, then it is crucial that the brand has a strong SEM program. Finally, if the goal is to build more brand advocacy, then emphasis on social media may be the right strategy.

Exhibit 19.1 is an example of how different media impact various points of the brand purchase funnel. In this example, media channels are organized by paid, earned, and owned categories. Within each aspect of this framework are individual media channels. By organizing the media planning strategy to match the purchase funnel dynamics, the planner directs media channels that are appropriate to the task at hand.

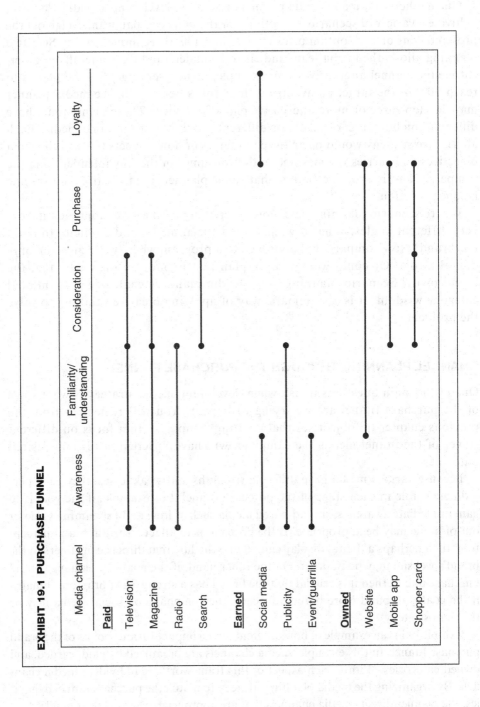

EXHIBIT 19.1 PURCHASE FUNNEL

Most media planners today employ sophisticated software tools for their strategic planning. Using a host of research options in combination with algorithms, planners can create or purchase both attribution models and predictive models that empower their decision making. Attribution models provide impact weights for each media platform or even vehicle in a considered media plan. For example, although most transactions in a campaign seem to have happened immediately following a consumer's exposure to a search ad, an attribution model can tell the planner how much of a factor the other elements such as the video ads that ran two days earlier were in motivating that sale. Predictive models can go even further to not only create a system for weighing media options based on previous campaigns, but they can also help play out potential outcomes for plans prior to them being activated.

CHANNEL PLANNING FUELLED BY THE COMMUNICATION PLATFORM

You may remember our previous discussion about the importance of a well-written communication platform to inspire the entire communication team? Here is where that simply stated phrase helps drive media decisions. Using the communications platform as a center point for all media decisions not only makes sure that the media team is considering the overall trajectory of the campaign, but also allows them to significantly explore and create unique contact points and combinations of media vehicles that tie all things together in a more creative, inspired, and motivating way. It also keeps the media team in step with the other teams working on campaign development, which fosters a more collaborative, customized, and integrated overall solution for the brand beyond just a "typical" or "one size fits all" media plan. No matter how "fun," "new," or "widely used" a strategy or tactic is, if it does not fit within the framework established by the communications platform, it either needs to be retooled or removed from consideration.

CHANNEL PLANNING FUELLED BY THE CONSUMER JOURNEY AND EMPATHY MAP

Just as important as the communications platform, so too is leaning into the consumer journey and empathy maps that should be a part of the campaign brief from the outset of planning. Rather than reviewing media based only on the brand's viewpoint through the purchase funnel, the media planner should consider both the consumer journey and empathy map that were completed earlier.

Just like the brand purchase funnel, the customer journey is a set of interrelated actions that consumers take when purchasing the brand. For example, the first stage of a home improvement project may be inspiration. Consumers see something on Pinterest or in a magazine or go to a model home that inspires them to take action. The second stage may be research. Here, consumers actively seek information about the project from online searches, magazine articles, and blogs. They may review similar projects on YouTube. The third stage is shopping, where the consumer goes to a variety of stores both in person and online to get a sense of the costs involved in a proposed project. Stage four is purchasing the products. Stage five is actually doing it. Stage six may be posting pictures of the finished project to their Pinterest board or to Instagram or other social media platforms.

Walking through the process like a consumer allows the planner to see which types of media may be important to consider in the strategic planning process, while using an empathy map to understand what the consumer is thinking, feeling, saying, and doing at each step on their journey keeps the focus of the planner on the consumer and their needs, which results in a truly authentic outreach plan.

MEDIA TACTICS

Media tactics are the details of your media plan. Tactics become the action plan that is executed in the market. You cannot implement strategies without them. Perhaps most importantly, the consumer will never truly see your media strategies, which are detailed only in internal documents. Rather, they will see the media tactics that are the manifestation of your strategies when activated. For this reason, it is important to map each tactic back to a specific strategy. It is also important to detail the use of each media channel. One way to provide such a framework is to include these four components: *description, cost, audience delivery*, and *audience impact with rationale*.

Description

The description details what you are recommending. In the case of print, it would be the specific publications, the creative unit placed, and the purchase frequency. For example, if your strategy is to schedule women's magazines, a tactic would be to schedule six full-page four-color ads in *Good Housekeeping*.

Descriptions vary by the medium chosen. So, in the case of broadcast, a tactic written in a media plan would include the types of stations, the dayparts to be purchased, and the creative unit to be used. It may or may not include the specific programs at this juncture because they have yet to be negotiated. This is done once the plan is approved. It could be done simultaneously, though, if the marketer has "bought off" on the broad direction of the media strategies. Outdoor media include the type of unit, the number to be purchased, and the general locations for the ads. Specific details are conveyed upon the final purchase. Online display contains the sites, the creative unit, and the dayparts to be purchased. Search engine marketing would include the general Ad Groups and associated pool of keywords to be tested as well as the geography of the test.

Cost

All tactics include detailed costs. Costs are provided at the category level and at the tactic level. For example, you may allocate a budget of $2.5 million to streaming video. The plan would itemize each provider's cost, which would then be added together to reach the $2.5 million streaming video budget.

The cost for each element in the media plan should reflect the agency compensation agreement. If the agency is working on a commission basis, then the media should contain the appropriate commission. If the agency is working on a fee basis, then the media should be shown in net dollars. At the tactic level, the marketer will want to understand the specific costs that he or she will be billed. The tactical cost aspect of the plan becomes the financial road map for the marketer in working with the brand's internal accounting.

Audience delivery – Reach, frequency, impressions, TRPs, clicks, etc.

All tactics will include the specifics of the audience delivery provided by each tactic. The list of metrics here would include delivery measures such as reach, frequency, impressions, TRPs, clicks, views, video completes, downloads, shares, etc. As communication plans contain a greater variety of elements from paid media to digital media to promotions and more the planner is moving more toward impressions as the combined measurement standard for reach in tactics. This is the simplest form of showing reach and the easiest to use across any form of communication.

Audience impact with rationale – KPIs and other support

As previously discussed, there are a large number of ways of executing a media strategy. Therefore, the tactics you recommend should contain a detailed rationale. The rationale for a media tactic focuses on how it creates the desired effect in terms of KPIs, how it reaches the target, how cost efficient it is, and how it may benefit the brand through association. For example, your rationale for selecting *Disney+* could be as follows:

- Streaming video is the best choice for carrying a sight-and-sound message to a consumer within relevant content on their schedule to support an upcoming promotion to a broad family audience.
- *Disney+* has the highest coverage of our parent target within the streaming video platforms.
- *Disney+* has a cost per thousand (CPM) that is 20% below average for the other over the top (OTT) options considered.
- Our brand's support of *Disney+* will appeal highly to our consumer who appreciates the family-friendly content and watches regularly with their partner and children.

This is a strong rationale for why *Disney+* should be a part of the streaming video plan. Each media tactic should have a similar rationale. Not all tactics will have all of these components. The important part of writing a rationale is to answer two big questions – why is this the best use of brand resources and why use this specific vehicle instead of another?

SUMMARY

Media strategies should accomplish the delivery and impact objectives designed for the campaign at the start of the planning process. These objectives lead to strategies that then inspire specific tactics. If you find that you have strategies that do not match an objective, then you should reconsider those strategies. Brands or planners should not entertain or decide to invest in any tactics out of order or risk spending valuable resources that may not ultimately deliver the right audience, at the right time or place, or for the right amount of investment.

There are many factors that play into which strategy and tactic would be considered the most viable. In addition to considering where in the purchase funnel the campaign is aiming, the planner must consider other critical components such as the communications platform, the consumer journey, and the consumer empathy map to be certain all efforts are as coordinated and consumer-centric as they should be.

Once a recommended strategy is provided, planners should consider or benchmark alternative plans to be certain the best approach is selected with which to move forward. The act of finalizing and acting on media strategies and tactics is both complex and challenging, but it also provides the opportunity to change the fate of a brand once activated.

Super Bowl advertising

The Super Bowl – the championship game of the National Football League in the United States – isn't an innovation per se – it's been around for decades. And as long as there has been a Super Bowl, there's been Super Bowl advertising. But the Super Bowl deserves a special mention for several reasons:

- It is one of the only programs in the United States that garners tens of millions of viewers. The 2021 Superbowl on CBS had almost 100 million viewer – almost a third of the entire US population. And the 2021 ratings were the worst ratings in 15 years.
- Ad costs are incredibly high: in 2022, NBC was pricing some ads at $6.5 million for 30 seconds.
- Brands generally produce new creative for the Super Bowl and often use the program to introduce new products. Film studios buy space to promote new movies. Some brands keep their commercials secret until air time, other brands "tease" their new ads through social media channels in the weeks prior to the big game.
- Super Bowl ads get additional traction through the dozens of media and advertising pundits who critique the ads in the days after Super Bowl Sunday.

CHAPTER 20

Learning the language of media planning

···

TALKING THE TALK SO YOU CAN WALK THE WALK

Once the strategies of a campaign have been determined, planners will need to deal with publishers and other media providers to finalize specific tactics. These can be broadcast programs, magazines, websites, or myriad other media platforms and vehicles. Each media category has its own language, yet there are some terms that are shared.

To understand how any business operates, one must know the language of that business. It is the same in media. By knowing the terms and concepts of advertising media, you can contribute your own ideas and precepts, envision how the entire advertising campaign fits together, and be accepted as a knowledgeable, contributing partner in the campaign development process.

Media terminology is not difficult or complicated. No one tried to create complicated terms or abbreviations to describe how the media work. Instead, the terminology just developed along with the industry, so much of the language makes logical sense. It is important that planners understand the straight-forward and not-so-straight-forward way to think and talk about media so they can converse on the same level as the rest of the team, but also so they can fully understand the concepts behind the words to make the most informed decisions and contribute in the most strategic ways possible.

The rest of this chapter is designed in simple and direct language not only to define the terminology planners will need to be successful in media, but also to illustrate and provide examples of the fundamental concepts these words define.

MEDIA, MEDIUM, AND MEDIUMS

We can start with the term *media*. The *media* are go-betweens, the facilitators that make it possible to deliver a message to a brand's community. The term *media* is plural with the singular being the word *medium*. The alternate plural, *mediums*, refers

DOI: 10.4324/9781003258162-20

to fortune-tellers and seers who make a living looking into crystal balls, not to be confused with the media industry even though media planners are often asked to predict the future.

MEDIA CLASSIFICATIONS AND HIERARCHIES

The terms *media class, category,* or *platform* are all words largely used interchangeably as the umbrella terms to include whole groups of media options such as video, audio, out of home, paid social, or search engine marketing (SEM). A single media outlet, such as a specific magazine title, a search engine, a streaming audio service, or a specific newspaper title is called a *media vehicle.* The specifications of the individual advertisement are considered the *advertising unit,* and a single placement in a vehicle is called an *insertion.* For example, if your media platform of choice is video, your vehicle might be *Hulu,* and your advertising unit might be a :30 spot. Because you find this to be an efficient and effective choice, you might choose to run multiple insertions here such as 25 times, or 25 individual ads, within the campaign period.

A campaign is typically broken down into multiple periods of time that are classified as active or inactive meaning that no brands run advertisements every single day or even every single week. In fact, as discussed in an earlier chapter, many brands choose to be inactive more days and weeks so that when they are active, they can be in-market at more aggressive budget levels. The periods of time that media is active is called a *flight.* A media flight is centered around a single message, has its own delivery and impact goals, and is scheduled with a start- and end-date over a period that typically spans between one to four weeks total. For example, Amazon may plan a back-to-school message for a flight that runs from August 1 to August 20 to reach 85% of parents with children 5–12 years old in order to increase their share of online school supply sales by 3% over last year.

A *media schedule* is what happens when you string together all of the insertions you have placed within one media class in a single flight. For example, you might talk about the paid social schedule that Amazon ran during the just mentioned back-to-school flight. This would include total investments and insertions in all social platforms that Amazon used during that window. In this example, let's say that Amazon's paid back-to-school social media schedule included investments in Facebook, Instagram, and TikTok.

Finally, the term campaign is typically reserved as the overarching term to indicate all of the media activity or insertions a brand has across all media classes. So, in summary, insertions in vehicles within in flights combine to make schedules, and all schedules combine to make annual campaigns.

THE BASICS OF CAMPAIGN AUDIENCE DELIVERY

When talking about media vehicles to be considered for schedules and campaigns, there are a few basic concepts that are commonly used. Let's look at each of these terms and concepts in detail.

Reach

There are two kinds of reach: *numerical* and *percentage*. Numerical reach is the raw number of individuals in your target community that have seen your message at least once within a given campaign window. Reach percentage is that same group represented as a ratio or percentage of the total target community. For example, if there are 35 million college students in a brand's target community and a campaign reaches 10 million of them, this campaign has a 28.6% reach.

Accumulated audience

As we have just seen, reach measures the size of an audience, but confusion can result between the reach for a single advertising insertion and the total reach for time period or a full campaign. To reduce this confusion, the term *accumulated audience* (also called *cumulative audience*, or *cume*) is used to refer to the audience of a series of advertising placements or of an advertising campaign (see Table 20.1).

If a series of advertisements is run in a single media vehicle, the total number of audience members reached is the accumulative audience. For example, let's say three advertisements are placed in the *New York Times*. The accumulated audience is the total number of different people who have been exposed to the brand's message in that single media vehicle. Each audience member is counted only once, no matter how many times he or she may have seen the advertising.

Unduplicated audience

Similarly, if advertisements are placed in a combination of vehicles, the total audience size is called the *unduplicated audience*. Again, each audience member is counted only once, no matter how many times he or she may have heard or seen your advertisements; counting a person again would inflate unduplicated audience figures.

Let's say a campaign is executed in the Google Display Network and on *NBC Nightly News*. Whether audience members see ads on Google or hear them on the nightly news or both, they are each counted only once.

The unduplicated audience is very much like the accumulative audience. The difference is that the accumulative audience involves the total number of different people

TABLE 20.1 New York Times accumulated audience

Insertion #	New readers
1	500,000
2	100,000
3	50,000
Total	650,000

Note: New readers are those who have not seen the advertising before.

who are exposed to advertising through a combination of advertisements in a *single vehicle*, whereas the unduplicated audience is the total number of different people who are exposed to advertising through a series of advertisements in a *combination of vehicles*.

Frequency

There are also two kinds of frequency: *frequency or number of insertions* and *frequency of exposures*. Frequency of insertion describes the number of times an advertisement appears in the media vehicle chosen for investment. Often, frequency is described on a per-week basis, rather than the frequency per year or the frequency during the course of a campaign. So, advertising might be running 25 times per week on a radio station during a 13-week campaign.

However, just because ads were placed frequently does not mean that the audience will see or hear the advertisement every time. In fact, it is unlikely that any member of an audience will ever be exposed to every insertion. With a frequency of insertion of 25 times per week, the average audience member may see or hear that advertisement only three or four times each week, which would be frequency of exposure. A good way to think about this is to consider an archer shooting arrows at a target. Every time a new arrow is launched it can be considered the equivalent of an insertion or an attempt to connect. Of course, not every arrow shot will hit the target. The actual number of arrows that do so with success would be the equivalent of frequency of exposure.

When scheduling multiple advertisement insertions, audience members are likely to be reached with varying degrees of frequency. For example, if ten advertisements are placed, perhaps only 20% of the audience members will see all ten of them, while 50% will see only one. One method a media planner uses to analyze the delivery of an advertising media schedule is to look at a frequency distribution of the exposures.

There are different schools of thought on how many times consumers must see or hear an advertisement before it registers in their minds. The concept of effective frequency as previously discussed in Chapter 17 determines a specific frequency number, such as 3.0+, which is when it is believed that a consumer will be more likely to retain the message.

Impact or response

The *impact* or response a media placement has on the audience is the result of a number of factors, many of which relate to the creative assets used in the message or the physical specifications of the ad unit chosen. Did the ad message resonate with the target? Was the ad size chosen large enough to stand out in a competitive environment? Was it a strong execution of the comms platform?

The media contribution to impact comes from matching the appropriate vehicle with the message to be delivered, the level of audience attention and engagement of each vehicle, and the ability of the media planner to time the message delivery in the most appropriate way to create the biggest effect. Did the delivery of the message sync with the purchasing funnel stage that consumers were in? Was the geography of the ad appropriately aligned with the purchasing behaviors of the community? There really are too many factors to list here, but the idea is to be as certain as possible that the potential of a campaign achieving its desired outcome is increased by investing media dollars in this way.

Continuity

Continuity involves the scheduling of the advertisement. A planner will want to schedule the pattern of advertising so that subsequent messages build on top of the gains made by previous insertions. If the insertions are scheduled too close together, the audience will experience message fatigue and perhaps be turned off or even angered by the constant interruption by the brand, which can actually move consumers farther away from a positive experience or sale. By contrast, if the insertions are scheduled too far apart, the brand may be losing ground because the message is not frequent enough to break through. If scheduled optimally, each subsequent insertion will appear before the effects have worn off from previous one, so there is a cumulative effect. Proper scheduling like this can provide continuity.

Recency

Recency is the idea that an advertising exposure is most potent when it occurs close to a purchase occasion. For some brands, arguably, even one exposure placed at an optimal decision-making time can influence a purchase decision. Recency explains why some pizza restaurants advertise their delivery service late at night, when people staying up late are hungry and might not want to leave the house for something to eat.

AUDIENCE MEASURES BY MEDIA CLASS

Now let's break things down a bit more granularly. Different media classes measure, value, and price their audiences in different ways. Let's look at measurement practices by media class.

Print media audiences: Magazines and newspapers

The gold standard for measuring audiences for newspapers and magazines is circulation. Although most have heard this term before, it is one of the most misused words in media. First, let's start with what circulation is not. This term is neither the number of copies printed, nor the number of readers of a publication. Circulation is the number of copies that were received or picked up by an audience during a given publishing cycle. For example, if a monthly publication printed 250,000 copies, and only 225,000 of these were distributed via subscriptions and news stand sales, the circulation would for this publishing cycle would be 225,000. The remaining 25,000 copies that were not picked up by consumers would not be included. Because more than one person can read each copy of a publication, or perhaps a copy was sent out but never actually read, circulation is not a good measure of readership. It simply measures the number of copies printed and received or picked up. This is where it gets confusing. Because most publications do not actually have more accurate measures for their actual readers, circulation is used as a surrogate or substitute for the number of readers. Doing so is an industry-accepted practice albeit a convoluted one.

This is not to say that all publications are lacking in more detailed audience information. Some invest a significant amount in researching their readers to better understand and be able to write for as well as sell ad inventory toward. One measure that a readership study will show is a publication's *readers per copy*. For example, most newspapers can average two readers per copy, while certain coffee table magazines that are on display in doctors' offices and other public waiting spaces may have a much larger number of readers per copy. If desired, a planner could estimate the total audience for a publication by multiplying their circulation by the readers per copy. Thus, in print media such as newspapers and magazines, the circulation is the number of copies printed and actually put out in distribution, whereas the audience or readership is the number of persons who read those copies of the publication.

Broadcast media audiences: Video and audio

Let's begin with defining what video measurements are based on. First, it will help to understand what is meant by a *television household*, abbreviated as TVHH in the media business. A household is a group of people who live together, most often a family, but also a single person living alone, partners sharing living quarters, or roommates. A TVHH is a household that has an operating television set; the set may be on or off, because the term *operating* means that the receiving set works, not that it is being used at any particular moment. Audience numbers are provided for all TVHH, but also for individual target segments.

Another common term is *households using television*, abbreviated as HUT. It refers to the television households with a set turned on as a percentage of all TVHHs or a particular target segment. The major radio ratings service reports on *people using radio*, abbreviated as PUR, which is persons listening to the radio expressed as a percentage of all people with radios by target segment.

Ratings

In linear TV, a rating refers to the persons who see or hear a particular program, station, or network expressed as a percentage of the target audience with sets, whether they have a set on at that moment or not. The rating can be for a local market area – called spot markets or designated market areas (DMAs) – or it can be aggregated for the entire country – called national or network TV.

Similarly, a radio rating describes those persons tuned to a particular program, station, or network expressed as a percentage of all the households or target segments

TABLE 20.2 An example of ratings and shares

Television station	TVHH sets on	Rating	Share
KAAA	12,000	$\dfrac{12,000}{250,000} = 4.8$	$\dfrac{12,000}{54,000} = 22$
KBBB	15,000	$\dfrac{15,000}{250,000} = 6.0$	$\dfrac{15,000}{54,000} = 28$
KCCC	18,000	$\dfrac{18,000}{250,000} = 7.2$	$\dfrac{18,000}{54,000} = 33$
KDDD	9,000	$\dfrac{9,000}{250,000} = 3.6$	$\dfrac{9,000}{54,000} = 17$
		21.6 HUT	100%

$$HUT = \frac{54,000}{250,000} = 21.6\%$$

that have operating radio receivers. All radios are counted, including those in use and those turned off at that particular time.

Share of audience

Again, using linear TV as an example, the share is those persons tuned to a particular program station or network as a percentage of all target households with sets turned on at that time. This means that in contrast to rating, share is not a percentage of the total target population, but rather a percentage of the HUT or target households watching something at that time. Like ratings, share can be determined nationally or locally within a particular DMA. A radio share follows the same practices.

To summarize, both rating and share involve the same people, those tuned to a particular program, station, or network at a particular time. Rating refers to those persons as a percentage of all target households who could potentially be reached while share describes those same persons as a percentage of all those with sets on at that moment (see Table 20.2.)

AN EXAMPLE OF RATINGS AND SHARES

Palookaville has four television stations serving its population of 250,000 TVHH. For 8 P.M. on Wednesdays, when 54,000 TVHH have their sets on, here are the ratings and shares for the four stations.

Here's another example. Let's say that there are 100,000 TVHH in Erie, Pennsylvania. Suppose 60,000 of those households have their television sets on at 8:00 P.M., and 20,000 of those households are watching a particular station in Erie. The station's rating would be 20% and its share would be 33%.

COMBINING REACH AND FREQUENCY FOR AUDIENCE VOLUME TOTALS

Beyond reach and frequency as stand-alone measures, it makes sense that campaigns be evaluated on their total combined volume. If reach is a measure of unique audience exposures or conversations, and frequency is a measure of repeated audience exposures or conversations, then combining reach and frequency would give us a measure of *total conversations* also referred to as *media weight.* Media weight can be measured in two basic forms: weight as a raw number and weight as a percent.

Media weight or total conversations as a number: Impressions

When combined, reach as a number and frequency measures the volume or weight of a schedule or campaign as a single figure called *impressions* or IMPs. Impressions are referred to as total conversations expressed as a raw number. Table 20.3 shows an example of how impressions can be calculated.

In this example, there is a frequency of 5 with an average of 25 million audience members for each insertion. This makes the average reach number 25 million. Impressions measure both numerical reach and frequency in a single figure.

$25 million\ R \times 5F = 125 million\ impressions$

So, *reach* (as a number) multiplied by *frequency* produces *total impressions.*

$R\# \times F = IMPs$

Weight as a percent: Target rating points TRPs

The sum of the ratings for a certain period of time is measured as *target rating points,* or TRPs. Let's say five advertisements are run each week on a television network, and the different ads garnered ratings as shown in Table 20.4.

Five spots have been run for a total of 50 TRPs, which means the average spot performed a rating of 10%. In this example, 5 is the frequency (F) and 10 is the average rating, or the average percentage reach (R). Thus, 50 TRPs gives an average of 10% reach or an average rating of 10 combined with the frequency of 5. As seen here, the TRP

TABLE 20.3 Calculating total impressions

Frequency	Target audience reached in millions
1	27.5
2	20.0
3	30.0
4	25.0
5	22.5
	125.0 impressions

TABLE 20.4 Example ratings for an ad campaign

Spot	Target audience reached as a % (rating)
#	
1	11
2	8
3	12
4	10
5	9
Total	50 TRPs

gives a combination of reach (10% in this example) and frequency (5 in this example) in a single figure. Note that when working with TRPs, reach is represented as a percent.

$$10R \times 5F = 50GRP$$

So, *reach* (as a percentage) multiplied by *frequency* produces *target rating points.*

$$R\% \times F = TRPs$$

It is important for to keep in mind that a single rating, called a rating point, reaches 1% of the audience. *It is also critical to remember that because ratings are percentages, they should never be added across media classes, across different targets, or across different geographic areas. As long as these three variables remain consistent, ratings can be added indefinitely.*

AN EXAMPLE OF REACH, FREQUENCY, TRPs, AND IMPRESSIONS

A furniture store realizes that it cannot achieve 100% reach in its local community of 50,000 population, but it would like to get close to reaching every target member possible. Table 20.5 shows the advertising results from 11 weekly advertising insertions.

TABLE 20.5 Reach for a print campaign

Insertion	Reach %	Reach #
1	11	5,500
2	8	4,000
3	9	4,500
4	6	3,000
5	13	6,500
6	5	2,500
7	17	8,500
8	10	5,000
9	8	4,000
10	6	3,000
11	6	3,000
F = 11	99 TRPs	49,500 impressions

With 99 TRPs, did the store get close to its goal of 100% reach? It is unlikely, unless no audience member was exposed to more than one advertising insertion, which is doubtful. More likely, the average audience member was exposed to perhaps three of 11 insertions, so the percentage reach would be about 33%.

IMPRESSIONS AS THE COMMON MEDIA STANDARD

Now that it is has been shown how total conversations or impressions can be derived from the dimensions of reach and frequency within broadcast, it is important to look at media weight more inclusively. The concept of measuring audiences as impressions has been modified and adapted for almost all platforms to become the common currency or standard. Media classes such as SEM, online display, paid social, out of home (OOH), and gaming all report audiences in IMPs.

More recently, video and audio have been more often reporting their audiences in impressions to stay consistent. In fact, the term impression has the same basic meaning across media classes, and since they are raw numbers, impressions are the single audience measure that can be added together across platforms. When this is done, it can create a combined estimate for the total conversations of a campaign, a number that can be quite impressive for sure. However, it is important for planners to remember a few things.

First, although impressions can be added together across platforms to create a sort of thud factor, not all impressions or conversations have the same value. For example, every time an audience member drives by an OOH board on their way to work, an impression is generated. By comparison, every time an SEM ad is served up, another impression is generated. It is quite evident that the attention the audience gives to their repeated daily exposure to a passive OOH board is not as valuable as that of a customized SEM ad that is driven by a unique search inquiry with intent.

Second, what constitutes an impression across platforms is not consistent. For example, an impression in linear TV is measured as a potential exposure to an ad, an impression in print is the equivalent of circulation, and an impression in an in-game dynamic ad means that the ad is seen for a minimum number of seconds. Because what constitutes and impression in each platform is different, and attention levels are not included in the calculation of impressions, adding impressions across platforms or media classes together should be done with caution.

DIGITAL MEDIA AUDIENCES: SEARCH ENGINE MARKETING AND DISPLAY

With digital ad spending now accounting for at or above 50% of most brand budgets, it is a space where planners must be well versed. Although digital platforms such as SEM, digital display and paid social have adapted a significant amount of the concepts and terminologies already discussed in this chapter, this space also has a complex language of its own. It should be noted that the reason for much of this complexity is that digital platforms have significant advantages over the offline world in terms of metrics because the measurements are more behavior-based. Here are a few of the most important additional terms, concepts, and differences for a planner to know about digital ad investments.

The online term for unduplicated audiences is *unique audience or unique visitors.*

In digital platforms, ratings are specifically for ad units not just their surrounding content. Although there are new measures being introduced that better define ad unit ratings in other offline platforms, it is certainly not yet a standard within the industry.

Because of the ability to observe and follow audience interactions within the digital realm, many other measures are possible beyond the idea of ratings to measure audience actions and reactions. One such example is as an *ad click*, which is a user's response to an ad that causes a redirect to another web location or another frame or page within the ad. From here, *click-through rate* can be determined. This is the number of clicks divided by the total number of ad impressions served. There is a plenitude of other quite self-explanatory concepts and possible measurements within digital platforms such as *time spent on site, video or audio completes, page views, downloads, app installs,* and *shares* to name a few. The idea is that once an audience member has interacted with online content or an action has been taken on an ad, the steps that follow can be monitored all the way to the end result. That is called a *conversion* or *response* where people take action based on content or an ad to fill out an application, go to a website, or make and e-commerce purchase (see Table 20.6). This level of detail in terms of response is why online advertising is so popular among advertisers.

That said, this is an opportune time to mention the hugely negative impact ad fraud has on digital campaign measurement. It is estimated that as much as $1 out of every $3 spent in on-line ad campaigns is essentially lost to fraudulent activities such as click bots, domain spoofing, or geomasking. All of these and more are highly sophisticated approaches hackers use to create fake or misrepresented audience interactions. So, as planners and brands get excited about the significantly advanced measurements that digital campaigns provide, they should also beware of considering those metrics infallible.

There are many kinds of advertisements available online, and some of them are listed in Exhibit 20.1.

TABLE 20.6 Prototype online campaign

Item	Number
Total impressions	10,000,000
Click-through rate	.02%
Clicks	200,000
Sales Transactions	50,000
Conversion rate from click-through	25.0%

EXHIBIT 20.1 TYPES OF CYBER ADVERTISEMENTS

- Banner ads
- Rich-media ads (e.g. animated)
- Pre-rolls
- Pop-up ads
- Interstitials (appear in a separate browser, streamed)
- Superstitials (same as interstitial, but cached)
- Extramercials (must scroll sideways to see ad)
- Video banners
- Webmercials
- Advertorials/infomercials

SUMMARY

Having a strong base in media terminology and basic concepts is critical. These concepts on their own are not difficult to understand, but they can become difficult to use in a practical sense. It important to think about these concepts when using them to fully question comparisons and challenge those who want to simply go by the numbers.

For example, reach and frequency can be elusive tools even though they seem straight forward because each medium can have very different universes upon which they base their information. As one who controls the media budget, it is crucial for a planner to understand the numbers on which negotiations are being based. For example, since it is a percentage, a rating in a very large DMA is far different than the same rating in a much smaller DMA. By comparison, a 5 Household rating in city of New York, the largest DMA, is approximately 367,431 viewers, while a 5 Household rating in the smallest DMA of Glendive, Montana is just 219 viewers.

Here is another example of how planners need to think about the concepts of audience management beyond taking them at face value. Radio stations are likely to tout their ratings based on a metro or standard metropolitan statistical areas (SMSA). Most metros are considerably smaller than television DMAs, so when comparing a rating between these two media classes, a planner will need to establish common ground for a meaningful comparison.

Additionally, when attempting to improve the click-through rate of an SEM campaign, on the surface the thought might be to simply increase budget to garner more clicks. However, if thought through more diligently, it becomes apparent that rather than spending more, a brand might want to first optimize their budgets more effectively to improve the accuracy and response they are getting with the existing funds. By being more analytical and implementing better investment strategies, it is possible to greatly improve responses such as click-through as a ratio to impressions delivered without spending any additional funds.

Finally, when looking into impressions generated by a digital display campaign, it would be important to ask big questions such as if there was a distinction made between total impressions served in a campaign and impressions that were actually viewable on-screen?

A familiarity with and working knowledge of the terms and concepts discussed in this chapter are both key, but really applying critical thinking when planning and using them is equally crucial.

Gloss Media turns beauty time into money

In today's constantly connected world, it's almost impossible to find a place where advertisers can find a captive audience. Before cell phones became commonplace, advertisers could reach travelers in airports with ads running on television monitors installed at departure gates. Similarly, the waiting room at doctors' offices used to carry magazines especially designed for people who only had ten or so minutes to spend looking at the magazine.

Now that we all have cell phones, though, we can easily entertain ourselves while we're waiting. There's really no type of location where we can't use our phones, right?

Well, spend time in any beauty salon or nail salon and you see a lot of customers looking for something to do. It is tough to keep looking at your smartphone when you are having a manicure. We've trained ourselves to keep our minds busy so we always have our phones at hand, so what happens when we can't?

That was the insight that Gloss Media used to develop a niche broadcast network for beauty and nail salons. Gloss provides both the televisions and the content. Salon owners get televisions for free and in exchange, Gloss Media schedules their network of salon televisions with programming and advertising designed for that 30- to 60-minute trip to the salon.

According to Gloss Media, there are more than 50,000 nail salons in the United States, with each of them having about 3,000 client visits each month. The vast majority are women, and while they're a captive audience, they're also relaxed and pampered. They are also likely to be close to a shopping center.

It's a great atmosphere to place a message for this audience, and it's a win-win for salons and Gloss Media.

CHAPTER 21

Learning about media costs

....

GETTING THE BEST DEAL IS RELATIVE

Once you understand the audience of a medium or a media vehicle, the reckoning of media planning comes about when you assess its value. Media planning and negotiating are based on judging how efficient media are and comparing the cost of one media vehicle with another.

In the advertising industry, there are *absolute costs* and *relative costs*. Absolute costs, sometimes called unit costs or vehicle costs, refer to the out-of-pocket price you are going to pay for placement in a specific media vehicle. A full-page black and white advertisement in the national edition of the *Wall Street Journal* costs approximately $240,000. Running a 30-second commercial during the Super Bowl costs approximately $4 million. Buying a local radio commercial during a popular morning show in Sherman, Texas, might cost $40. So, unit costs vary widely and are based largely on the total number of impressions that the individual media vehicle delivers and the value that advertisers place on those impressions.

That brings us to relative costs. It is important to understand the relative efficiency of the Super Bowl and the *Wall Street Journal*. Without such an understanding, how would you know what the best value is? To compare one media vehicle to another and one medium to another, the gold standard in media cost comparison is *cost-per-thousand*, or CPM.

COST-PER-THOUSAND

In advertising, the number 1,000 can be abbreviated as K (*kilo*) or M (*mille*). Most often, K is used for money and M is used for audiences. Because 1,000 × 1,000 equals a million, we use MM to mean a million. (Do not be confused by media headlines, which often abbreviate million using just one M.)

DOI: 10.4324/9781003258162-21

All this is a bit of background to explain the abbreviation of "cost-per-thousand" as CPM rather than CPT. With that little history lesson under our belt, we can put the CPM term to work. CPM is a mainstay for comparing one media vehicle to another, as well as comparing one medium to another. Let's start off by looking at how to use CPM to compare one media vehicle to another.

It can be difficult to compare one media vehicle to another because you must consider the advertising unit rates or prices along with the reach or impressions that they deliver. This is comparable to looking at the average cost/gallon of gas from different gas stations, or the cost/square foot of different homes for sale to determine which is the best deal.

Let's do a CPM example to show relative cost in media in action. Say that you are looking at two different magazines that have different unit rates and different circulations. Say that Magazine A, with a circulation of 2.1 million, charges $23,500 for a full-page advertisement, and that Magazine B, with a circulation of 1.2 million, charges $13,500 for the same full-page ad. You might expect that the magazine with the larger circulation charges more because costs rise as you reach more people, but is it the more economical way to reach your audience?

This is where CPM comes into play. Instead of trying to compare the cost and circulation at the same time, we assume that each magazine has a circulation of only 1,000. We compare the cost for each 1,000 in circulation by dividing the advertising rate by the circulation to get the cost of advertising in a single copy of the publication. Then we multiply the answer by 1,000 to compare the cost of a thousand-copy circulation.

Here is the CPM for Magazine A. Doing the same for the other publication, Magazine B, gives a comparison CPM.

$$Magazine\ A = \frac{\$23,500}{2,100,000} \times 1,000 = \$11.19\,CPM$$

$$Magazine\ B = \frac{\$13,500}{1,200,000} \times 1,000 = \$11.25\,CPM$$

So, according to this CPM analysis, Magazine A has a CPM (based on its circulation) of $11.19, whereas Magazine B has a CPM of $11.25. In this case, the CPMs are virtually identical. Because Magazine A has a 75% higher circulation than Magazine B and is priced at relatively the same cost as the smaller circulation publication, Magazine A seems to be the better value of the two.

CPM is used in every media analysis from print to broadcast to digital display. The only difference between the various media is the method used to calculate the audience. Raw circulation figures are typically used as a point of comparison for print, whereas audience estimates are used for broadcast and online audience figures. Still, the same analysis can be performed whether you are comparing two websites or two television programs. And like with the examples above with cost/gallon of gas or cost/square foot for a new home, the lower the resulting CPM number, the better the deal is.

TABLE 21.1 Average market media CPM based on adults

Medium	Average market CPM
Magazine	$140–1,300
Google SEM	$38.40
Network TV	$20–30
Out-of-home	$13–22
Newspaper	$10–$45
Radio	$10–20
Paid social media	$12.12

Source: Top Draw Inc. via topdraw.com, March 2021

CPM AS AN INTERMEDIA COMPARISON ANALYSIS

It is difficult even for the most seasoned media professional to compare advertisements in different media. Is a full-page, four-color bleed advertisement in a magazine the equivalent of a 30-second network television commercial? Or is the placement in a video game worth the same as a banner ad on a gaming enthusiasts' website? These are difficult questions, and although there is some research in the area of intermedia comparisons, much of it remains proprietary, meaning the research is generally owned by a medium itself (such as a video game company), and often they choose not to share.

In the case of intermedia comparisons, CPM is a standard to apply but certainly should not be the only analysis that a media planner uses. The following is a general CPM estimate for a wide variety of media.

As you can see in Table 21.1, if you were selecting based on CPM alone, radio would be the medium of choice for every advertising campaign. Yet, of the media listed in Table 21.2, radio has one of the lowest media impacts or advertising revenue within this hypothetical consumer packaged goods example.

As a brand manager looking at the media landscape, you will need to work with your media group to determine the impact of each medium for your particular

TABLE 21.2 Hypothetical consumer packaged goods CPM adjusted by media impact weights

Medium	CPM	Media impact	Adjusted CPM
Magazine	$140–1,300	50	$280–2,600
Google SEM	$38.40	70	$54.86
Network TV	$20–$30	80	$25–37.50
Out-of-home	$13–$22	10	$130–$220
Newspaper	$10–$45	20	$50–$225
Radio	$10–20	30	$33.33–$66.67
Paid social media	$12.12	65	$18.65

Note: Media impact score 1 to 100.

category or brand. The impact value of each medium can then be compared to the CPM or used to weigh the CPM for a more definitive analysis.

Table 21.2 is an example of weighing CPMs based on an impact score for each medium for a hypothetical packaged-goods brand such as a toothpaste. Let's look at how this might be applied for this brand. Based on this chart, if the media decision makers for this toothpaste brand feel that a radio ad has the same impact as a targeted Google search engine marketing (SEM) ad, then they can purchase considerably more radio impressions for their dollar than with SEM. However, since this chart shows their information weights targeted SEM is worth more than double the value of radio ads, then radio may not be such a bargain for this brand.

The CPM is the standard measure for comparing media, but it should not be used in a vacuum. It provides the basis for determining value but is not the only aspect of assigning value to a medium.

COST-PER-POINT

CPM is the main cost comparison criterion when looking at a variety of media, but planners working with broadcast costs on both a national and local basis often use a standard called *cost-per-point* (CPP). A cost-per-point compares broadcast vehicles on the basis of how much it costs to reach 1% of the audience. Remember that a 1% reach is the same as a rating point, so we call this comparison cost-per-point.

Let's take a look at how you might use a CPP in comparing two radio stations. Radio Station A costs $5,300 per commercial unit and reaches 2.2% of our audience (the rating). So, we simply divide the cost by the rating to derive the CPP.

$$CPP = \frac{\$5,300}{2.2\,Rtg} = \$2,409\,CPP$$

Now look at Radio Station B, which charges $6,200 per unit and achieves a rating of 2.5 percent. Its CPP would be as follows:

$$CPP = \frac{\$6,200}{2.5\,Rtg} = \$2,480\,CPP$$

In this example, Radio Station A is slightly more efficient in reaching a rating point (1% of the audience) than Radio Station B. When media negotiators are rapidly calculating hundreds of programs and stations, the CPP is a key measure for efficiency. Think of it as the currency for local broadcast negotiations.

The reason CPP is used in broadcast planning instead of CPM is that CPP is a much simpler method of assessing costs across various markets or across various dayparts. CPM is a great analysis tool to determine value, as is CPP; but CPP allows for the quick addition of costs across various markets. If you are planning to advertise in the top five media markets in the United States in daytime television, you would not want to add up all the hundreds of possibilities of unit costs for this television period across all these markets. The CPP allows you to quickly figure costs by taking into account the size of the market, because 1% of the population of New York City is a lot bigger than 1% of the population of Boise, Idaho.

ONLINE COST ANALYSIS

As we said earlier, the online media world offers much deeper diagnostics than most other media. CPM is the initial standard for all online analysis, whether it is in SEM or in online display advertising.

The second layer of cost analysis beyond the CPM is the *cost-per-click* (CPC). The cost-per-click is calculated by simply dividing the media cost by the number of clicks obtained within a certain time frame. Most online media professionals analyze their online plans after a week or two of activity to determine what sites and what creative executions are producing the lowest CPC. Then adjustments are made to the subsequent schedules to (1) add more impressions to proven performers, (2) eliminate poorly performing sites, or (3) add contingency sites to the campaign.

Depending upon the category, online media planners negotiate with the websites on either a CPC or on a *cost-per-lead* (CPL) basis. CPL is the cost an advertiser pays for an explicit sign-up from a potential consumer interested in the advertiser offer. For example, if the advertisers know they will make money if their campaign hits a certain cost-per-lead target (say, $20), then they will negotiate with the web publishers to pay that much for that target response, but not pay for leads above that threshold. For established categories with known conversion rates, such as auto insurance, this is a standard method for online placement. It also ties in nicely with SEM pricing, which is done on a bid basis for selective keywords: the more popular the keyword, the more it may cost. For example, the insurance business is highly competitive online, so a keyword such as "auto insurance" could command as much as $200 per click. On the other hand, a lower-interest category, such as hazardous waste hauling, may be only $10 per click.

Some online media planners also use the terms *cost-per-action* or *cost-per-acquisition* (CPA) to describe the cost of generating a sale, acquiring a customer, or making some sort of transaction. Other terms sometimes used interchangeably here are *cost-per-order* (CPO) and *cost-per-transaction* (CPT), both of which measure the cost of media placement to generate a final sale. Again, this is calculated by dividing the online campaign cost by the action that it is designed to generate.

ONLINE PRICING

Advertising online uses some of the same pricing approaches, such as CPM, as does advertising in other media. Nevertheless, there are additional systems used within the online space that do not apply to other advertising media. As Table 21.3 shows, the most common pricing systems include techniques such as counting the number of click-through searches, where Internet users go beyond a website by clicking on an icon or some other connection that takes them to another site. Total time spent on a

TABLE 21.3 Primetime TV local cost per point

Market	DMA rank	Women 18–49 daytime CPP
New York, NY	1	$5,952
Tampa, FL	11	$1,117
Austin, TX	39	$422
Eugene, OR	117	$86
Anchorage, AK	147	$101
Total		$7,678

Source: Service Quality Analytics Data (SQAD).

site is another pricing approach, but it can be misleading because a person may access a website and then leave the room while still connected. That would add up to a large amount of time viewing, even though no viewing is actually occurring. Size-based pricing is dependent upon the size of the advertisement as a portion of the web page, but many if not most Internet ads are full-page insertions so that measure may not be very reliable. CPT charges only if an actual purchase is made, which would diminish the role of common Internet searches that do not result in buying behavior at that particular time. Most Internet advertisers now use a combination of these other approaches, known as *hybrid deals.*

PAID SOCIAL MEDIA PRICING

One big myth of social media is that to use it effectively as a brand has a zero cost. Although having an organic social presence does not have a message placement cost, a number of years ago all social media platforms migrated to a pay-to-play system, which means for a brand's message in social to be boosted and show up in news feeds now has a set associated cost often with a minimum buy in levels. Social media such as Facebook, Twitter, and others often use paid pricing systems adopted from other media, especially from various online methods such as CPM or CPC. Some examples of these pricing options are illustrated in Table 21.4.

Much advertiser use of social media is not actually involved with placing messages, but rather with using social media to track how often the company and its products and services are discussed, and whether such discussions are favorable using techniques such as *content analysis* and *sentiment analysis* to gauge the nature or tone of conversations consumers are having about a brand.

TABLE 21.4 Some systems used for Internet advertising pricing

- Cost per thousand (CPM)
- Click-through rates
- Time spent listening/viewing/visiting
- Size-based pricing (more space or more pages, the higher the cost)
- Cost per transaction
- Hybrid deals (combinations of other approaches)

PRODUCTION COSTS AND WORKING VERSUS NON-WORKING DOLLARS

In addition to the costs of media space and/or time, there is a cost for producing the advertisements. Production costs should always be considered when planning media campaigns as many of these costs are fixed and can be quite sizeable investments. The more media categories and platforms involved in an outreach plan, and the more complex the production process for each, the larger the budget for production will need to be. To help overcome some of the inherit costs of content creation, many brands build assets that are more adaptable and optimized for the most critical media environments in the campaign.

Because being in market and in front of consumers with as much budget as possible is the goal of most brands, many have guidelines or even caps on what are considered working and non-working dollars. *Working dollars* is money spent on message placements that are actively "working" to reach consumers, where *non-working dollars* is money spent on creative asset production. A common ratio for a large national brand is to have 80% working dollars in market to 20% non-working dollars in creative asset production.

Cost-plus

Many advertising agencies that handle production for their clients simply take the production costs and add a certain marked-up percentage, commonly 15, 18, or 20%, depending on the type of work and the contact needed between the agency and the advertiser. Such an approach can work, but there are other approaches that may provide a more realistic reflection of the actual work involved.

Time-based

With time-based production compensation, some hourly reimbursement rate is established and then simply multiplied by the number of hours spent on this work. An approach like this reflects the investment by the agency in the production work, but it is easy to spend a lot of time on details that the advertiser may not want. Unexpected problems often arise in advertising work, which makes advance budgeting difficult or inaccurate. Thus, although time-based pricing may be somewhat more reflective of the actual costs than simpler cost-plus pricing, it still poses problems.

Performance-based

This approach tries to measure the outcome of the advertising and then base reimbursement on the performance; simply put, the more sales generated by the advertising, the more the production costs. But such an approach is difficult to establish, and perhaps even more difficult to measure. It may, for example, be difficult if not impossible to measure what role the advertising played in the marketing work, or how much the advertising came into play in swaying the purchase decisions.

Value-based

In this case, the value of the overall work is measured and then the agency reimbursement is calculated. A print advertisement of a certain size is considered to have a certain value, and a television commercial of a certain length is considered to have a certain value. By setting these values in advance, both the agency and the advertiser know what compensation will be accrued. Some productions may take longer, or require more investment than others, which is difficult to predict and to account for using this system. It may encourage agencies to do work rapidly rather than well, or to prepare more versions of an advertisement than might otherwise be warranted.

Other fees

The costs of public relations work are most often based on the time spent working on the account. However, like advertising costs, some work has more value and some measure of outcome needs to be considered.

Other common fees include campaign set up, campaign monitoring, reporting, and optimization. There are also fees for all sorts of other services, such as overnight delivery, attending special seminars or training sessions, or even entertaining the top executives of the client company. The idea is that a company needs to consider all costs associated with doing business when budgeting funds for outreach campaigns.

COST TRADE-OFFS

Going back to the beginning of this chapter, we discussed the two kinds of cost analysis: the initial analysis is absolute costs and the second is relative costs. These two pillars of media value analysis are used by media planners in their ongoing determination of the best media plan for the dollar.

As a brand manager in charge of media dollars, it is important that you ask a variety of questions regarding media costs. The first question is, "What can I do effectively for the dollars that I have to invest in media?" This is not asking what the best CPM is, but what the best media plan is.

Let's take a look at an example for a national packaged-goods brand on a $1 million budget. Here are three plans developed for the same product by different media agencies:

1. Plan A was developed by a CPM-driven agency, which said that the brand should schedule national television spots for eight weeks within the daytime television daypart, with approximately 40 target rating points, or TRPs, per week, or 15 to 20 commercials per week.
2. Plan B recommended only magazines as the support plan. Their plan consisted of six months of support using six publications with four insertions per publication or a total of 24 insertions.
3. Plan C recommended allocating the dollars to the six best markets for the brand to develop a television and print support plan that would cover 75% of the year with activity.

All three plans included paid social, and similar significant investments in SEM.

Based on the question of effectiveness, *which of these plans do you feel meets the criteria?* Do you get the same answer if you ask the *which plan is the most cost efficient?*

Common sense would tell you that whereas Plan A might be cost efficient, it may not be very effective. On the other hand, Plan C may be the most effective, but it might be too limiting in terms of sales and efficiency. And so, there you have the trade-offs that happen with every media plan and negotiation. There is always a trade-off between what can be done well and what is most efficient for the brand.

SUMMARY

Working with media costs is a very important skill set as it is the responsibility of the media planner to be as diligent and accountable for every dollar they spend. Using measures such as CPM, CPP, CPA, and CPO, planners can determine the relative cost and potential impact of the investment choices they are faced with. It is also critical that other factors be included beyond just budget efficiency. In the end, the best media plan for your brand may not be the most efficient plan. It is for this reason that as media plans and investment options are assessed, it is important to understand the fundamentals of cost analysis, but it is even more important to understand the fundamentals of trade-off analysis and other measures of media effectiveness.

CHAPTER 22

Evaluating opportunities

....

APPROACHING DIFFICULT MEDIA INVESTMENT DECISIONS

Identifying the optimal media vehicles for the media plan is a key component of the planner's job. This process involves comparing one medium to another as well as stacking up
one vehicle against another. Should an advertiser use magazines or television? Should
an ad be purchased on a search engine or as an online display ad? In addition, knowing
how different vehicles work together is another important aspect of a planner's work.

There is no single way to make good decisions. In fact, we do not know if a media investment decision is a good one until after the ad has run. So, how do we move forward to
make the best possible decisions we can? Most media planners utilize a number of different
perspectives, including the research findings provided by rating sources and by a specific
medium, and their own experiences that inform a subjective appraisal of the media vehicles.

ALIGNMENT WITH AUDIENCE DELIVERY GOALS

Planners will need to analyze the audience potential, including measures such as reach
and frequency of the different vehicles under consideration when making investment
choices. The media plan will contain specific reach and frequency goals, and the
planner will evaluate which vehicles best achieve those goals, either alone or working
together. Rarely does one medium do the job on its own, which is why it's important
to construct an integrated plan that takes advantage of individual audience deliveries
as well as the scale needed to create the brand's desired outcomes.

ALIGNMENT WITH IMPACT GOALS

Part of selecting the right media investment is understanding the overall messaging
and campaign goals and how different media or even vehicles can strongly influence
the impact a brand is able to achieve there. For example, even though social media

DOI: 10.4324/9781003258162-22

has a significant amount audience loyalty and time spent is only increasing, in general, most turn to social media for things other than shopping. Although research indicates that social media users are showing an increase in their follow up to ads viewed in their longer-term shopping strategies, most view ads within their social feed in the moment as highly annoying and easily overlooked. By contrast, social is a great platform for engagement. So, for a brand seeking immediate transactions, social might not be the best choice, but for one looking for deepening the brand's conversation and relationship with its community, social could be ideal.

When it comes to matching brand goals with potential media audiences, other syndicated sources like Kantar Media SRDS or Mediamark Research Inc. (MRI) can also be utilized to understand a bit more about how a specific target audience matches the vehicle's known audience. These syndicated sources can tell you, for example, which audio genres, platforms or even specific podcasts Peloton users prefer. Understanding how a very specific user audience interacts with a particular vehicle can help rationalize higher CPMs in a media plan if necessary to prove that effectiveness outweighs efficiency in certain cases.

Finally, to better connect media and vehicle choices with desired brand outcomes, planners can use other measures such as analyzing results of previous campaigns, attribution modelling from outside vendors, or even sales modelling based on the brand's own proprietary data. Looking at the impact previous investments have created helps planners move forward more informed about future investments.

ALIGNMENT WITH CONTENT RELEVANCY, AUDIENCE RECEPTIVITY, AND ENGAGEMENT

When it comes to audiences consuming media and, thus, to brands choosing strong investments, good content is key: It is one of the biggest indicators of consumer mindset while ads are being delivered. Understanding and evaluating the content surrounding a brand's message as well as the audience's engagement with the medium and the content there must be considered. Is this relevant content that seems to lend a sense of connection or authority, such as an ad for our new natural anti-aging eye cream, running within an article titled *Nature's Best Beauty Secrets*? Are audience members using this vehicle or content to entertain, educate, or connect with each other? For example, would my ad for tax relief planning be appropriate in a space where my stressed-out entrepreneurial audience member is attempting to briefly escape from the financial issues they are facing with their budding business? Depending on the mode of operation of the audience of a vehicle and the planner's understanding of the consumer, the brand message may be extremely relevant and well received or might show up as an uninvited or highly unwelcomed intrusion.

ALIGNMENT WITH MESSAGING SCALE NEEDS: COST EFFICIENCY

Because it is critical each media dollar be spent not only to create impact, but to ensure that impact is at scale, investment decisions cannot be made without serious consideration of efficiency as well. The best "apples-to-apples" comparison is a cost-per-thousand (CPM) comparison. CPM was discussed in detail earlier in Chapter 21. You will remember CPM is the cost to expose the message to 1,000 people in the target audience. This measure celebrates media investment choices so that relative cost comparisons can be made between media platforms and vehicles of many different audience sizes and price structures. CPM breaks down options to the least common denominator level to see which venue truly provides the most audience for the smallest investment. Although important, remember that the most efficient plan or option may not be the cheapest out of pocket and may also not prove to be the most impactful. Striking a balance between efficiency and effectiveness again allows impact to be realized but at the scale it is needed.

ALIGNMENT WITH TIMING NEEDS

The specific period of time over which a campaign is to be spread and the various periods of active windows within the campaign will, in part, dictate the best vehicle selection. The mix of vehicles chosen for the campaign should allow for some consistency of advertising exposure over that time. Some campaigns "front load" a message to seed the message strongly with a target early-on during the campaign. Others put more dollars behind making sure that there is more distributed consistency in the campaign. Either way, fully understanding purchase cycles including when consumers begin their brand research, when they start to narrow their brand considerations, and when they are most likely to make their purchase will be critical.

Message timing needs can also be more micro in nature. Some brands have different calls to action at different times of the day and media vehicles might need to be scheduled around those for more impact. For example, a coffee shop might see 85–90% of their business during the hours of 5 A.M. and 10 A.M. In order to talk with their consumers during those peak purchase hours, vehicles that will allow for customized messaging for coffee to run only during that time window, such as social media posts run only in the early morning newsfeeds with a 10 A.M. cut off, might take priority.

By increasing the odds that a brand's message is in front of the consumers at every stage in the purchasing process during which they hope to reach them will greatly improve outcomes. They key is finding vehicles that can connect brands with consumers just before and during each of these stages.

ALIGNMENT WITH GEOGRAPHIC NEEDS

The necessary footprint of the vehicles and how their distribution and audiences align with the geographic needs of a campaign is an important variable when considering investment options. For example, if a quick-service restaurant brand such as Chick-fil-A experiences big differences in consumption from market to market or even from different neighborhoods within markets, a planner can create and activate uniquely geofenced search engine marketing (SEM) ad groups with keywords tailored more to each region, local market, or even ZIP code. Highly localized digital Out-of-Home can also be added in the key neighborhoods of local markets of the campaign to reinforce the message for the restaurant including customized calls to action, such as special meal deals. By contrast, if Chick-fil-A has other requirements that dictate a truly national footprint for their branding campaign with a much less customized message to drive overall brand favorability, becoming the lead sponsor of a top-rated national TV event such the Chick-fil-A Peach Bowl and using a much broader SEM footprint would be more appropriate.

The key to choosing vehicles with the right geographic flexibility is finding the right vehicles to not only reach and engage the intended audience, but also to be certain that the vehicles chosen can do so with as little wasted exposures across geographies as possible. Finally, it is important to mention that as illustrated in the example above, brands can have many different geographic needs within the same campaign.

CONSIDERING THE 70/20/10 RULE

To continue to explore and future-proof brands while not walking away from tried-and-true media channels from their previous efforts, many media planners will follow at least roughly what is referred to as the 70/20/10 rule. This directive states that a brand should plan to spend approximately 70% of their budget on media platforms and vehicles that have previously be the cornerstones of their success. Another 20% can be spent on additional platforms and vehicles that the brand may have tested on a smaller scale to a point where they have empirical evidence that rolling more investment out in these areas would very likely show incremental effect. Finally, the last 10% of a brands budget should be considered for purely test-and-learn investments in media platforms and vehicles that the brand has not previously used. This manner of investing is a way for brands to experiment significantly without jeopardizing their established stance within the marketplace.

EMPLOYING AN OMNICHANNEL APPROACH

Have you ever heard the saying the whole is great than the sum of its parts? If so, you already have a keen understanding of planning media using an *omnichannel approach*. The idea around this approach is to plan and activate various media in combination with each other to reinforce one another while taking advantage of each channel's strengths and compensating for each channel's weaknesses. This concept is even more important when you consider that consumers experience campaigns in their totality and do not necessarily notice or separate out the various platforms or vehicles being used.

When brands use a truly omnichannel approach, they choose a combination of vehicles and align messaging across them all in a carefully choreographed manner. Media planning like this is much like composing a masterful music score for the brand's message where different instruments play their part and sometimes even take on a key solo role, but still all moving toward creating a united story, mood, and tone for the listener to experience in aggregate. Rather than isolating or creating one-off media plans, using this coordinated approach when choosing vehicles can truly be felt and experienced by the brand's community with much greater result.

SUMMARY

Clearly, media planning is not just a detailed-oriented science, it is also an incredibly creative artistic skill. A media planner's aggregate experience along with their empathetic understanding of their brand's community, their investigative knowledge of potential media vehicles available, and their resourceful approach to new creative and technical possibilities combined with statistical data all come together to provide optimal recommendations for the brands and causes they serve.

Hulu lets you choose your ad

Let's face it, when you're immersed in binging your new favorite show, advertising can be seen as an uninvited guest to your viewing party. For most consumers, advertising is seen either as a necessary evil (so they don't have to pay for the content) or it is a downright annoyance. This is often due to the interruption coming from a product or service you would never have any intention of buying.

What if you could choose what ads you wanted to see? Would that make a difference?

Hulu used that simple insight to develop the idea of choice-based advertising. Choice-based advertising gives the consumer control over their advertising experience. Prior to starting to watch a program, consumers are asked to pick the ad they would most likely want to see. Then that ad is served to them. It is a win-win. Consumers see something that they want and the result for advertisers is a 40% lift in commercial recall. Choice really pays off.

CHAPTER 23

Video media

···

SEEING IS STILL BELIEVING

When we refer to television and radio, we generally call them *broadcast media*, even though today they are not always transmitted by broadcast. Television and radio can be sent by satellite transmissions or digitally via the Internet, and television can be sent via cable. Nevertheless, the traditional term *broadcast* is still used when referring to these advertising media.

It is important to note that many changes have happened in this media space where video is viewed. A big case in point, the word television used to represent both the device and the content being viewed. To be specific, when someone was watching television, this meant they were viewing content from TV providers on the box that was in their living room. The two were not really separated. However, as television and other video-based content is now viewable on a variety of device screens, such as smart phones, desktops, and laptops, as well as on a TV set, the industry has adopted new terminology.

In general, the word video now represents the content being viewed, with each device on which it is being viewed called out as a separate screen. To give this context, let's look at the term fourth screen. What exactly does that mean? At its beginning, video content viewing started with large scale movie theatre screens also known as the "silver screen." This was the first time audiences could have common experiences viewing recorded content where both their eyes and ears could be engaged. Literally, seeing was believing as consumers could see shared images from around the globe. The silver screen gave birth to a whole new way for consumers to entertain and inform themselves and ad revenue soon followed. Cinema advertising was born to carry sight and sound messages for brands as well as public service announcements.

Years later as broadcast technology came about, and video images could be distributed simultaneously on a mass scale to individual homes around the country,

DOI: 10.4324/9781003258162-23

society adopted second-screen technology via their TV set. Decades later, the third screen came along with the birth of computers and the expansion of video to the Internet. Here is where the division between video content and devices began. On the third screen, consumers had the ability to control more of what video they watch, and when. Finally, with the advent of mobile devices such as smart phones, gaming consoles, and tablets, society adopted fourth-screen technologies. Here, complete customization of video content can be achieved on a schedule purely determined by the audience.

Regardless of the screen on which it is viewed, when all forms of video advertising are grouped together, it is the single largest advertising platform in terms of ad expenditures. Although the share of the media pie that traditional TV, referred to as *linear TV*, controls has diminished somewhat recently, as newer third- and fourth-screen devices take a larger part of the total advertising investment, video is still the number one investment and clearly the trend is heading in an upward direction. The power of sight and sound that video provides looks to be a strong brand investment for the foreseeable future.

LINEAR TV INDUSTRY STRUCTURE

Linear TV is synonymous with traditional TV. Viewing linear TV means watching programming at its scheduled time via a TV set. To create and distribute linear TV content takes two components – TV networks and their station affiliates. Traditionally, the networks create original content and provide this programming to local stations in each Designated Market Area, or DMA. As a result, stations are called network *affiliates* when they reach an agreement with a network and are then legally bound to carry the network's content as scheduled. Many local television stations are joined together in chains to make up the footprint of their parent network.

The "Big Four" US linear television networks are CBS, NBC, ABC, and Fox, and they have affiliated stations in most of the US television markets. The public television network PBS is a rather informal affiliation in which the stations are less obligated to carry network programs and may choose to air them at different times. By its non-profit nature, PBS does not carry paid advertising in the same manner as the Big Four, although it does have companies that help underwrite program expenses. Many of the underwriting messages of PBS sponsors, however, look identical to commercials that air on other networks.

Brands can sponsor linear TV content at a local level by placing ads with the local affiliate stations or at a national level by placing ads with the networks directly. Because of this, national TV is often referred to as network TV while local TV is called spot TV because it is being shown only in local spots around the country on a DMA-by-DMA basis.

Once a network has aired its original content, a program episode can have a second life. The Big Four networks often rerun their content multiple times to get the most out of their production investment. In addition, the rights to later air specific episodes or even whole seasons can be sold to other video providers by placing this content into a system called *syndication*. There are some programs specifically produced for syndication, but most syndicated content is made up of reruns of older network programs. A good example is the Comedy Central cable network airing all 180 episodes of the hugely popular 1990s sitcom *Seinfeld*.

CABLE AND SATELLITE TV

Cable TV networks are not really broadcast networks in the traditional sense. Instead, a cable network may have only one channel of programming that is distributed via cable and satellite systems. Just as in linear TV, planners can place ads in cable and satellite tv systems on both a network (or national) and spot (or local) market basis. Although cable TV was introduced in the late 1940s and the first satellite TV content became available in the 1960s, both came to sizeable popularity in the 1980s and 1990s. Since the advent of the Internet and the growth of third and fourth screen devices, video audiences have been shifting how they spend their time with video. Today, we see more audiences leaving behind their cable and satellite TV subscriptions. This group is referred to as *cord cutters*. In addition, even more growth is happening with younger audience members that are never signing up for cable or satellite subscriptions once they leave home. This group is called *cord-neverers*.

CONNECTED TVS, STREAMING, AND OTT

So where are cord cutters and cord-neverers going? Enter the age of digital TV.

The Internet allows different ways for individuals to find and watch their favorite programming, also known as *original content*. For example, The Big Four networks make some, if not all, of their programming available online on their own properties including websites, apps, and other subscriptions. For example, NBC's website, nbc.com, provides full episodes of current programs such as *This is Us* as soon as the day after its original linear TV airing. Audiences can also catch other episodes on NBC properties via the video streaming app, Peacock. Advertisements in these streaming video on demand (SVOD) environments air before and during the programming in a format known as a *pre-roll*. Some ads can be skipped, while others cannot. This depends in part on the subscription a viewer has as well as the agreement that the streaming provider holds with the brands it hosts.

Additional services like Hulu are a subset of SVOD and part of a growing content provider space known as *over the top* (OTT). OTT allows members to add content over-the-top of their regular viewing options by watching selected programs from multiple networks as well as other original programming via their smart devices. Hulu is similar to other digital channels in that it offers both a "free" service with commercials and a "subscription" service with a reduced number of commercials. Video audiences can also view a host of original content via YouTube, including content produced by individual influencers who host their own YouTube channels.

To make things even more complex while bringing us all back together again, both linear TV and streaming video can be viewed on a singular device much like a "traditional" TV set in your living room. This would of course be only if your TV is a *connected TV*. A connected TV is a device that looks like a traditional set but has *smart TV* capabilities embedded, creating a true convergence of video screens in a single device once again.

TYPES OF VIDEO COMMERCIALS

Large advertisers once sponsored entire linear TV programs. Because advertising has become more expensive and advertisers want to reach a wider variety of audience members across a fragmented marketplace, sponsorships of this nature in linear TV have greatly decreased. However, this idea of sponsored programming has received a new application in some OTT video programming today.

The standard advertising unit in video today is a 30-second ad, abbreviated as :30. Many video formats also offer fractional units but on a smaller scale such as :15 and :10 spots. Occasionally, brands who have a significant budget and want to make a really large campaign impact will run spots that are :60 or more, but typically these same campaigns include a number of shorter edit spots as well. By contrast, curing certain lower-rated time periods, some video networks and stations offer unique opportunities. For example, infomercials are program-type commercials that take up a full 30 or 60 minutes and center completely around a single brand or product.

Ads in video platforms such as streaming and OTT are similar in many ways. As mentioned previously, these ads most often take the form of pre-rolls before and at set times within the content.

VIDEO ADVERTISING RATES

The costs of video advertising depends on the size of the audience, which varies by station or program as well as by time of day and the length of the spot. In an average television show broadcast on a network like ABC, there is a limited amount of time available for advertising; the amount of time is regulated by the Federal Communications Commission (FCC). Buying television advertising time depends on availabilities (often called *avails*), which is the television broadcast time still available for purchase. An advertiser can pay a full rate and guarantee having that particular time in which to advertise or can risk paying a preemptible rate that is cheaper but that can be taken away by another advertiser who is willing to pay more.

As a broadcast time approaches, a strange thing occurs because of the economics of supply and demand. Time that has been sold at a preemptible rate goes up in price as other advertisers express a willingness to pay more to gain that time slot. But unsold time decreases in price as the station or network tries to sell it at bargain prices rather than having no advertising to run in a particular time slot.

On linear, cable, and satellite TV networks, the highest-rated time is prime time (8:00 to 11:00 P.M. Eastern Standard Time) in the evenings, with other categories grouped into *dayparts,* which are scheduled programming times throughout the day. The standard dayparts are shown in Exhibit 23.1. Times for the Mountain Time Zone vary more widely.

VIDEO AUDIENCE MEASURES

The basics of TV audience measurements were covered previously in detail in Chapter 20. In addition to these concepts, several additional measures need to be added here to encompass digital video.

Nielsen has been tracking digital video recorder (DVR) viewership since 2005. The service reports these ratings estimates for live viewing plus all DVR viewing until 3:00 A.M. after the program first airs. This is called Live+SD for live plus same day, and for live viewing plus all DVR viewing for three days (Live+3D) or seven days (Live+7D) after the program first airs. This can increase ratings anywhere from 30 to 75%, which is not surprising given the reason most audience members use DVRs is for delayed viewing.

Many brands also rely on the Nielsen C3 or C+3 rating, which is the average commercial viewing during a show for live viewing and up to three days of DVR viewing. Advertisers requested these commercial ratings to find out how many people are watching their ads, as opposed to how many people watch a program. Nielsen's Extended Screen system captures viewing on TV and computers and reports it into a single C3 rating. This requires an episode or broadcast to have the exact same commercial structure on-air as online. Nielsen has recently announced it will be is replacing its C3 measurement with a newer technology that will track and measure actual viewership of individual linear TV ads by tracking ad watermarks that work almost as an individual fingerprint for each ad message produced and aired.

Streaming video as a whole is also measured by Nielsen where measures are expanded to include metrics such as *video completes* as well as time spent in-app or on-platform.

EXHIBIT 23.1 TELEVISION DAYPARTS

	Eastern/Pacific time	Central time
Daytime	Before 5 P.M.	Before 5 P.M.
Early fringe	5–6:30 P.M.	5–6:30 P.M.
Prime access	6:30–8 P.M.	6:30–7 P.M.
Prime time	8–11 P.M.	7–10 P.M.
Late fringe	11–11:35 P.M.	10–10:35 P.M.
Late night	After 11:35 P.M.	After 10:35 P.M.

Advantages and disadvantages of television advertising are listed in Exhibit 23.2.

EXHIBIT 23.2 TELEVISION ADVERTISING

Advantages

- Impact; combination of sight and sound
- Mass coverage
- Extensive viewer time; people spend a lot of time in front of the television set or other video devices
- Repetition; better and easier than for print
- Flexibility of coverage and commercial content
- Prestige of the medium
- Versatile: Sound effects, color, motion, stills, voices, etc.
- Harder to tune out a commercial message
- Personal involvement of audience members
- Techniques of television advertising are so effective they are used for educational purposes (e.g. *Sesame Street*)

Disadvantages

- Cost can be very high
- Message wear out is high as commercials get old quickly
- A very fragmented space with so many options is often needed to get the scale required

---

BUYING VIDEO ADVERTISING

The commercial break when commercials are run is called a commercial *pod* and can consist of as few as two and as many as eight different commercials. Networks tend to rotate advertisers through a pod so if you bought one spot in a weekly program for seven weeks, you may have the first pod position the first week, the second during the second week, and so on. The first or last pod position is generally seen as the "better" positioning, as there is a great chance someone will see at least part of the ad before changing the channel or before returning to the program after leaving the commercial pod for some other reason. The more ads in a pod, the more the viewer is exposed to *clutter*, which reduces overall ad recall because of ad *message fatigue.*

If your commercial is run improperly, such as without sound, or if there is a mechanical problem with your commercial, you will usually be offered a *make-good,* which is the opportunity to run the commercial again in an equivalent time slot. You are not obligated to take the make-good, and you can cancel the *buy* instead; you will not yet have paid anything for the spot. After all, if you were running a political advertisement on the day of an election, for example, you would not want a make-good at some future date after the election is over.

THE FUTURE OF VIDEO

As the leading ad format, video is showing no signs of slowing down. New technologies are driving this growth. For example, if a consumer has a connected TV, most video providers can offer *addressable TV* options. This is where ad content is customized to individual audience behaviors on a device-by-device basis, an alternative that has been on the market for several decades but that many believe the market is finally ready for at scale in the near future. But this is only one of many new developments on the horizon. According to analysts at Statista, growth in live broadcasting, 360-degree panoramas, and virtual reality videos will continue to push the space of video to new experience levels, driving interest for both audiences and brands alike.

SUMMARY

Although now far from its early days as a medium, TV, transformed today to become video, is still the preferred format for many brands when connecting with their audiences. The options have grown, and greatly diversified with the branching of linear TV into many digital formats across a wide variety of devices.

No longer does video achieve mass reach of singular audiences as it did with programs like *I Love Lucy* in the 1950s, which is still the top-rated TV show of all time boasting a rating of nearly 70%. Still today, audiences respond tremendously to the impact of sight and sound messaging that only video can provide. And although there is a strong decline in linear TV viewership among younger audiences, total time spent viewing video in its various forms still constitutes the largest time spent across target communities.

Dog TV means TV is literally going to the dogs

Between walks and playing fetch, dogs have a lot of downtime. Just like us, they get bored. Unfortunately, dogs don't have cell phones to keep them entertained. If you've ever had a bored dog, you know that they might be whiny, destructive, or just simply depressed.

No more.

Dog TV has taken to the air. It is a television channel designed especially for dogs. It's available on multiple streaming systems including Apple+ and Fire TV, and also on apps for cell phones. It's also available via computer.

Over 2,000 three- to six-minute programs have been developed to keep Fido happy. Programming content ranges from exciting Frisbee watching to more calming Reggae music. No matter what your dog's mood, Dog TV a program for it.

In addition, the network carries programs for dog owners, including shows about different breeds and some how-to programming (such as how to make healthy treats and meals for your pup).

While you think that much of television has gone to the dogs, this channel has dog owners shelling out nearly $10 a month to keep their puppy happy. In addition, newsletters sent out to subscribers allow advertisers to offer special promotions to these pampered pups. Now that is some dog devotion.

Media innovations: Teaser campaigns

A teaser campaign, or a "pre-launch" campaign, is a type of ad message that shares enough information about an upcoming advertising campaign to build consumer anticipation. From a media perspective, a teaser campaign features a series of related media placements pointing to the eventual "reveal" – or launch of the ad campaign. Teaser campaigns can appear in any medium: From photos on social media, to billboards, to television.

Teaser campaigns can be effective for several reasons, including:

- People are naturally curious, and we want to answer the puzzle that the teaser is presenting to us. This will encourage people to seek out the campaign when it airs.
- Other people like to feel that they are the "first to know" about the upcoming campaign.
- People tend to love the feeling of anticipation – think about how you felt as a child on the night before your birthday.

UK food delivery brand "Just Eat" had a successful teaser campaign in 2020 using rapper Snoop Dog. The teaser ads, placed on a variety of social channels including Snapchat, TikTok, YouTube, and the gaming platform Twitch, showed Snoop Dog considering rewriting Just Eat's ad jingle. This raised awareness for the campaign releasing the new jingle. Studies in the UK showed that after the teaser and the new jingle campaign aired, awareness of Just Eat surpassed its competitors Deliveroo and Uber Eats.

CHAPTER 24

Audio media

....

CAN YOU HEAR ME NOW?

The space of audio has greatly diversified and increased in popularity significantly with today's consumers. The first big reason audio has seen such a dramatic increase in audience is the vastly growing number of available options within audio content. This content is also highly customizable to specific tastes and preferences. Individuals can create their own playlists and curate their own audio content to consume on their terms via a variety of devices. A second big reason for the large growth in audio audiences is the ability for this medium to be consumed anywhere, anytime, and simultaneously with other activities such as driving, working, studying, exercising, and even cleaning house or doing yard work. Audio is no longer limited to simply music or traditional talk shows either. Today, audio adds a plethora of additional options from audio books to podcasts of almost any genre providing something for everyone of any age, background, language, or interest.

The audience growth and platform flexibility, particularly within the streaming audio space, makes this increasingly desirable in today's media mix. Let's take a closer look at better understanding this changing and attractive media channel.

TERRESTRIAL RADIO

This type of audio is radio as most people know it traditionally. In many ways, terrestrial radio operates much like linear television. Radio networks are similar to TV networks in that stations affiliate with a content provider. Often, the content is fairly specific. For example, there are radio networks for sports fans such as the Dallas Cowboys Radio Network and Fox Sports Radio, along with other niches such as the Business Talk Radio Network and Univision. Some of these networks provide significant levels of programming while others such as the Cowboys Radio Network only provide specific coverage that may be seasonally driven. And many of these

DOI: 10.4324/9781003258162-24

EXHIBIT 24.1 RADIO SCHEDULING TERMS

Morning and evening drive time (known as A.M. drive or AMD and P.M. drive or PMD)	The highest-rated radio listening times in most markets, during morning and evening commuting periods
Shift time	A high-rated radio listening time in some markets where factory work shifts constitute a large part of the driving commutes.
Morning and noon news	News programs when people are preparing to go to work or school and when they drive to lunch; evening news is more highly rated for television than for radio.
Sports	Programming at any time when sports programs are aired or during regularly scheduled sports scores and news.
Late evening or overnight	Listening periods for talk shows, call-in programs, and similar scheduling, often after the television has been turned off for the night.

---

networks provide what would be considered syndicated programs such as *All Things Considered* by NPR radio.

Although terrestrial radio and linear TV have much in common, there are some differences that merit discussion. Network programming is less prevalent in radio. There are greater numbers of independent stations in radio than is the case with television. Individual radio personalities such as the on-air announcers and hosts are in some cases an important factor in attracting audiences. And terms such as *prime time* and *fringe* do not apply to radio, but rather, other time periods dominate the listening periods, with different terminology, as shown in Exhibit 24.1.

SATELLITE AUDIO/RADIO

This form of audio includes digitally encoded material that is broadcast to receivers from either an orbiting satellite or from a repeater station. Listeners of satellite radio do so via a special satellite receiver such as one built into new vehicles. Subscriptions are sold to either the entire network or to specialized networks such as music, kids, talk, sports, and the like. The service provides a wider variety of musical programming than terrestrial radio stations, and programming contains far fewer commercials since revenue is primarily subscription based. SiriusXM is the provider most associate with satellite radio. The company also now offers streaming audio options that can be consumed via web browser or app.

STREAMING AUDIO/RADIO

In addition to the live streaming of terrestrial radio stations over the Internet, audio streaming programs like Pandora and Spotify are Internet-only offerings that feature a personalized experience and comprehensive selection. This is audio classified as *over the top* (OTT). Pandora and similar stations allow users to create their own "radio channels" based on the artists the user selects where the channels intuitively generate upcoming songs based on user endorsement of selections. Spotify and similar stations differ in that they provide unlimited choices that are selected by the user. Some of the other top providers of streaming audio today include Apple Music, Amazon Music, YouTube Music, and Idagio. Services are generally available with advertising for free, or with reduced advertising for a monthly fee ranging from $5 to $10. Advertising opportunities include traditional audio ads as well as visual banners to accompany them.

One of the hottest areas of growth within streaming audio is the space of podcasts, audio programming in the form of series of episodes focusing on a particular topic, theme, or genre. Many podcasts are documentaries or are similar to other more traditional radio talk shows with hosts and guest panelists who serve as experts on the episode topic being explored. Subscribers to podcasts can listen to episodes on their own schedule, with many using this OTT format to binge listen to multiple episodes in one session.

Another final streaming audio option is audio book services such as Audible that provides the listener access to virtually unlimited published works including books, newspaper articles, magazines, as well as podcasts.

Strengths and weaknesses of radio as an advertising medium are found in Exhibit 24.2.

EXHIBIT 24.2 RADIO ADVERTISING

Advantages

- Can be an economical investment at a relatively low CPM
- Penetration into all homes and all rooms; dorms, kitchens, as well as on the go
- Complements other media very well, especially to build frequency; can reiterate and supplement other campaign elements
- Useful for reaching specialized audiences and passion groups with both broader and niche interests
- Strong on-air personalities can build a large audience of listeners and drive authentic conversations
- Daily continuity is possible, which may be too expensive in other media
- Penetration into urban, suburban, and rural areas
- Can make excellent use of slogans, music, and notable sound effects
- High timing flexibility for in the moment impact and no competition; especially good for small retailers
- High geographic flexibility and transportability. Especially strong for broad local-market messaging.

- Good for merchandising and promotional connectivity
- Highly customizable content curation on the listener's timeline
- Provides both terrestrial and digital coverage options

Disadvantages

- Perishable
- Rate policies not standardized; must deal with each individual station or provider
- Advertisements can be easily ignored or skipped

TYPES OF ADS

Radio stations traditionally sell their inventory in packages of 30 or 40 or more ads each week. But for many advertisers, those patterns may not reflect the best radio advertising opportunities. In retail, for example, if a big sale is planned, the best pattern is to run 60–70% of the radio commercials for the first big selling day and then save the balance to promote the next biggest selling day. For a sale that runs Wednesday through Sunday, use the bulk of the money to promote the Wednesday opening and put the rest toward Saturday, which is likely to be the next biggest sales day.

In any advertising medium, the most important buying consideration is choosing the times and spaces that best match your needs, not necessarily those that the sales representative is pushing or that have an attractive packaged price.

GEOGRAPHY OF AUDIO ADVERTISING

Most audio advertising occurs on local terrestrial radio stations or with localized geofencing in place for satellite or streaming services creating extremely localized market coverage. This is known as spot or local market audio. When using terrestrial radio, media planners can find the best stations to reach their target audiences, with most campaigns being a mix of four to ten stations. This number varies significantly according to the size of the market, with larger markets generally having more stations from which to choose. Many local stations also live stream their content via the Internet, either on their own websites or through other digital service providers as discussed above. Often, buying a terrestrial radio schedule with a local market station provides inventory on these streaming platforms as well.

AD FORMATS OF AUDIO

Audio ads are either produced spots or live reads. Produced spots are most common across terrestrial, satellite, and most streaming platforms, where content is either created by the brand, their agency, or even the station. Pre-recorded audio ads allow for the use of music, sound effects, and jingles plus provides a level of control over the content that many brands prefer.

By contrast, in a live read ad, the on-air announcer reads an advertiser's spot on the air. This can be delivered via a script, a fact sheet, or ad-libbed from the announcer's personal knowledge. Live read ads are viewed as being more authentic and can also be an endorsement when the on-air announcer personally recommends an advertiser's product or service during the program.

Most podcasts are most known for a live read format within each episode, which has shown to be extremely impactful. Because listeners put so much trust in their podcast hosts, recent research from the Super Listeners 2021 Report reveals that 86% of podcast listeners remember hearing ads while 76% report having taken action such as visiting a site, conducting more research, or even making a purchase after hearing a podcast ad. These statistics rank podcast ads as potentially the most response-generating ad opportunities available.

In some situations, produced audio spots may have a period of silence in the middle of the ad. This is known as a donut where set content opens and closes but allows the local announcer or another pre-recorded segment to be added in the middle to provide customized local market content during the actual ad spot.

AUDIO AUDIENCE MEASUREMENT – CUME, AQH RATINGS, AND TIME SPENT LISTENING

Audio ratings are generated by a company called Nielsen Audio, which collects data by selecting random samples of populations throughout the United States and providing respondents with a diary to record their listening habits over a designated period (generally, seven days). Respondents are paid a small cash incentive for their participation. Nielsen Audio releases this data several times a year. The company also uses streaming measurements and affidavit reports from local stations in addition to Portable People Meter or PPMs, which are wearable devices. Recruited consumers wear their PPM meters each day for between a year and two years, with data released monthly. The PPM electronically gathers inaudible codes that identify the source of a broadcast that a user listens to (i.e., the specific radio station). PPMs are in use in 48 radio markets.

The key audience data Nielsen Audio provides includes the *cume*, the cumulative number of unique listeners over a specific period of time; the *average quarter-hour (AQH) rating*, the number of people listening in a specific quarter hour or 15-minute period; and *TSL*, time spent listening, which is the amount of time an average listener spent listening to a station at one time before changing the channel or turning off the radio. The cume counts a listener one time, while the AQH rating is a product of cume and TSL. For example, if you looked in a room and saw that your brother and father were listening to a podcast on a smart home device, then 15 minutes later looked in and saw that your brother had left the room and your mother had walked in, the cume would be 3 (dad, mom, brother) and the AQH would be 2 (an average of two people were in the room in a given 15-minute period).

AUDIO DAYPARTS

Unlike television, which sells specific programs, radio stations sell dayparts. Dayparts include the morning drive, known as A.M. drive or AMD (5:30–10 A.M.); midday (10 A.M.–3 P.M.); afternoon drive, known as P.M. drive or PMD (3–7 P.M.); evening (7 P.M. to 12 midnight); and overnight (12 midnight to 5:30 A.M.). Though the schedule of dayparts can vary slightly from station to station and market to market, most stations run similar daypart line-ups and sell their advertisements accordingly. The two most popular dayparts are morning and afternoon drives, when people are commuting. As a result, advertising rates are likely to be higher during these times.

Rates might also change given the time of year. Since more people are out and about during the summer months, listenership is higher, and rates might reflect that. Ad rates also vary based on the spot length. Availabilities include a 60-second spot, which is standard in the industry, a 30-second spot, and even 10- and 5-second commercial units. The latter are known as "blinks." It is typical to represent audio ads as :60s, :30s, :10s, and :05s.

SUMMARY

Today, many media planners and brands wonder if audio as an advertising medium will survive given other more affordable and interactive options. Not only has terrestrial radio continued to be a key player in many media plans for retail businesses that have a need for highly localized market messaging such as car dealers, banks, and fast-food outlets, but the addition of satellite and streaming OTT audio options have drastically increased audience following and bettered audio user experiences. With high customization as well as a wide variety in geographic and timing options available, these trends should only strengthen. While it is clearly a medium in flux, we predict that audio will continue to increase in both audience size, influence, and impact moving forward.

Closing the deal

Advertising can build awareness of brands, provide information that differentiates one product from another, and create an emotion bond between brands and consumers. Now, advertising can also push people toward making a purchase, via audio out-of-home (OOH) ads.

Audio OOH ads reach consumers when people are making purchase decisions in stores. In particular, audio OOH is terrific for consumer package goods since often consumers can be persuaded to make a purchase when they're in store if they hear about a good price, an interesting new product, or even if they're hungry. Hungry shoppers who hear an ad for tortilla chips on a grocery store's sound system are likely to throw a bag into their cart.

One grocery store found that airing a message for the store's inhouse sushi bar increased sushi sales by 2%. Measurement is very straightforward since the store controls when the messages will air, and can compare days when the message airs to days when the message doesn't air. Flexibility and customization make audio OOH a great choice for many retailers.

Influencers: Beyond digital

More and more brands are working with influencers to help promote their brands. When we think of influencers in today's digital age, we immediately think of national or international YouTube or TikTok sensations. Digital influencers can attract hundreds of thousands of views for their videos, reaching people all around the world.

At the same time, one universal truth of our industry is that all marketing is ultimately done at a local level. Someone living on a specific street in a specific town makes a decision to purchase something. While that person may enjoy a good TikTok video, did the message really appeal to that person given their current life situation?

Ralston Purina solved that problem. Ralston seeded its new premium brand dog food with local radio announcers across the country. However, these weren't random announcers. Ralston looked for people that not only had a dog loving audience, they had to be dog lovers themselves.

Ralston gave the announcers the new dog food for their own dogs. Then the announcers talked about the food on the air. And taking it one step further, the announcers demonstrated the new brand at local grocery and pet stores. The impact was immediate. This helped propel the new brand to record heights.

It is all about finding the right audience and influencer. Think about a product that you purchase every so often. What type of influencer would appeal to you? When would you be most receptive to a message from that influencer?

CHAPTER 25

Print media

....

PRINT MAY BE IN DECLINE, BUT IT STILL SERVES AN IMPORTANT ROLE

When learning about the various types of media, it is important to keep in mind that many media types overlap with others. For example, newspapers are a traditional print medium, but newspaper content can be read online as well as on tablet or mobile devices. In fact, many newspapers have a larger online audience than a traditional printed audience. So, when we talk about print, it is really the origin of the content that we are talking about.

This chapter explores printed media: newspapers, magazines, and similar publications.

NEWSPAPERS

When we think of a newspaper, we usually think of the typical daily news. A daily paper is published at least four days each week, but most dailies come out all seven days of the week, or perhaps every weekday, or weekdays plus one weekend day. A weekly newspaper is a newspaper issued three or fewer days per week. A local newspaper that is published twice a week is still considered a weekly. Publishing may be a combination of online and print or just an online version of the original printed newspaper.

There are other types of newspapers, too, such as college newspapers, neighborhood or community newspapers, foreign-language newspapers, and "shoppers," which are often free-distribution papers filled with local classified advertising.

Kinds of advertisements

Two kinds of advertising dominate the commercial print side of newspapers: Display advertising and classified advertising. Perhaps it will be easier to differentiate between the two types if we start with classified advertising.

DOI: 10.4324/9781003258162-25

Classified advertising is so named because it is organized by classification. Also known as "want ads," classified advertisements are the smaller advertisements, usually toward the back of the newspaper, organized so the potential buyers can easily find the category needed, such as used cars, part-time jobs, lost pets, and garage sales. Although online products such as Craigslist and Facebook Marketplace have taken a large bite out of the classified marketplace, it remains a strong revenue stream for many newspapers.

Display advertising is the regular advertising, marked by larger sized ads that are found throughout the rest of the newspaper. The boundaries between types of advertising are disappearing, though, and these days most newspapers will accommodate "classified display," which are larger announcements, like other display advertisements, but still in the proper categories with other classified advertising.

One problem with placing advertisements nationally using many newspapers is that there is no uniformity in the page size of newspapers. Some use five columns, some use six or seven or eight, and the lengths of columns vary as well. This wide variety makes it difficult to prepare a single advertisement and have it appear in many newspapers. To help solve this problem, the standard advertising unit (SAU) was developed; it lists several standard sizes of newspaper advertisements so that an announcement of a certain size will fit into most newspapers, although in some there may be extra space around the advertisement. Using the SAUs, regional and national advertisers can run advertising placements in almost all US newspapers, without the need to re-size the advertisements for each individual paper (see Exhibit 25.1).

The other aspect of newspaper advertising is digital ads. Newspapers offer a variety of digital advertising units plus the opportunity to sponsor pages of content. The typical digital ad units include skyscrapers, vertical and horizontal banner ads, and squares. Newspapers also offer rich media options in the form of video on their sites which typically are pre-rolls prior to being able to view content. Finally, many newspapers offer their content via mobile application, which creates advertising opportunities to engage with the newspaper audience in more dynamic fashion and to create more customized experiences based on user behaviors.

Print advertisement specifications

Newspaper print space is usually sold by the column-inch, which is a space measurement one column wide by one inch high. Thus, an advertisement that is six inches high and three columns wide would total 18 column-inches (6 columns × 3 inches = 18 column-inches).

But remember that different newspapers have different column widths, which means that the size of an advertisement may vary from one newspaper to another; that is precisely why the SAU was developed. What the advertiser is buying is space; do not think of the ad size as type, because some of the space may be left blank. Newspaper advertising can also be purchased in larger quantities, such as quarter-page, half-page, and full-page ads. Again, these sizes vary from one newspaper to another.

EXHIBIT 25.1 STANDARD ADVERTISING UNIT (SAUs) FOR NEWSPAPERS

Depth in Inches	1 COL 2-1/16″	2 COL 4-1/4″	3 COL 6-7/16″	4 COL 8-5/8″	5 COL 10-13/16″	6 COL 13″
FD*	1xFD*	2xFD*	3xFD*	4xFD*	5xFD*	6xFD*
18″	1x18	2x18	3x18	4x18	5x18	6x18
15.75″	1x15.75	2x15.75	3x15.75	4x15.75	5x15.75	
14″	1x14	2x14	3x14	4x14	5x14	6x14
13″	1x13	2x13	3x13	4x13	5x13	
10.5″	1x10.5	2x10.5	3x10.5	4x10.5	5x10.5	6x10.5
7″	1x7	2x7	3x7	4x7	5x7	6x7
5.25″	1x5.25	2x5.25	3x5.25	4x5.25		
3.5″	1x3.5	2x3.5				
3″	1x3	2x3				
2″	1x2	2x2				
1.5″	1x1.5					
1″	1x1					

* FD=Full depth

Advertising rates and discounts

Most advertising media offer discounts to advertisers based on a variety of factors. For all media including newspapers, a *flat rate* indicates that no discounts are available; no matter how much advertising is purchased, the rates will not change. An *open rate* indicates that discounts are available, although an open rate is not a discounted rate; it is the highest rate charged before discounts begin to be applied to the cost of an advertisement. When advertisers see an open rate, they know that – eventually – discounts may be earned.

For all media, the advertising rates are listed on a rate card, whether there is an actual printed card or only an online listing of advertising prices. Because costs can be very high and most newspapers are intended to attract local advertisers who have more limited budgets, saving dollars while investing is important. A combination rate applies if a single publisher owns more than one newspaper, offering a lower advertising rate to advertisers who use multiple papers in the chain.

If an advertiser signs a contract for advertising space, the eventual anticipated discount may be figured into the contract. If the advertiser fails to earn the discounted rate in the contract, the advertiser must pay the difference in costs, known as a *short rate* – that is, money paid from the advertiser to the newspaper because the advertiser failed to advertise enough to earn the contract discount rate. Similarly, if the advertiser uses more advertising than anticipated and earns an even better discount than was stipulated in the contract, there may be a rebate paid from the newspaper to the advertiser. Short rates and rebates are terms that apply to all media, not only newspapers.

For all media including newspapers, quantity discounts are based on the amount of advertising purchased over time; as an advertiser uses more advertising space or time, larger discounts may be earned, leading to reduced advertising costs. Frequency discounts are earned for advertising often. Continuity discounts may be earned for regular advertising. Frequency and continuity discounts are similar; frequency applies to the total number of ad placements, while continuity applies to regular placements, such as every week or every day. Dollar volume discounts are also a way for newspapers to reward advertisers who increase their spending either in print or online as digital and terrestrial print is being bundled in most media plans today.

Special charges

In print media, color costs extra because it involves extra steps in the printing process. Black ink is included with the advertising space, and then one or two or three extra colors cost more; full-color printing is black plus three colors, known as a four-color process (even though black is not considered a color in printing). Color can be added in advance (known as a preprint) or during the regular printing process (known as ROP color, for run-of-paper or run-of-press). Spot color is just exactly that: a few spots of color, such as a border or headline. Process color uses tiny dots of color to make a color picture.

Position in the printed issue may mean an extra charge for an advertiser who may be willing to pay more to be sure that a specific ad is in a particular place or section of the newspaper. Position on the page may also cost extra; most advertisements are on the bottom half of the page, so an advertiser may be willing to pay more to be sure that an ad is not "buried" or surrounded by other advertisements.

See Exhibit 25.2 for advantages and disadvantages of newspaper advertising.

EXHIBIT 25.2 NEWSPAPER ADVERTISING

Advantages

- Timely
- Contents vital to audience; thus, good readership
- Broad reach; appeal to all kinds of people
- Localized circulation; can target geographically
- Complete coverage; almost everyone reads newspapers
- Edited for all ages; can reach adults, teens, men, women
- Frequent publication; daily advertising results in continual impressions
- Can handle emergency situations; short ordering time
- Can tie in advertisements with news
- Can direct customers to stores
- Advertising budgets of all sizes can use newspapers
- Quick results
- Can include many different items in a single advertisement
- Reader controls exposure (as opposed to radio or television)

Disadvantages

- Many differences in sizes, deadlines, etc., so advertiser must have separate dealings with each newspaper; can be costly to change mechanical specifications for each
- Great variation in production quality
- Color may be of poor quality or difficult to use
- Short life
- Declining readership and interest of audiences

Circulation and audience

As mentioned previously, circulation is the number of copies of the publication that are actually distributed and picked up by the community. There will be some extra copies that are returned as unsold, and some free copies that are given to advertisers to prove that the advertising appeared as ordered. Advertisers are usually interested in the paid circulation – that is, the number of copies that were delivered to paying readers. Advertisers are also interested in the size of the audience or readership if available. This is the number of persons who actually read the publication.

Many large newspapers offer city-zone editions, which are distributed in the central city and any contiguous areas that appear to be the same as the city itself. There may be separate suburban editions in other areas.

Oftentimes, planners want to know the circulation within the retail trading zone (RTZ), the entire area where people live who shop for major purchases in the city zone. Others may by trying to achieve total market coverage (TMC), with advertising reaching every household in the market.

Newspapers also measure the number of unique visitors to their digital platforms. It is a key measure of the newspaper's overall reach. Total audience for the newspaper is provided through third-party research services. Scarborough and Alliance for Audited Media are two measurement services that provide readership information for print. These sources allow advertisers to better understand the audience dynamics of newspapers for both the printed and digital versions.

Mechanical print considerations

As mentioned before, a brand may sign a contract to indicate how much and how often they foresee placing messaging with that medium. Whether or not there is a contract, each advertising placement is accompanied by an insertion order, telling how and where and when the ad is to appear. These terms are used with all media, not just print.

Newspapers offer advertisers a tearsheet, which is a page torn from the actual newspaper that contains the particular advertisement that was run. Do not confuse a tearsheet with a proof. A proof is an advance copy either of the advertisement or of the page provided, so the advertiser can check the ad for accuracy.

Buying advertising space

Recall the following definitions: *frequency* is advertising often, and *repetition* is using the same ad more than once. It is possible to have frequency without repetition and also to have repetition without frequency. Few advertisements work when run only once or a few times, so frequency is often an important factor. Larger-size advertisements attract greater readership than do small ads. The idea is that a planner must weigh the space options available along with these trade-offs.

Many advertisers believe that an advertisement on a right-hand page of a publication draws more attention than one on the left-hand page. Similarly, they believe that an advertisement in the front of a publication is better than one in the middle or back sections. Thus, they often specify "right-hand page, far to the front," although research shows that these factors are not significantly better in newspapers.

We have already seen that an ad on the upper half of the page may have less competition from other advertising. Whether or not the advertisement is near the "gutter" (the center of the layout where two pages meet) does not matter with newspapers.

Timing for newspaper advertising depends on the shopping patterns of the audience members. For example, most newspapers can tell you what day is their "best food day," when national food advertisers along with local grocery stores run the most advertising. Auto tires may do best on a Saturday when more readers have time to shop for tires.

Pre-printed inserts

In addition to typical newspaper ads printed within the actual paper content, most offer the option of included materials that are printed in advance and inserted as stand-alone pieces. These are referred to as pre-printed inserts that are typically retail sales pieces placed in the daily or Sunday newspaper. In effect, the newspaper becomes a delivery vehicle for other advertisements. The popularity of pre-printed inserts among retailers is a driving force in their importance. Pre-printed inserts can account for up to 70% of the total revenue for the Sunday newspaper. Since advertisers can deliver preprints by the newspaper's carrier route, they are able to tailor sales messages to various geographical parts of a city or town. Research has shown that consumers value pre-printed inserts. Some consumers buy the newspaper largely for access to these inserts.

CONSUMER MAGAZINES

There are several types of magazines. Consumer magazines are covered in this section. Business publications are also magazines, but they differ somewhat in use and structure from consumer magazines, so they are covered separately. Farm publications are often an amalgam of consumer magazines and business publications, so they have some traits of both categories.

Consumer magazines are either general-interest or special-interest publications. The days of general-interest magazines are largely over, with only a few survivors. Most magazines today are special-interest publications with a magazine to cover almost any interest, from model trains to retirement locations to gaming. The largest circulation category for magazines are women's interest publications, entertainment, and health and beauty publications.

Subtypes of magazines include regional and metropolitan (metro) editions, which are circulated in limited areas within the wider national circulation of large magazines. International editions of several publications are available, sometimes simply translated and other times completely reedited. Special-audience editions are also published, such as college-student editions of news or sports magazines carrying advertising that might not interest a more general audience.

Just like newspapers, magazines have pushed largely into the digital arena. Most large circulation publications offer both repeat and new online content as well as tablet and/or mobile editions. Some have gone as far as moving all of their content online in lieu of a printed version.

Circulation and audience

Circulation of magazines, like newspapers, is measured by the number of copies distributed, either to subscribers or through newsstand sales. The primary audience is defined as those persons who receive the publication because they subscribe to it or buy it, and the secondary audience, also called the "pass-along audience," is defined as those persons who get the publication from someone else.

Several audience concepts apply to all advertising media but are perhaps easiest to understand when applied to magazines. The accumulative audience (the cumulative audience, or *cume*) is the total number of persons who see or hear an advertisement at least once in a single media vehicle (in this case, in a single magazine), even though the campaign may appear in multiple vehicles. The unduplicated audience, measured as *net reach*, is composed of all the persons who are exposed to an advertisement at least once in a combination of vehicles, for example, when four magazines are used in a campaign. The duplicated audience (also called *dupes*) is defined as those persons who are exposed more than once to an advertisement in a campaign. If we add up every time the advertisement is seen by the entire audience in all the media vehicles, that figure is referred to as *total impressions (IMPs)*. The average number of times that an audience member is exposed to an advertisement from the campaign is called the *average frequency* or *average exposure*.

Through several large third-party audience measurement services such as Mediamark Research Inc. (MRI) Simmons Market Research (SMRB), a media planner can learn about the audience dimensions of a wide variety of publications. Since MRI also collects brand-buying habits of its respondents, a media planner can develop an analysis that details approximately how many brand users read a specific publication. This type of information can be crucial to making a magazine purchasing decision.

Frequency and repetition

Like newspapers, consumer magazines measure frequency as the number of times people see or hear an advertisement during the campaign, whether or not the same advertisement is repeated. Repetition refers to using the same advertisement more than once, whether or not it is done frequently (see Exhibit 25.3).

Advertisement position

Again, as with newspapers, many advertisers ask for their ads to be on a right-hand page, far to the front of the publication. In fact, research shows that in consumer

---

EXHIBIT 25.3 CONSUMER MAGAZINE ADVERTISING

Advantages

- High quality of production and color; can show package
- Flexible scheduling: weeklies, monthlies, etc.
- Selective readership; permits market segmentation
- Prestige of the medium, in many cases
- Advertising message retained for a long time; has long life
- Better audience data than from most other media
- Flexibility in format: size, foldout, insert, color, smell, etc.

Disadvantages

- Waste circulation, especially in general consumer magazines
- Advertisements easily ignored, compared to television or radio

magazines, left-hand or right-hand page placement makes little difference, and place-ment at the front, middle, or back of the issue also makes little difference. It does not matter whether the advertising appears in a thin or thick issue of the publica-tion. What determines readership of an advertisement is the subject of the ad, the interests of the audience, and the size and frequency of exposure to the advertising. Remember, these characteristics are for consumer magazines; later in this chapter, how the outcome differs when business publications are involved will be discussed.

Magazine ad specifications

Most magazine ads units are common terminology both familiar and largely self-explanatory. Full-page, half-page, one-third page, and quarter-page are the regulars in the schedule. Planners can also choose often if their content runs vertically or horizon-tally. Visualize the difference between a vertical one-third that would run like a column, versus a horizontal third that would run like a banner ad. Planners can also choose to invest in covers, both inside, and back. Some publications offer "false" covers, which are ads that are temporarily fixed to the front of a publication when mailed out to subscrib-ers. Other options include spreads, which are two-pages that read as one large page, fold-outs, and pre-printed inserts that are bound into the publication spine while on press.

Sectional editions

To test various versions of an advertisement, an advertiser may ask for a *split run*, when different versions of the ad go to various divisions of the audience. By meas-uring the sales response, the strength of the advertising appeal or message can be gauged. Split runs can be used for various sections of a city through a local newspa-per or for different sections of the country through regional editions of magazines.

Advertising deadlines

The deadline for placing advertising in a magazine may be months in advance of pub-lication. The publication issue date is when the magazine is printed and distributed – often first to newsstands and then to subscribers. The cover date is typically set a few weeks or a month in advance to tell newsstand operators when to take the issue off sale and to expect a newer edition.

BUSINESS PUBLICATIONS

Business publications and farm publications are similar to consumer magazines in most respects, so it is not necessary to repeat all the information that applies for all of them. Nevertheless, there are some differences for business publications that should be observed.

Business publications are categorized as (1) vertical publications, those that reach all levels within a single industry, such as *Advertising Age*; and (2) horizontal publi-cations, those intended for a single job function within a cross-section of industries,

---

EXHIBIT 25.4 BUSINESS PUBLICATION ADVERTISING

Advantages

- Often read during business hours; reader's mind on business
- No distractions; no other news or entertainment material
- Produces direct inquiries, from people who have that concern and responsibility
- Flexibility in timing and format, same as consumer magazines

Disadvantages

- Lots of other competitive advertising

---

such as *Sales & Marketing Management*. Sometimes business publications are categorized as industrial publications, those that appeal to a certain industry; institutional publications, intended for those employed in institutions such as prisons, clubs, or colleges; professional publications, aimed at certain professions; and merchandising publications (also called trade papers), to aid in marketing efforts. These categories may not be mutually exclusive; *Advertising Age* is an industrial publication, a professional publication, and a merchandising publication (see Exhibit 25.4).

Business publications can become true thought leaders in their respective industries. For example, the *Electrical Engineering Times* is the standard bearer for the integrated circuit design industry while *Progressive Grocer* leads as the top publication for grocery-industry news and information. Business publications can become a trusted industry source and carry significant weight as a marketing vehicle.

As can be imagined, there are thousands of specialized business publications making it difficult for anyone investing media dollars to be familiar with all of them. Many business publications feature a media data form that provides insights into the publication, its readership, and its editorial and advertising policies, which can help the media buyer determine how well the publication matches the target group and advertising goals.

Advertising rates

And like other media, business publications offer quantity discounts, which are often called bulk rates, and frequency discounts, sometimes known as frequency rates. Many business publications are published monthly and offer per-issue rates, based on the number of issues used – not to be confused with frequency rates, based on the number of advertising insertions.

Most advertising media offer rate protection policies so that advertisers with a contract will not have their rates increased during the term of the contract, although they may benefit if rates are lowered.

Magazines usually charge premium prices for ad placement on the outside front cover (Cover 1), the inside front cover (Cover 2), the inside back cover (Cover 3), and the outside back cover (Cover 4). There are sometimes other preferred positions as well.

An advertisement that is inserted into the publication rather than appearing on a regular page also usually costs more. Inserts can be bound into the publication or can simply be inserted between some of the pages.

Color rates, short rates, and rebates may all apply, as they do with other kinds of publications.

Business publications offer a variety of other marketing services. We previously mentioned that helping develop a trade show presence is one aspect of certain publications. Because a business publications audience is highly prized, these publications market their subscriber lists to advertisers to carry out direct marketing campaigns.

Circulation

Many business publications are distributed for free, with the income coming solely from advertising (called free circulation). Others charge for subscriptions and single copies (called paid circulation). Some publications control who can receive their publication (controlled circulation), while others do not. A publication sent to customers by a business may use franchise circulation, or "distribution paid," the latter being when a publisher sells the magazines in bulk to the business, which then provides them free to good customers.

Checking

A checking copy of a magazine serves the same purpose as a tearsheet of a newspaper: to prove that the advertisement ran as ordered. Many publications include reader-service cards, which can also help measure audience response.

Frequency and repetition

Frequency is essential for successful advertising in business publications, just as it is in newspapers and consumer magazines. Studies have shown that frequent and steady business publication advertising helps increase readership and recognition, produces buyer inquiries, and helps build brand preference.

In addition, business publication advertising can help increase an advertiser's share of voice (SOV), which is the percentage of messages within an industry category that come from a particular advertiser or firm.

Business publications have special patterns of monthly and seasonal response, so advertisers need to be aware of the readership patterns within a certain industry as well as for a particular publication.

THE FUTURE OF PRINT

As it currently stands, print as a media class continues to show decline in physical distribution and consumption, which is somewhat offset by digital audiences. Even still, overall readership is down year-over-year. For example, according to *Editor & Publisher*, total audience for weekday newspapers peaked in the mid-1980s whereas

Sunday newspapers peaked in the early 1990s. Since then, there has been a significant and quite consistent decrease in audiences for both. However, if we isolate digital circulation, in the last year, we can actually see a significant increase of between 25–27% there. These promising digital numbers have again offset the overall decline in print, which is one of the key factors behind more and more publications adopting a digital-first mentality.

One key trend that continues is that revenue for print publications has been increasingly coming from subscription-based circulation rather than advertising revenue. As with most media, print revenue has historically been heavily weighted toward advertising. However, in the past few years this shift has been increasing, with 2019 marking the first time in history where advertising revenue was supplanted becoming the second largest revenue stream for publications.

A second related trend is for more and more of the dollars print publishers are making from advertising to come specifically from their digital assets. According to Pew Research, this growth has continued to increase each year at a ratio that has doubled in the past 20 years.

In part due to these overall shifts, most publishers now realize that providing free online content is not the road to success. More and more titles are moving to digital subscription plans and have adopted digital paywalls. Once a consumer samples a few free online articles each month or has access to read the first few sentences beyond a free headline, they must pay to read more. It is likely we will continue to see publishers continue to build out their digital presence and unique offerings to keep up with audiences, especially as their readers demand tried and true sources of reliable information in a growing age of fake news.

SUMMARY

In short, few media categories have seen more volatility and morphing than print, yet it is a medium here to stay. As with other media, content may be distributed in a number of platforms, but print publishers still provide very highly desirable content. While there is a movement toward digital publishing, both newspapers and magazines continue to have their place in the media landscape. According to the Alliance for Audited Media and confirmed by Pew Research, newspapers continue reaching nearly 25 million audience members every single day while magazines continue to serve highly specialized interest groups. It is clear the print game has shifted, but it continues to be one of significance.

CHAPTER 26

Out-of-home media

....

OOH! LOOK AT THAT IMPACT

Many of the major advertising media reach into the home. Video, audio, newspapers, magazines, Internet, and social media can all be delivered to the home. Yet there are several types of media that are available primarily outside the home – commonly known as out-of-home media – reaching consumers when they are traveling, waiting, shopping, or otherwise out and about. Otherwise known as outdoor advertising as well as OOH, out-of-home is one of the oldest forms of media, and the influx of digital technology has created new opportunities for consumer reach, customization of messaging and engagement within the platform. Additionally, planners can take advantage of in-the-moment highly creative executions to make brand messages in OOH.

OUTDOOR ADVERTISING

Printed (or static) outdoor advertising consists of billboards, which can be changed periodically, and permanent signs, such as those for a nearby motel or business. The standard-sized billboard is called a 24-sheet or 30-sheet poster, because once it required many sheets of printed paper to cover it. Today these billboards can be covered by just six, or even three, sheets of paper or one single large sheet of printed plastic made of flexible polyethylene film. Billboards smaller than the standard size are commonly referred to as junior panels.

OOH billboards are purchased in *showings,* or *gross rating points* (GRPs), both an adaptation of the concept of rating or percentage of audience exposed. Although similar to ratings, OOH showings or GRPs are not target specific. So, ratings are percentages of targets, showings and OOH GRPs are percentages of populations.

Billboards are usually purchased within a market zone. Once a year, the average daily circulation of cars, buses, trucks, and pedestrians is measured for each billboard location. This information helps formulate how many billboards are required

DOI: 10.4324/9781003258162-26

EXHIBIT 26.1 OUTDOOR ADVERTISING GRP

A purchase of 100 GRP of outdoor advertising is intended to result in an audience that achieves a reach of:

- 90% of the local adult population, with a
- frequency of slightly more than once a day
- over a period of 28 days

---

within a market zone to achieve a certain audience level. In outdoor advertising, the standard buy is 100 GRP over a four-week period, which results in the audience levels shown in Exhibit 26.1. Other levels of advertising (25 GRP, 50 GRP, 150 GRP, and so on) are available, but only as divisions of multiples of the number of billboards used to achieve 100 GRP; there is no guarantee that a billboard buy of 200 GRP will achieve twice the audience impact as 100 GRP – only that you will be using twice as many billboards. Billboards near shopping centers can also be purchased through a shopping-center network (see Exhibit 26.2).

Of course, there are outdoor advertising signs that are not billboards. Painted bulletins stay up for several months, sometimes for years. It has become increasingly popular for brands to paint entire sides of building walls with messages or build three-dimensional structures to enhance messages. These murals or free-standing art installations are often used to engage with consumers, who will commonly snap selfies or group photos with them a background or prop and share this content via social media to give the message a viral life beyond the original exposure. Cities small and large across the US have many of these iconic branded OOH locations.

Spectacular signs such as those in Times Square in New York City are another way to used OOH advertising to make a larger-than-life statement. LED signs and digital billboards allow messages to be quickly changed and are much more visible and engaging. Some of these boards even provide an interactive experience. For example,

---

EXHIBIT 26.2 OUTDOOR ADVERTISING

Advantages

- Reaches potential customers close to point of sale
- Communication can be quick and simple
- Repetition is easy in high-traffic areas

Disadvantages

- Short message may limit creative breadth
- Despoiling the landscape; may earn public's enmity
- Legal restrictions

---

bus shelters in major metropolitan areas might have thermostats installed to change messaging along with the daily weather, or in-store cosmetic kiosks might provide customized skin care product information based on the consumer's skin type as picked up by small in-screen cameras.

Brands can also use large-scales projectors to illuminate brand content onto other structures such as buildings or bridges within municipalities. Such messaging can be very timely, easy to set up, and highly impactful. In order to participate in these types of activities, planners must work with local municipalities to understand all rules and requirements, as well as secure any permits needed.

Going the oppositive direction, brands can use OOH on a small scale. From posters around construction sites, to stickers or even sidewalk chalk, messaging can be very accurately and locally placed. For example, there are companies today that specialize in what is referred to as reverse graffiti. This is a technique where a plastic template is created and laid on the concrete. The company then power washes the concrete with high pressure water, cleaning the concrete except for area screened by the template. This leaves behind a more eco-friendly and longer lasting message.

OOH can also receive a big boost from technology with the addition of servers, cameras, and other digital technology to create messaging that moves or changes such as video screens. This type of OOH is often referred to as *dynamic media*. These morphing displays can be placed in stores, sports arenas, shopping centers and restaurants, along roads, and in similar public places. Sometimes kiosks and other accessible locations are used for interactive addressable video screens.

When using OOH, brands are almost always renting the locations for their messaging, although there are exceptions where long-term purchases allow messaging to remain indefinitely. Because the options are so numerous, there are a plethora of local and regional providers of outdoor boards. However, there are a number of national firms that have OOH availability across the United States.

TRANSIT ADVERTISING

Transit advertising makes use of both the inside and outside of transit vehicles, as well as transit stations. Inside buses, subway cars, and commuter trains, the signs above the windows are called car cards. These are usually 11 inches high, although signs above doors must be shorter, and the widths vary. The exterior of buses and cars can be wrapped with messaging printed on strong adhesive but temporary vinyl masks. Posters inside train or subway stations and in airline terminals can vary a great deal, depending on the exact location, the need for illumination, and the pedestrian traffic patterns.

Transit advertising is similar to outdoor advertising, sold by a showing, or a *run*. A full showing or full run has one car card inside every vehicle in the transit system; a half showing or half run would allow for one car card in every other vehicle. Because passengers usually stay in one car and often in one seat, double showings (double runs) and triple showings (triple runs) are common, providing two or three – or possibly even more – car cards within every vehicle.

EXHIBIT 26.3 TRANSIT ADVERTISING

Advantages

- Economical: Very low cost per thousand
- High repetition
- Continuous exposure, day and night
- Limited number of competitive messages

Disadvantages

- People are not thinking of advertising; hurrying elsewhere
- Advertisements subject to mutilation and vandalism
- Some doubts as to quality of the market

Signs on the exteriors of taxicabs are usually displayed on the rear trunk or perhaps on the roof of the cab. Trucks can also carry advertising, with some trucking companies offering vehicles with lighted signs for nighttime viewing (see Exhibit 26.3).

Transit advertising offers a huge audience with an approximate cross-section of the area population. Because people are mobile, the opportunities for repeat exposures to an ad are quite possible.

OTHER OUT-OF-HOME MEDIA

The types of OOH media possible today are truly too numerous to count. Almost any surface or area can become a canvas for an OOH message. This can include such things as skywriting or airplane-towed banners, mobile billboards, benches and other street furniture, signs on gas pumps and at rest areas, public gardens, and grassy fields. Again, the creative imagination of a media planner is almost the only limitation here provided with the available budget and legal approval needed to do it. And as technology advances, even more types of out-of-home are coming to market, many of which may offer better audience selectivity and higher cost efficiencies. Most of these new types of opportunities take advantage of interactivity. For example, some digital offerings use touch-screen technology or integrate mobile and social activation technologies such as QR codes. For instance, a poster at a bus station could have a QR code that connects a passenger to a mobile application such as a clothing store or newsstand. Using OOH media to capture consumers while they are waiting for something might be the next "killer app."

SUMMARY

Whether it is referred to as outdoor, out of home, or OOH, this class of media options lives up to its name of being on the go and highly impactful. OOH provides high levels of audience exposure to brand messages with very good efficiency. With the use of technology, it also offers highly customizable targeted options that can be sensitive to location, time of day, weather, as well as consumer behaviors or characteristics.

One of the biggest benefits of OOH is the highly creative nature of the medium. Because of this, many brands are taking advantage of converting many of the spaces they own into OOH messaging opportunities inside their physical stores and locations as well. With so much growth and such variety here, a later chapter will cover these in-store options in greater detail.

Murals

If there's a non-descript building with a blank wall near your campus, there's a good chance that soon you may see a mural painted on it. A mural is a painting that is painted directly on the outside wall of a building. A small one can cover 100 square feet and a large can be on the entire side of the building.

One new use of murals is to raise awareness of underrepresented creative communities. A campaign called "Represent: Black Arts" serves several purposes. First, the murals raise awareness of the stories of Black communities in the cities where the murals are painted (the Lower East Side in New York City and Sunset Boulevard in Los Angeles).

Additionally, the murals help to build an equitable and inclusive creative culture by highlighting the works of Black artists, such as Karen J. Revis. Finally, the murals build awareness of the Black Artists + Designers Guild, hopefully opening up new paths for its members.

These murals received an AdWeek Out Of Home Impact Award in 2021.

Charging station network

As the world is turning to electronic vehicles (or EVs) to help combat climate change, one entrepreneur saw an opportunity to support this burgeoning technology and provide a new media channel. Scott Mercer launched Volta Charging, which has more than 2,000 charging stalls nationwide. Many of these stalls are at shopping centers, providing a convenient place for drivers to top off the charge in their vehicles. Charging your EV at a Volta Charging stall is free, because the costs are covered by advertising revenue from digital ads at the stall.

Volta Media, also owned by Mercer, installed 55-inch digital screens on either side of the stall. Advertisers can reach an audience of consumers who are concerned about the environment and have taken steps to address their own carbon footprint. Retail stores in the shopping malls can direct customers to their stores, or share public service messages. In addition, Volta Media allows advertisers to switch up messages quickly, perhaps based on special offers, weather forecasts or traffic patterns.

CHAPTER 27

Search engine marketing

....

HELPING PEOPLE FIND YOUR BRAND WHILE THEY ARE ACTIVELY LOOKING

Search engine marketing (SEM) is a media placement tactic that promotes a client's website by increasing their visibility in *search engine result pages* (SERPs). Search engines have existed since the early days of the Internet, even before the World Wide Web, in order to help people use keywords to find what they were looking for. After the web browser was invented, search engines morphed into graphic interfaces and were monetized. SEM can be a valuable part of a media plan, as a variety of advertisers can benefit from this direct communication with consumers, whether the consumer has an acute need that a brand can solve, is in need of information for a highly involved purchase decision, or is looking for a great deal. It is because of this ability to place a highly relevant message in front of a consumer who is literally seeking out information about a brand just before making a purchase that SEM is often considered one of the most valuable conversion media classes available today.

In the search engine marketing arena, the key player is Google. According the Oberlo and GS.Statcounter.com, this singular search giant accounts for 87% of US online queries, rising to over 90% of all online queries globally. On average, Google processes over 3.5 billion searches each day, of which approximately 63% were from mobile devices. It is estimated that 84% of the world's population conducts a Google search three or more times each day. With this undeniable dominance in a highly desirable platform, it is no wonder that Google garners nearly $150 billion in ad revenue annually, which accounts for approximately 30% of all digital ad spending. It is important to note that Google has grown well beyond being a search engine only. With their acquisition and monetization of YouTube, development of their own network, and build out of other technologies including proprietary devices, the brand has continued to diversify greatly. Never-the-less, the largest income generator for the Google media titan remains SEM advertising.

DOI: 10.4324/9781003258162-27

SEM BASICS

The discipline of search engine marketing includes *paid search results* and *organic search results.* Paid advertising is accomplished using tools like Google Ads or Bing Ads with a variety of formats, placements, and payment structures. These are the inquiry results that show up at the top or to the side of the page and are marked as paid ads. By contrast, organic searches, which fall into the realm of *search engine optimization* (SEO), are the other natural results that happen often and are considered unpaid advertising. To be clear, natural indexing as it occurs in search engines is not for sale. Instead, SEO is frequently improved by ensuring that the text on a page or site matches the types of searches that people undertake. Additionally, SEO considers the number of links on a site as well as where users to the site come from, along with other types of behaviors displayed by consumers as well as the manner in which a site's content is officially passed along and valuated.

HOW SEM WORKS

The basic concept behind SEM is straightforward. Similar to using a filing system to organize and easily locate information, individuals go to a site like Google and enter search words in order to find the information they need. Technology allows search engines to constantly "crawl" through the Internet and index websites. Indexing websites means identifying the keywords that would describe that particular site's content. The inquiry results that follow connect individuals searching for something to the pages that are likely to provide the information that they need. In addition, while providing this information, the search engines also show paid placements also called *sponsored content, sponsored links,* or *paid ads* from companies that have purchased keywords matching the users' needs. Search engines use highly complex, proprietary algorithms to make these matches and are constantly updating and refining their algorithms to make the best matches for both organic and paid content. All of this happens in near real time.

WHY SEM IS DIFFERENT AND COMPLEMENTARY

The consumer mindset while using a search engine is somewhat unique from other types of media behaviors since it indicates that the person is actively looking for information. When consumers are the ones explicitly driving the conversation about a product or service, it is likely that they are engaged at a particular level within the purchase cycle, making them very strong prospects to purchase a specific brand. For this reason, providing branded information via a search engine inquiry is different from other types of advertising messages in several key ways:

- SEM is fairly nonintrusive and invited, as it reaches an individual when they are actively seeking information.
- SEM derives from a voluntary, consumer-driven search, where the consumer actively selects to respond to a specific link.

- The process of matching consumer inquiries with paid SEM content is intuitive and responsive, staying current with consumer behaviors and requiring no additional consumer action.
- SEM fine-tunes the user experience by minimizing the chances that a consumer will be exposed to what they would consider worthless results.

It is important to point out that there are often a large number of other message exposures that did the lifting and motivated the consumer to create a search inquiry, particularly if it is a *branded search* where the name of a company or product is included in the search. For example, a consumer might see a video ad earlier in the day regarding discounted tickets on Southwest Airlines or might pass a billboard on their drive home promoting this same campaign message. However, it might not be until later that evening when the consumer can log on and search for information by typing "Discounted tickets Southwest Airlines" into their Google search bar and ultimately making flight reservations. Although the search for the tickets happened last in the transaction, it was in large part due to the earlier exposures in video and outdoor that led to the search in the first place.

PLANNING SEM CAMPAIGNS

Selecting appropriate keywords can be a challenging aspect of planning media, requiring significant research and strategic planning. A planner should begin by looking closely at their brand's own consumer insights, communications platform, calls-to-action, and key performance indicators (KPIs). From there, Google provides some important tools to expand keyword considerations. One of these free tools is Google Trends (www.google.com/trends/), which provides up-to-the-minute information on the search terms currently trending. It also provides snapshots of search term popularity, including a tool where a search term can be entered to examine interest over time, regional interest, and popularity of related searches.

Additionally, the Google Keyword Planner allows a planner to identify potential keywords for a new SEM campaign or expand on keywords for ongoing SEM campaigns. Performance metrics on the different keywords are also provided, so planners can assess which keywords are very popular (and possibly more expensive), as well as which keywords may be *long tail* keywords meaning they do not have a high search volume but may be more likely to lead to clicks and conversions. Finally, the Google Keyword Planner offers assistance in advance-targeting needs. For instance, this tool could help identify the keywords that are most attractive to people who live in Chicago and speak French, if that is what you are looking for. Keyword Planner is available to anyone once a free Google Ads account is established.

Most search engines have regulations that advertisers must follow regarding both the keywords bid on and the content of the landing page, which is the branded website where the consumers' click would take them once they left the search results page. Specifically, the keywords and the landing pages should be well matched to ensure a good consumer experience. If a company selling pet supplies bid on the keywords "concert tickets" or "cheap airfare" to direct people to their site, you can see how the consumer would be disappointed and the process of SEM matching would be compromised. By contrast, most competitive keyword bids, often referred to as *competitive blocking*, are allowed. In other words, Pizza Hut can bid on the keywords "Domino's Pizza Deal" when running a special promotion that directly targets consumers who typically would prefer Dominos.

Pricing for *paid placement* is different from other types of media placements. SEM is based on a bidding system as opposed to the typical negotiation method that many media planners are familiar with. The bidding process assumes that multiple advertisers want to reach the same group of people at the same moment within the same search inquiry. Rather than negotiating to hold and place their spot, advertisers offer a bid on how much they want to pay to reach these buyers. With SEM, the higher the advertiser bids on a keyword, the higher in the rankings their ad appears, and the more likely it is that web searchers will see the ad. Ranking means visibility, though a brand does not have to be at the top of the rankings or make the highest bid in order for prospects to see the ad and click on it. The goal is to get the lowest cost-per-click (CPC) and the highest quality clicks for the budget, which means sales and leads for the brand.

To add to the complexity of SEM, there are different types of pricing structures that advertisers can use for their bids. One popular type is the aforementioned CPC, where payment of the ad only applies if the brand's link has been clicked on. Other advertisers are more comfortable using a *cost-per-thousand* (CPM) payment, where advertisers pay for every exposure to an ad, even if it is not clicked on.

LOCAL SEARCH AND GEOFENCING

Search engine marketing is not only for large national and global clients. On the contrary, SEM provides extreme geographic flexibility, allowing brands to bid on keywords based on the brand's physical or geographical location. In addition, SEM can add another variable such as where the consumer is in-the-moment. This type of search is called *micro-moment searches,* which account for a vastly growing number of inquiries. An example of a micro search is a consumer using their mobile device to inquire about "great pizza near me." Google has classified micro moments into four groups: I want to Know, I want to Do, I want to Go, and I want to Buy. By combining highly geofenced location-based information with micro moments, it is clear how impactful an SEM message can potentially be.

Because this level of geographic customization is so appealing, many more local search marketing services have been developed. Some of the more popular apps and providers in this space are Google Maps (Google+ Local), Yahoo! Local, Waze, and Citysearch.

TESTING

Given the high price of media placements, advertisers can burn through their SEM ad investments quickly. In order to get the results needed and be the most diligent planner possible, it is very important for media planners to constantly test and assess different keyword combinations in order to efficiently drive traffic. For example, bidding $1,000 per click might generate a lot of clicks, but will also cost a lot of money. SEM involves understanding the fine line between a bid that reaches a lot of people and a bid that results in ads that are never seen. As previously discussed, it is the act of strategically making decisions to increase metrics such as SEM click-thru-rates, not simply spending more money that will create more desirable responses

SUMMARY

Providing a deeper understanding of brand communities and the ability to match brand messaging to consumer information needs based on their location, state of mind, and place in the buying process are the biggest driving forces that make SEM a powerful platform. It is important to consider the trade-offs when choosing keywords and all SEM investments, including making sure that a planner is considering all of the exposures that ultimately lead their consumer to search for information.

Although SEM is often the last step in the consumer's buying journey, search activity is often a result of a number of prior exposures across many other media platforms within a campaign. Because of its immediate results, customizable messaging, and ability to conduct strong test-and-learn scenarios, SEM is a critical tool for most brands today, especially when used as a part of a total omnichannel plan.

CHAPTER 28

Online display advertising

....

MEETING CONSUMERS WHERE THEY LIVE: ONLINE

The Internet is one of the most depended-upon tools in people's daily lives. According to Statista, 91% of Americans are online an average of eight hours a day, and 82% of the population uses social media. There has been a steady yearly increase in overall digital usage in the US from 2011 to 2022. People between the age of 16–24 spend more than three hours per day on social media and adults 25–34 spend an average of two hours and 37 minutes a day on social media platforms. Usage locations include home, school, and work. Smartphones enable Internet usage from anywhere and at any time. An important point to remember when developing a communication plan is to understand why people are using specific sites on the Internet. What purpose does the audience have for going to those sites or apps? Without that understanding, we can continue to add to the plethora of ads that interrupt people rather than provide information they might be interested in.

ADVERTISING AND ONLINE BEHAVIORS

Many people spend time online for a directed activity; in other words, they were searching for or intended to visit sites for news, entertainment, or for a variety of types of information. Ads are placed in most of these sites including through search engines such as Google. Ads appear in social networks and in online games, providing revenue for companies who provide the content as well as providing opportunities for brand exposure for companies that place the ads.

One of the primary purposes of digital advertising is to direct people to online sites that are interesting and valuable to them. Some digital ads direct people to branded sites and online retail sites (e-tail sites), where people can learn about and or purchase products. Other ads might take people to rating services where there is rating information and reviews of products in different categories.

DOI: 10.4324/9781003258162-28

There are numerous digital advertising options and creative units, and finding a mix that efficiently builds reach and frequency against a specific audience can be challenging. Millions of different websites accept advertising and finding sites that are "sticky," (sites that have visitors that stick around and don't hurry off to another website), can be tough. Finally, the different types of rate options can be confusing to some clients and some agencies. Should ads run on site-based and pay-based impressions or click-throughs or based on action taken toward buying the product? There usually is no right or wrong answer but information in this chapter should help you understand more about the complex world of digital advertising.

Digital (classified, video, banner, and search) advertising spending has increased significantly every year. It is projected to grow from $34.28 billion in 2020 to $63.3 billion in 2025. The top category of digital advertising is retail, followed by automotive, financial services, telecom, and packaged consumer products.

Display and banner ads embed advertisements in different web pages. These ads can include text and images and, like search engine marketing (SEM), attract traffic to an advertiser's website via a link. Generally, the online user needs to click somewhere on the ad to be redirected. Audience response is usually measured in exposures, clicks, or action taken on the site.

Rich media ads provide an interactive online experience for the user. For example, some ads expand and provide a new online context when users click or roll over the ads. Other examples of rich media include embedded video ads or ads that seem to "float" over the page itself. Such ads arguably gain more attention than a static ad (such as a banner ad) and often do not force users to leave the site they are currently on. Depending on the ad, different types of audience behaviors can be tracked (e.g. the amount of time spent viewing a video).

Most of these types of online advertising are placed through advertising content networks. These are companies that connect advertisers to websites that want to host advertisements. The key function of an ad network is to aggregate available ad space from online publishers and match it with advertiser demand. There are three types of online advertising networks.

VERTICAL NETWORKS

Vertical networks clearly identify which websites are part of the network, and advertisers always know exactly where their ads will run. These types of networks are priced slightly higher than other networks. The higher price is due to promoting a more qualified audience, thus, there can be more demand for the sites by relevant marketers. In general, vertical networks offer two types of media placement: run-of-site (ROS) advertising across specific channels, e.g. travel, concerts, or movies. Advertisers can also use specific sites within the category.

BLIND NETWORKS

Blind networks offer lower costs than vertical networks but do not provide information on where ads will run prior to the flight; hence, the media planner is "blind" to the content where the ads will run. Most networks offer a "site opt out" method, which allows for certain categories or sites to be excluded. The networks usually run campaigns on a run-of-network (RON) basis, across a range of different sites that are part of the network. Blind networks are priced lower as they often utilize remnant space or space in sites that were not purchased by advertisers who purchased vertically.

TARGETED NETWORKS

Targeted networks focus on specific targeting technologies such as search-based, contextual, or behavioral targeting. Targeted networks specialize in using consumer click stream data to enhance the value of the inventory they purchase. As in traditional media planning, the planner must carefully identify the key audiences for the digital advertising campaign. To make these decisions, planners determine whether to use search-based targeting, contextual targeting, or behavioral targeting.

Search-based targeting derives from SEM. Conducting searches online is a popular activity, and most online users are familiar with these kinds of ads that are connected with search. Google is the most popular search engine at 91%. Yahoo search is at 31% and Bing is utilized 27% for search.

Contextual targeting provides users with ads about a subject that is of particular interest to them. Instead of basing the ads on what customers are searching for, contextual advertising looks at the content customers look at as they navigate through the Internet. To market to consumers, true contextual advertising relies on relationships between online advertisers and web publishers. The high degree of an ad's content relevancy promises the potential for a higher click-through rate and an increase in sales and profitability.

Behavioral targeting monitors the behavior of an individual as they move from site to site. Ads are then generated to correlate with this behavior. For example, when using behavioral targeting, the online fashion site American Eagle can identify users who visit their website. Then, when the users visit other sites that are part of the network where American Eagle has purchased ad space, those potential customers will see an advertisement enticing them to purchase clothing from American Eagle. Behavioral targeting allows advertisers to appeal to consumers with different ads based on their past behavior, even as different consumers view the same web page; while one consumer is seeing the American Eagle ad, another might be seeing an ad for Nordstrom. The downside is that behavioral targeting has been considered by many to be invasive. Due to changes in the use of cookies (system for tracking an individual's internet use), people visiting American Eagle or other sites are asked if they want to opt in or share their data. Advertisers are constantly exploring new ways to enable consumers to advance their behavioral and contextual data collection with the deprecation of the third-party tracking cookie. At the same time, it opens up new opportunities for web advertisers to collaborate with different partners and digital ad buyers and planners.

MEASUREMENT

Measurement of online users involves large samples as well as passive technology. Participant data is collected whenever the participants use their computers. The data are transmitted daily to the measurement service. Two of the leading services are Nielsen//NetRatings and Comscore. Nielsen//NetRatings is a division of the same company that calculates television ratings. Nielsen has a ratings service that will track online viewing of digital media, which is a blending of their online and traditional television metrics. In order to deal with the move away from cookies, Nielsen has developed a new measurement system called *Nielsen One*. This system uses different data sources such as streaming use and first-party data. *Unified ID 2.0* and *Identity Sync* are also developing cookieless measurement systems. New methods of tracking digital use should address consumer privacy concerns, according to eMarketer insider intelligence.

Comscore focuses on all types of digital measurement, including search engine optimization and mobile marketing.

Many websites track their own statistics using a system such as Google Analytics, which provides daily counts of visits to the site, identifies the country of origin of a visitor, and determines whether the visitor is new or returning (based on IP [Internet protocol] addresses). These analytics programs can also indicate the amount of time a user spends on different pages that make up a site. In-depth demographic information is generally not available, though, and as a result, media planners might use multiple data sources for evaluating web properties. However, people will increasingly have to opt in and agree to be tracked.

PLANNING DECISIONS

In addition to making decisions about how best to reach the audience, the planner must be involved in two other key decisions: The advertising creative format and the payment method. Questions regarding the advertising creative format include, will the ad be text only, a clickable image, or rich media? Will it be placed in an environment that is most likely to be seen on a computer, on an iPad, or on a smartphone? Should the ad be adapted for different devices? Questions regarding the payment method include: Will budget decisions be made on an impression (cost-per-thousand, or CPM) basis, or on a bidding (cost-per-click, or CPC) basis? Digital advertising revenue is generated from both CPM (impression-based) and performance (CPC) measures. Negotiated CPM advertising is analogous to other types of advertising: The planner or buyer estimates the number of impressions that an ad will generate against their audience and a cost is assigned to the impressions. With negotiated CPC, the advertiser will only pay for the people who click on the advertisement. For example, one ad might cost 40 cents on a CPM basis or $2 on a CPC basis (see Table 28.1). In this case, the advertiser would set a daily or weekly budget and once the goals are reached, the ads would stop running. One key thing to remember about planning and costs is the costs can be negotiable.

TABLE 28.1 Cost comparisons for digital advertising

	Impressions: .40 CPM	Clicks: $2 per click
Daily budget: $20	Total daily impressions: 50,000	Total daily clicks: 10 Approximate click-through rate: 10/50,000

THE FUTURE OF DIGITAL

"Big Data" has become an integral part of communication planning. Big Data are collections of data sets so large that they are difficult to process and understand using traditional tools. The trend toward larger data sets was spawned by consumer media usage habits that allow for companies to collect a wide range of information; this information, in turn, allows researchers to spot trends and patterns among different types of activities. Couple this with the ever-expanding number of advertising channels and the result is that advertisers can better understand consumers' buying patterns – where they shop, how much they spend, what they need in their lives, where they spend time, and what they do in the digital space. Big Data can help advertisers home in on audiences in a way never before imaginable. Planners are always looking for the "right data." In other words, the data have to relate clearly to the audience we want to reach and be pertinent to why, where, and how they are using the Internet. Planners also need to match the digital choices with the personality of the brand for which they are planning. Kantar, a data analytics and consulting group, has developed a Media Reactions study that identifies places where users are most amenable to ads and are less inclined to react negatively to them. As audiences become more digitally active, as there are more sites to visit, and as there are more apps to use, engagement with communication becomes more important. Pricing for ads is evolving to this model of engagement over impressions, CPMs, or CPCs. Real-time bidding (RTB) is a method of automated buying of advertising placements. The key idea behind RTB is that ad impressions should not be sold in bulk; rather, each ad impression is regarded as unique, and advertisers know the best prospects for their messages. The media planner provides a set of demographic and psychographic parameters to one of many digital trading desks, along with a bid for an impression for an exposure to someone who meets the parameters. When someone matching those parameters visits a website that is part of the ad network, the advertiser with the highest bid has their message shown to the individual. "Programatic" computer programs assist this buying process, which would take an inordinate amount of time if done site-by-site by the media buyer.

Augmented reality (AR) provides digital advertising opportunities inside events like baseball games or hockey games. Ads can be placed digitally on walls or boards and replaced with other ads but appear as if they are part of the environment.

Brave.com offers a unique look at a possible future for digital ads. Users are given a choice of whether they want to see ads or not. They can select how many ads they are willing to look at in an hour and users are paid for every ad they see.

Brands are looking at new formats and applications due to the growth of 5G. The speed of 5G provides more options for interactive and streamed content. "More than 90% of marketing professionals worldwide expect 5G to have an impact on their industry over the next decade," according to eMarketer.

SUMMARY

The digital world is constantly changing, and planners must keep up with the changes in order to best serve their clients. In addition, the more communication planners and brand planners can daily pay attention to those changes, the better they can anticipate what those changes might be and provide the best opportunities for brands and clients.

Netflix and merchandising

If you're like us, you might wonder how Netflix makes so much money. As one of the few streaming services that accepts no advertising, it relies on subscription revenue alone. Until now.

Netflix has gone all-in on merchandising. Starting in 2021, the Netflix.shop website started offering merchandise related to some of its biggest Netflix-produced hits. Want a pair of Elegorgon socks or a *Squid Games* hoodie? What about the soundtrack from *The Harder They Fall* or a side table inspired by *Lupin*? The Netflix.shop has you covered. Netflix also offers a variety of merchandise branded with the Netflix logo or the word 'Chill.'

A new offering is a plush pillow-like doll that looks like the default profile photo used by Netflix members. These fuzzy, neon pillows, called chilleez, come in many different colors. Netflix users can also now change their profile pictures to an image of a chilleez, creating synergy between the shop and the streaming platform.

These offerings promote the overall brand of Netflix as well as raise awareness of its offerings.

CHAPTER 29

Mobile

....

The prevalence of smartphones is often the quickest channel to reach audiences online.

Most media are fixed or stationary. Mobile is a tool that stays with us. It goes everywhere with us, going step by step with us and recording our personal histories. It's a portal to each person's best and worst moments. It is the most deeply personal medium.

OH NO! I FORGOT MY PHONE!

Mobile has become an important, albeit indispensable, part of the media landscape worldwide. People often feel slightly uneasy if they have left home and forgotten to take their phone with them. More than 50% of college students with smartphones check them automatically if they wake up in the middle of the night. The smartphone is an integral part of life.

The prevalence of smartphones is often the quickest channel to reach audiences online.

Most media are fixed or stationary. Mobile is a tool that stays with us. It goes everywhere with us, going step by step with us, recording our personal histories. It's a portal to each person's best and worst moments. It is the most deeply personal medium.

Smartphone ownership continues to grow with more than 6 billion people owning one. Over 95% of the smartphone ownership is adults 18–49. The ubiquitous nature of smartphones enables media planners to reach audiences in very specific situations and requires ads designed specifically for mobile. People can be deeply engaged with their phone whether they are standing in line, commuting on public transportation, or any number of activities or quiet moments.

The Pew Research Center reports that 97% of Americans own a cellphone of some kind, 85% of Americans own a smartphone, and 78% of adults in the UK own a smartphone. Korea leads smartphone ownership at 94%. In China, 66% of the population have a smartphone and 88% of the Japanese own smartphones.

DOI: 10.4324/9781003258162-29

Brands are investing more money on mobile and shifting dollars from traditional media channels to mobile display ads, apps, and games. Mobile commerce and mobile digital payments have helped enable growth of mobile marketing and sales. Global expenditures on mobile advertising grew 71% despite Covid-19.

Because consumers rely so heavily on their phones for so many things, it follows that they rely on the phone in their customer journey. So, planners need to research and understand how and why the mobile device is used as well as when. Ideally, the planner can reach people at an optimum time with information that is useful rather than annoying.

One important aspect of mobile devices is being able to reach people in geographic areas close to where someone might have access to a specific brand. For example, Starbucks can send a special offer to a phone that has opted in to receive notices when that phone is within a certain geographic area of a Starbucks store.

Mobile is often used in "micro moments" or very short times during the day or night. Thus, with such a short amount of time to make an impression and engage with someone, the message should be as personalized and optimally localized as possible and quick. The Mobile Marketing Research Association discovered that it takes less than half a second for two-thirds of mobile ads to be recognized. The advertiser has less than half a second to make an impact with an audience on mobile. So there needs to be a discernable and emotional call to action.

TYPES OF MESSAGES

A variety of messages are available. As is all Internet usage, mobile Internet is divided primarily into search or search engine optimization (SEO), which means paying for a high ranking in search outcomes based on specific word choices, as well as online classified and display (banners, buttons, overlays, interstitials, and popups).

Video and streaming video are a big part of mobile usage. Specifically:

- Streaming video advertising (pre-rolls, mid-rolls, post-rolls)
- In-stream videos
- Out-of-stream (self-play video on a social network, embedded in advertising content)
- Contextual video advertising (branded video players)

Other examples of advertising that appear in mobile are newsletters with ads, interactive TV ads, in-game advertising, sponsorships, and advertising within games.

AD EXPENDITURE

The expenditure on mobile advertising has consistently grown. It is currently more than $95 billion, which is up 2730% since 2012. The spend by the end of 2022 is expected to be more than $134 billion. This is more than 70% of all Internet ad spending and more than 50% of all ad media expenditures.

BRAND COMMUNICATION

People interact with their phones, usually, in short bursts throughout the day and night. In order to enable messages to cut through, brands can employ the five Ps of mobile engagement:

- Presence – understand the channels the audience is accessing and when, and ideally, why so the message is delivered at the right time
- Personalization – compelling to the audience specifically by using their name or making the ad location based
- Presentation – the ad is developed for the smaller phone screen and its functionality
- Peer-to-Peer – much of the use of phones is for socializing and sharing content with friends. Content that can be shared is more likely to attract interest.
- Performance – when the ad has consistent and fast delivery, is easy to interact with, and is intuitive, this helps maintain consistent attention.

Chick-fil-A sales had never declined until the Spring of 2020 when sales dipped due to Covid-19, where lockdowns caused some stores to close and others to switch to drive-through only. The company adopted stringent safety measures and then wanted to advertise to let people know their stores were open and safe. While dining rooms were closed, people could order from their phones, pick up at drive-through, or have meals delivered. Customers paid through the app. The result was 777% increase in curbside pick-up and a 291% increase in mobile drive-through orders. Customers shared the positive experiences on their social media and the brand received free press.

REWARDED ADS

Rewarded ads offer the viewer some kind of bonus if they watch a 15- or 30-second ad that can't be skipped. If done right, the ads reach the right people and the ads offer an immediate benefit that is valuable to the viewer. Some of these ads can appear in games. KitKat tied in with the game Candy Crush and launched a new product with rewarded, full screen ads. Brand recall was raised by 40%.

GAMING

To one degree or another, Gen Z is a generation of gamers. Games such as IRL (In Real Life) and Animal Crossing or Sims are easy entry points to more games and the metaverse.

According to eMarketer, 74% of mobile gamers in the US would watch a video advertisement if they were able to get in-app content in return. They also reported that 82% of mobile gamers would rather play free mobile games that include ads than pay for mobile games that are ad free.

Some of the main reasons given for playing games, according to Facebook Gaming, are to relieve stress, pass the time, to immerse themselves in another character or world, feeling accomplished for completing a challenge, and be dazzled by something unique. The reasons for playing mobile games are essentially the same as console or computer (PC) gaming, but mobile is much more accessible and intermittent.

TIKTOK AND OTHER SOCIAL PLATFORMS

TikTok grew quickly and then even more quickly during the Covid-19 pandemic. In fact, it grew to 700 billion users worldwide. The short form video app lends itself perfectly to mobile usage. There is always fresh content. Its popularity with Gen Z audiences has opened the door for entertaining shopping ecommerce. There are a variety of TikTok ad formats. Discovery page takeovers, in-feed native video, and sponsored lens filters work well to establish awareness.

The more a brand can connect with the life of its audience, the more it can cut through and resonate with that audience. Duolingo started using TikTok because it simply wanted to create trust with its audience. They weren't trying to sell anything, just entertainment. They gained a share of voice with their mascot-based content that was often irreverent and disruptive. Although the intent was not to start conversations, the conversations started organically. The messages weren't about trying to sell a product. The short videos hit tension points in the lives of the audience, and they could be safely shared. The smartphone was the obvious way to view and share those messages.

The app has worked with Shopify and Walmart and it has developed a self-service ad tool that can provide automated commissions to influencers who share product links in the US.

In the US, TikTok is used principally for entertaining video content. In China and other parts of Asia, the age span of users is more diverse, and the app is used often for information seeking. So if an advertiser is running a global campaign it's important to remember that the app is used differently in different countries and the age base can be different.

Shake Shack tied in with DoorDash and created a dating site named "Eat Cute" for Valentine's Day. The majority of dating sites are accessed on smartphones, thus the logical tie in with DoorDash and a dating site. The purpose for Shake Shack was to introduce their Buffalo Chicken sandwich. Couples are matched according to their shared love for the new chicken sandwich. Singles set up their profile by providing their name, uploading a selfie with pronoun choices and romantic orientation. They then indicate their preferred spice level from "lettuce be friends" to "too hot to handle." They can choose to share Instagram profiles and can choose to direct message each other. If the romance doesn't cook, participants will all get a promo code for a free Buffalo Chicken sandwich from Shake Shack on DoorDash. Users can also enter to win a $5,000 DoorDash gift card when they post a screenshot of their profile on Twitter with the hashtag "#EatCuteWithDoorDash." The campaign also included TikTok and some top influencers sharing their dating advice and their experiences on the platform.

Ads can be bought on TikTok by cost-per-click, cost-per-view, or cost-per-thousand basis. Audiences can also be more refined so the media planner can specify exactly who they want to reach. Hashtag challenges are the most popular paid ad format for Gen Z. Brands can engage with their audience by lip-syncing a jingle or verbiage from a brand message and posting with the brand hashtag. Hashtag-plus-challenge formats enable viewers to go from the videos with the brand hashtag directly from another tab on TikTok to purchase from the brand. A World Advertising Research Center (WARC) case study outlined the hashtag challenge "#TransformURDorm" with Kroger, the largest grocery chain in the US. Kroger worked with Dentsu, 360i, and TikTok. Students posted their "dorm room transformations" to TikTok using the hashtag. Influencers were enlisted to show how they "transformed their dorm" using video effects and music that is appealing to the audience. All the products could be purchased while still in the TikTok app. The challenge was participated in more than 477 million times.

One of the more important positive attributes of TikTok is the algorithm used to feed users what they want to watch and appropriate ads are then matched to them. Thus, ads are not interruptive and annoying. The ads match the feed.

THE FUTURE

Brands, culture, and technology, will continue to move faster and faster. Smartphones will get smarter. Attention may grow even shorter. Brands can stay connected by working with consumers and speaking with them, not at them. Mobile devices of different kinds can evolve, and the human connection needs to evolve with them in order to stay relevant. According to Statista, 37% of people in the US have landline phones. Obviously, the number of people with only a landline is much smaller. Occasionally, we use the smartphone as a phone, but usually the focus is on the computer capabilities of the smartphone. The personal nature of the smartphone keeps the door open for more collaborative opportunities between brands and their audiences.

As our smartphone holds more and more of our information and as technology advances, we will be able to walk into the Apple store, for example, and the information in our phone can be immediately shared with the people in its Genius Bar. It will transmit how old our phone is, any problems it might have, and it will supply the history of other Apple products we might have. One way a customer relationship management tool can enable us to get immediate, personal attention.

CHAPTER 30

Social media

....

IT'S ALL SO META

Social media advertising represents a blending of traditional and digital media with a dose of word-of-mouth thrown in for good measure.

Social media include most types of Internet-based applications that focus on interactivity and that allow the creation and exchange of content designed both by users and by brands. Social media sites not only support but also encourage interaction. Marketing messages on social media sites no longer focus on one-way, top-down messages from a brand, but rather provide an opportunity for open discussion between a brand and a customer. Social media can be a focal point of the marketing/brand planning rather than an add on or after thought.

This idea of interactivity differs from that of other types of digital advertisements. Digital messages such as banner advertisements want the online user to click on the ad and be directed to a branded website. Social media messaging can be used for that kind of directional interactivity and to provide purchase incentives, too. Social media advertising is also used to build communities of users focused on the brand. These communities develop positive word-of-mouth for brands.

There are several ways that social media monetizes advertising messages. One is by the brand inserting its message into the social media content. The second way stems from the social media producer becoming their own brand with a large number of followers. Some will display a product or brand but the producer can also collaborate with a brand and develop their own labels and products and then share marketing. For example, a "star" on TikTok could create a line of T-shirts and jackets that they design and then work with Columbia Sportswear to produce the clothing.

Social media is unique in that it includes paid, earned, and owned media. *Owned media* are social media that a brand controls, like a website, a blog, and its Twitter, Instagram or TikTok account. Owned media is often used to build long-term

DOI: 10.4324/9781003258162-30

relationships with customers and increase trust in the brand. *Paid media* – is the type of media a brand pays for to leverage a channel. It can include display ads on a social media site and search engine marketing. Paid media builds on the foundation established by owned media and often directs online users to the owned media properties. *Earned media* is when customers become the channel, sharing the content created by the brand. It reflects the brand's understanding of what customers are most interested in and willing to share.

SOCIAL NETWORKING SERVICES DEFINED

When we think of social media, we often think of social networking services (SNS). SNS have a goal of building and encouraging social networks or social relations among people, often people who share interests, activities, or offline relationships (see Table 30.1).

When your business is part of one person's network, your interactions with that individual can be seen by everyone in that network. What this means is that one individual's conversation can start a chain of conversations within that individual's social group or network, leading to positive word-of-mouth.

Many large and small brands have an SNS presence because large numbers of consumers spend time online. Facebook has 2.89 billion monthly active users. And almost 1.9 billion people are daily active users or 66% of the monthly users. Looking at the average number of Facebook friends; 40.41% have 0–200 in their network, 38.35% have 200–500 in their network, and 20.79% have 500+ friends in their network. In other words, if someone in the last group mentioned here posts something on Facebook, 500+ people can see that posting. Twitter has 429 million users worldwide and is projected to have 497 million users by 2025. The US has 84 million of those users now and is projected to have 100 million Twitter users by 2025. Japan has 70 million Twitter users and South Korea has 8 million. According to Statista (September 14, 2021), YouTube counted more than 2.1 billion users worldwide. As of February of 2020, more than 500 hours of video was uploaded to YouTube every minute. Pinterest reached ten million unique monthly visitors faster than any other site. They currently have 459 million monthly active users worldwide. Instagram is the second most-used social media channel for marketers worldwide. Instagram users number 500 million daily. The top three Instagram accounts worldwide, according to

TABLE 30.1 What is a social networking service?

Component	Explanation
Profile	A representation of the user including name, image, and list of interests
Social links	A way for users to connect with each other, such as "follow" on Twitter and "friend" on Facebook
Channel of communication	Method of sharing information (text, video, image, audio)

TABLE 30.2 Social media components

Component	Explanation
Profile	A representation of the user including name, image, and list of interests
Social links	A way for users to connect with each other, such as "follow" on Twitter and "friend" on Facebook
Channels of communication	Method of sharing information (text, video, image, audio)

Statista are: Cristiano Ronaldo with 306 million followers, The Rock with 255 million followers, and Ariana Grande with 253 million followers. Facebook and Instagram are both owned by Meta.

A social networking service has three overall components: Profiles, social links, and channels of communication. These are described in Table 30.2.

Social media sites differ in the type of benefit they offer. Some, like YouTube, focus primarily on video sharing, while a service like Nextdoor guarantees that everyone in the social network will be from the same geographic area. A summary of these sites is provided in Table 30.3.

New social media platforms are constantly being created, each involving ways for people and brands to engage with each other. The most popular social media site today can be replaced rather quickly by another, newer site.

Important types of social media that media planners should know about include:

- Blogs: The term *blog* comes from the term *weblog*, which is a website that is generally created and maintained by an individual and includes regular entries of commentary, descriptions of events, or other material such as graphics or video. Many blogs focus on commentary or news on a particular subject. Others more closely resemble personal online diaries.
- Review and opinion sites: These types of sites allow online users to rate products, services, and businesses (although currently retail stores and services represent the bulk of the reviews). Although these rarely accept advertising, companies can set up branded accounts to respond to user reviews and provide information about the brand.
- Geosocial networks: These are tools that use geographic services such as GPS to engage users who submit their location data to a service either through their

TABLE 30.3 Segmentation of social media sites by specialty

SNS portals	Micro blogging	Photo sharing	Video sharing	Blogging	Review sites	Geosocial
Facebook	Twitter	Shutterfly	YouTube	Wordpress	Yelp	Nextdoor
Reddit	Pinterest	Flickr	Twitch	Wix	Citysearch	BrightKite
Snapchat	Reddit	Instagram	Vimeo	Squarespace	Angi	
LinkedIn	Tumblr	Photoblog	Liveleak	Weebly	Glassdoor	
TikTok	Posteezy	Smugmug	Metacafe	CMS Hub		

computer or, more likely, through their mobile phones. Users can see where their friends are frequenting, and businesses can reward frequent visitors who "check in" at their location.

Within a single category, some sites offer simple and streamlined tools and applications; others offer ones that are more complex. Some appeal to younger people, some to older. Some are brand new, and some have been around for quite a while. Most of these sites have their own analytics systems modelled after Google Analytics. Tracking or using cookies to follow and track users on specific sites is now more complicated as users must agree to have their engagement and usage data released.

Because this type of media is changing every day, one role of the media planner is to be aware of the different social media offerings available, to track their popularity and their demographics, and to assess how well the medium would match the consumers. Working with others in the agency, the media planner also needs to assess whether there is a commitment to consistently providing content for the social networking site, as well as a commitment to responding to online interactions. Because there are multiple levels of involvement with social media, the media planner may also be responsible for negotiating the media placements in places in some of the social media they want to use.

INITIAL LEVEL OF BRAND INVOLVEMENT: AN SNS PRESENCE

Many brands jump into social media by setting up a simple site and populating it with some content. Examples include a Facebook page dedicated to the Wendy's Frosty brand, a Twitter feed that outlines new offerings from Barnes & Noble, or a YouTube video channel for the sports giant Nike. The key to success is to acquire a large number of followers and to maintain and grow the number of followers. Many online users will search for brands that they like and choose to join those social networks. Other online users will see that their friends in the social network like certain brands and will choose to follow those brands as well. What this suggests is that a social networking site can be set up with little to no cash outlay as long as some content is available to populate the site. The media planner, then, will be watching to see if there are increases in followers and monitoring the effects of different content.

SECOND LEVEL OF BRAND INVOLVEMENT: SNS ADVERTISING

Established SNS allow advertising on their sites. These ads work similarly to different types of digital advertising, discussed in Chapter 29. An overview of how several of the sites work is next.

Facebook

Advertisers can create highly pinpointed advertisements and present them to specific Facebook audiences. Facebook users provide information about themselves, not only demographic information but psychographics as well. Using the Facebook advertising tool, a media planner can select demographic characteristics for the advertisement including age, gender, and geographic location; advertisers can even choose to reach people on their birthdays. Additionally, specific audiences can be segmented based on what types of other Facebook sites they have affiliated with; that is, ads can reach people who like *Seinfeld* reruns on Netflix or "fly fishing." Ads on Facebook can direct people to a site on the Facebook network or to a site off the network.

Facebook is owned by Meta, which also owns Instagram. Similar targeting strategies are available on that site.

Twitter

"Promoted Tweets" are paid tweets from advertisers that appear at the top of a Twitter search results page. "Promoted Trends" are updates of the most popular Twitter topics that are promoted by advertisers. They initially appear at the bottom of the Trending Topics list on Twitter and are clearly marked as "Promoted." Users who click on a Promoted Trend will see Twitter search results for that topic, with a related Promoted Tweet from the advertiser appearing at the top of the page. Rates are impression based.

YouTube

YouTube's direct advertising plan includes video clips that begin 15 seconds after a viewer starts watching a video. Another option is placing Google Ads, where advertisers can select keywords or categories where their ads appear, or can target based on geography, interests, and demographics. Costs are based on cost-per-click (CPC) bids (see Chapter 21 for more information on bidding).

Pinterest

An important value of advertising on Pinterest is reaching people based on the topics they like. There are several ad formats available on Pinterest: vertical ads, square ads, and video. Products can be pins and multiple images in a single ad can be swiped through. Advertisers can also create a hybrid format that mixes lifestyle images and video. Pinterest has also created a shopping list feature. They collect a user's pinned shoppable products and then notify the user when there are price changes for those products. Pinterest is the third most popular platform for shopping behind Facebook and Instagram.

TikTok

TikTok is a video-sharing app that enables users to produce and share 15-second videos on any topic they choose. TikTok claims 100 million average monthly users in the US, (half of whom are under 34), and almost 700 million monthly users worldwide. The platform, however, is enticing people to interact based on interests, hashtags, or stories. Even though it is a global app, it facilitates and often emphasizes local content. Users can also connect with products and brands. The hashtag "#TikTokMadeMeBuyIt" has more than 2.3 billion views and TikTok Reviews has had more than 3.6 billion views.

THIRD LEVEL OF BRAND INVOLVEMENT: SOCIAL ADS

Innovative marketers are always looking for new and different ways to integrate a traditional type of advertisement with a social network, termed a *social ad.* According to the Internet Advertising Bureau, a social ad is an online ad that incorporates user interactions that the consumer has agreed to display and share. With this definition, then, a social ad is an ad that contains information about the user (such as a picture or name) associated with some ad content. As a result, this can be seen as a personal endorsement, almost like a word-of-mouth message. Examples include display ads with polls. Ads for feature films, for example, might ask, "Will you see this movie this weekend?" along with response options such as "yes," "no," and "not sure." Once the individual votes, the responses will appear in a new box along with the names of friends who have also voted in the poll.

Social advertising is always evolving the use of social media to generate new and interesting modes of consumer engagement. Cheetos (Frito-Lay, PepsiCo) increased market share by creating a branded art exhibit. They discovered that consumers were sharing oddly shaped Cheetos pictures online. They then ran a series of films on Facebook, Instagram, Twitter, and YouTube that led consumers to a branded site where examples of "Cheetos art" could be uploaded. Outstanding examples could win money. The next step was an online "Cheetos Museum" as well as a pop-up restaurant they called "The Spotted Cheetah.' To launch the museum, Frito-Lay partnered with Jimmy Kimmel Live!, which created a sketch about the "art" and the museum. This example emphasizes the importance of noting why people use specific media. Because the social media here were chosen by users for entertainment and the messaging used for Cheetos was also for entertainment, it enabled consumers to participate in something more than what they already shared.

PRICING OPTIONS

In addition to the traditional CPC and cost-per-thousand (CPM) pricing, discussed earlier in this book, some other pricing options are being considered and occasionally implemented by some advertisers. These include:

- Cost-per-install: With this option, which is similar to cost-per-click, the advertiser pays each time a user downloads and installs a widget or application on a computer or smartphone. While this guarantees distribution of content, it does not guarantee the user will interact with the content.
- Cost-per-action: The advertiser pays each time a user takes a specific action, such as becoming a fan or friend, posting to a profile, looking at a video, or playing a game. This works best when a single, specific action is desired.

- Cost-per-engagement: The advertiser pays each time an engagement takes place over a given time period, such as submitting branded user-generated content, interaction with such content, votes, reviews, and ratings.

FUTURE OF SOCIAL MEDIA

With new applications being invented all the time, it is difficult to foresee the future of social media. Many new SNS are in development, and it is important to see whether those succeed. As new SNS come online, keeping track of how they evolve from an advertising perspective is important.

Facebook and Twitter don't like to think of themselves as websites; instead, they see themselves as stand-alone applications that can organize a user's entire web experience. Facebook, in particular, has become a "hub," providing news and information and social sharing. Facebook Marketplace, an online buying and selling platform has one billion active users. There are plans to connect with and enable creators to earn money on Instagram also.

SUMMARY

Instead of interrupting a user experience, brands need to look for ways to be part of a user experience when they participate on SNS. The evolving digital landscape is a challenging yet fascinating environment that can allow for creative brands and for media planners to reach new levels of engagement with consumers.

Rethinking social?

In November of 2021, British cosmetics brand Lush announced its global Anti-Social Media policy. Basically, the brand said it would no longer post on Facebook, Instagram, Snapchat, or TikTok.

Instead, the brand stated it would grow its YouTube presence, create email newsletters, and utilize Twitter for customer service. For inspiration, it plans to use Pinterest posts. Lush also said they'd increase in-person events as well. They're also starting a print magazine called "Lush Times."

Lush joins large fashion brands like Bottega Veneta and Balenciaga who have begun focusing on ephemeral content (which are messages shown for a short period of time before they disappear).

Lush's decision was based on concerns about the negative impact of social media on user's mental health, particularly that of young girls. In today's society, mistrust of social media continues to grow. However, Lush is taking a risk by not participating in channels where their competitors are active. It will be interesting to see if Lush maintains their commitment to leaving social media, and whether other brands will follow.

CHAPTER 31

Role of social influencers

···

IT'S NOT ALL ABOUT THE KARDASHIANS

Influencers have been a part of brand campaigns for centuries. In the 18th century, Queen Charlotte, the wife of King George III, endorsed the Wedgwood pottery company with a so-called Royal Warrant, which indicated that she had purchased products from the brand. Many decades later in the United States, baseball great Babe Ruth was the first paid endorser of a product: Red Rock cola.

Endorsers' influence over brand purchases can be explained by Heider's Balance Theory. This theory posits that if you like an influencer, and that influencer likes a brand, then you will like the brand as well. Social media is one way that you can quickly know what brands that people you like also like. As a result, social media is the primary channel for influencer marketing, which now not only includes royalty, celebrities and sports stars, but also social media-savvy individuals who build a loyal following online.

Influencers are here to stay, but how the world of influencer marketing looks and operates has changed a great deal in a short time, and in five years may be drastically different from today.

WHAT IS INFLUENCER MARKETING

Influencers are individuals who have a dedicated following on one or more social media channels. They are also viewed as experts in their specific niche areas, such as fashion, beauty, food, and the like. These characteristics are the key reasons that brands wish to partner with influencers: to promote products and services to their followers. These followers trust them and, thus, the influencer's recommendation has a great deal of credibility.

Influencer marketing can be very effective, as many people, particularly younger audiences, are willing to buy products from influencers they follow. An influencer

DOI: 10.4324/9781003258162-31

doesn't necessarily have to be someone with thousands of followers. Influencer types can be broken into four groups:

1. Mega influencers are people with more than a million followers. These are often celebrities or people who are well-known through their successes outside social media, such as movie and television stars, musicians, and sports figures. These influencers can quickly build broad awareness of brands.
2. Macro influencers are people with between 100,000–1,000,000 followers. They are often people who have used their talents or knowledge to build highly successful personal brands, such as chefs or interior designers. Like Mega influencers, macro influencers can build broad awareness of brands.
3. Micro influencers have between 10,000–100,000 followers. These individuals tend to be focused on one or two areas of expertise, and these areas might be more niche areas, and often products are the only compensation they need. Their followers are more likely to engage with posts, which means they may have a higher likelihood to become purchasers of the brand.
4. Nano influencers have between 1,000–10,000 followers. These individuals tend to be newer to the social media sphere and are highly enthusiastic about building their personal brands. Like micro influencer followers, their followers are also more likely to engage with posts.

Regardless of the type of influencer, influence has three components: relevance, reach, and resonance. Relevance is the clear connection between a brand and the influencer. Remi Bader features body-positive content on her Instagram and TikTok feeds. Bader's work in both those platforms made her relevant to an inclusive-sized swimsuit brand called Adore Me. The brand hired Bader to promote their brand on her social platforms and also created ads on Instagram with Bader as the spokesperson.

Reach is the number of individuals in the influencer's follower base that could be reached through a partnership. While many brands want to partner with mega and macro influencers with large bases, other brands find that a smaller, more focused base from a micro or a nano influencer might be more effective.

Resonance is the potential level of engagement that a sponsored message from an influencer can create among their audience. Engagement can include likes, comments, and sharing of messages. In general, nano and micro influencers have followers who are more likely to engage with messages.

Influencer marketing is most associated with Instagram, and most brands see Instagram as the primary channel for influencer activity. However, other channels also have their own sets of influencers, who are often different from the influencers on Instagram. Snapchat, YouTube, and TikTok reach different segments of the population and so different influencers reign supreme in these channels.

If you're planning a global influencer campaign, remember that different countries have their own top influencers as well as different patterns of platform usage. In South America, for example, Facebook and WhatsApp are the top social media platform, while Instagram and Twitter are much less popular. Some countries have some unique platforms as well: in China, the platform WeChat is by far the most popular, and a number of top Chinese influencers are very successful on this platform.

INFLUENCER MARKETING COSTS

In the early days of influencer marketing, sending free products to influencers would often generate positive social content in the form of a product review authored by the influencer. Today, free products are merely a starting point, with mega and macro influencers commanding high payments for a single post. Prices in this industry vary greatly, and there's no standard rate card to plan costs. While some nano influencers may only require a free product in order to create a message about it, many other influencers have established rates and will negotiate via their agents. Mega influencers are likely to have a press kit or media kit describing their rates and the types of partnerships available.

When determining a budget, an influencer's cost is based around influencer's follower count and engagement rate. Engagement rate includes all the likes, comments, clicks, and shares on an individual post. Cost per thousand (CPM) is then affected by qualitative factors such as star power or access to a niche audience.

Mega influencer Kim Kardashian has more than 175 million followers, and it is estimated that she earned between $400,000 and $550,000 per post in 2021. Her CPM would be between $2.25 and $3.10. A less well-known person on Instagram is Liv B (itsLivB), who often posts about food. It is estimated she earns between $310 and $525 per post. Given her number of followers (about 102,000), her CPM is between $3.02 and $5.05. On a CPM basis, having Kim Kardashian for your spokesperson is somewhat more efficient than having Liv B.

However, Liv B's engagement rate is almost double that of Kim Kardashian. For each post, Liv B generates, on average, a 2.87% engagement rate, meaning that there are close to 3,000 likes, shares, comments, and clicks on each of Liv B's posts. The CPM for engagement would be between $103 and $171. In contrast, Kim Kardashian gets about 2.7 million likes, shares, comments, and clicks on each of her posts. The CPM for engagement would be between $148 and $203. On an engagement basis, Liv B is more efficient than Kim Kardashian.

Something else that influences cost is the platform. Exhibit 31.1 provides an index for CPM differences among different platforms, using the most popular platform, Instagram, as a baseline. TikTok and Twitter are less expensive than Instagram. This

---

EXHIBIT 31.1 INDEX FOR SOCIAL MEDIA INFLUENCERS CPM

Instagram	YouTube	TikTok	Twitter	Facebook
100	200	30	50	250

For example, you may find that a macro influencer with 550,000 followers would promote your new frozen food company and charge $8,000 for a post on Instagram. That cost translates to a CPM of $14.54 (8,000/550 = 14.54). A CPM on that influencer's YouTube could be estimated to be $29.09 (14.54/100*200). On TikTok, the CPM could be estimated at $4.36 (14.54/100*30) and on Twitter, the CPM could be estimated at $7.27 (14.54/100*50). On Facebook, the CPM would be estimated to be $36.35 (14.54/100*250).

is likely due to content limitations in terms of time and space with both of these platforms. YouTube and Facebook are priced higher.

CREATING AN INFLUENCER PLAN

As with any other type of media plan, considerable research goes into developing a strong recommendation. The steps in developing the plan include:

- Platform research: Investigate which platforms to use. Certain platforms work best for certain product categories. For example, beauty, fashion, and food brands tend to be on Instagram. Video games are on Twitch. Brands appealing to younger demographic groups focus on TikTok, and many influencers on Twitter work for the brands that they tweet about. Use social listening to identify how competitors and complimentary brands use different social media platforms. The third-party tool Hootsuite provides search streams that can monitor conversations relative to the brand and its industry.
- Decide on goals. As discussed earlier, some influencer categories are better for creating brand awareness, and others are focused on brand engagement. Understanding the specific demographic and psychographic targets and how they use social media should also be considered as goals are developed.
- Decide on the type of partnership. A relationship with an influencer can be more than a simple product review written by the influencer. For example:
  - Gifting: The brand can provide products for the influencer to give away to their followers.
  - Sponsored content: Creating content for posting on the influencer's social media.
  - Content co-creation: Creating content with the influencer that is featured on their social media as well as the brand's.
  - Influencer takeover: Allowing an influencer to take control of the brand's social media accounts for a specific time period.
  - Affiliates: Providing a sales code that gives influencers a percentage of any sales that originate from their post.
  - Discount codes: Giving the influencer a discount code that they can promote and offer to their audience.
- Establish analytics. You may wish to measure different types of engagement, as well as set up special direct links so you can track the number of people who arrive at your brand's website directly from an influencer's post. You may also wish to establish a unique hashtag for the campaign to track how the hashtag performs.
- Investigate influencers. Use social listening to identify influencers on your selected platform. Apps like Right Relevance can aid in this work. In general, the more you invest, the more you will want to investigate an influencer's work. Some things to look for in identifying potential influencers:
  - Does the influencer already post about things that relate to your brand? Restaurants should look for people who dine out, fashion brands should look for influencers who regularly review products, and the like.

- Is the influencer generating engagement? Click through multiple posts and see how many people regularly engage with the content.
- Does the tone of the influencer's posts match or compliment your brand voice?
- Have they worked with similar brands in the past? Mega and macro influencers may be able to provide a portfolio of their past work for this analysis.
- Identify how to reach influencers. You may be able to connect with a micro or nano influencer via a private message, while mega and macro influencers may list contact information on their profiles. Companies like Insense and Trufan can connect a brand with all categories of influencers.
- Gather costs and outline a calendar for posts with your influencers.
- Track campaigns and make adjustments based on performance. You may wish to integrate influencer posts with other social media activity, or have it stand alone during times when there is less presence in other media.
- Identify which third-party tools can be used to track campaigns. At this writing, several third-party tools can be helpful in tracking influencer campaigns.

RULES, REGULATIONS, AND ETHICS

Influencer marketing is regulated in many countries around the world. In the United States, the Federal Trade Commission (FTC) requires influencers to disclose if they are paid for a post that promotes a brand. This is also true of influencers based in the EU, the UK, Australia, and India. Even though these are clear regulations in these countries, this disclosure requirement needs to be built into any contract with the influencer.

In addition, most of the platforms discussed in this chapter require disclosure of paid partnerships. Instagram specifies that any branded content (must use the Branded Content tag to identify the relationship; TikTok has branded content rules similar to Instagram. YouTube requires that influencer marketing videos be labeled as paid promotions. Similarly, Facebook branded content is uploaded via a special tool that identifies the content as sponsored. As a result, even if an influencer in a country without disclosure regulations about sponsored content promotes your brand, the platform will likely require that disclosure.

Some influencers may be wary about putting the #ad or #sponsored hashtag right up front in a comment or even in the title of a post, as requested by the FTC. But that's where it needs to be, to protect both your brand and the influencer, as paid promotions not labeled as such would be considered deceptive advertising, which is against the law in many countries.

Brands also need to protect themselves in their contracts with social media influencers, given that influencers may make a misstep that might harm their own reputations and, as a result, the reputation of brands they support. From the supermodels who supported the disastrous FYRE festival, to a famous talkshow host's use of her Apple tablet to promote a Microsoft tablet on Twitter, to issues from the past haunting model Chrissy Teigan, influencers can quickly lose the credibility they work so hard to build. Having a way to extract a brand quickly from problematic issues is an important step to remember.

SUMMARY

Influencer marketing is an evolving type of promotion that has the potential to build brand awareness and encourage people to purchase products. Like any other media choice, significant research is necessary to understand the best path for a brand. The changing nature of social media means that today's top platform may fall out of favor tomorrow, so understanding the changing nature of platforms is also necessary for the development of a strong influencer program.

Innovation: Influencer marketing

For many younger consumers, Buicks aren't on their consideration set for a new car, thinking that the brand is more for older people.

The GM brand Buick recently wanted to appeal to younger people and decided to use an influencer campaign to do so. The brand asked ten bloggers who wrote about design, fashion, and food to create Pinterest boards that illustrate how one Buick model, the Encore, could help express their personal style. Each blogger wrote about the experience on their blogs and promoted their boards on Facebook, Twitter, and Instagram. The "Pinboard to Dashboard" campaign drove more than 17 million unique site visitors.

When GM was planning its campaign for its electronic vehicle titled "Everybody In," they also turned to influencer marketing to get the attention of younger consumers. Focusing on influencers who, according to GM, "defy expectations and represent all walks of life," they selected professional surfer and shark attack survivor Bethany Hamilton, fitness instructor Cody Rigsby, and gamer Erin A. Simon to promote the vehicles.

CHAPTER 32

In-store media

....

REACHING A CAPTIVE AUDIENCE

According to a Statista study in July of 2021, Internet users still prefer to shop in-store rather than online for a number of different categories. For example: packaged foods and beverages (72% versus 9% online), OTC healthcare (65% versus 13%), haircare products (64% versus 18%), household cleaning (64% versus 12%), replacement tires (53% versus 19%), and skincare products (48% versus 20%).

It follows then that in-store ads influence brand choices. In grocery store chains across the country, shoppers see brand messages from the moment they park their cars until they complete their purchases at the cash register. And it isn't just in grocery stores: Walmart, Target, Best Buy, and other big box retailers now embrace in-store advertising. These messages are valued because they reach consumers close to the point of purchase. A shopper may have a list with "butter" written on it, but he probably won't decide on the specific brand of butter to purchase until he is in the store. In-store advertising also can encourage impulse buys – those unplanned purchases that are stimulated by seeing the brand (or an ad for the brand) in the store.

Another value of in-store media is that consumers often buy on impulse, and some estimates show that about half of the total purchase at the grocery is spent on items consumers were not planning to purchase. Younger consumers, in particular, respond to in-store marketing. One study found that they were more willing to consider and purchase brands that they learned about via in-store marketing.

Given the amount of decision making going on in a store, it is not surprising that advertisers are trying to get their messages in front of consumers when they are making these decisions. From a simple "shelf talker" (a small sign on a shelf pointing the shopper to a product) to digital opportunities, in-store advertising

DOI: 10.4324/9781003258162-32

TABLE 32.1 Pros and cons of in-store media

Pros	Cons
• Recency: Brand message appears very close to point of purchase • Capitalizes on impulse buys • Register sales data available to connect exposures to sales • Ad can be located anywhere – in stores, next to merchandise, on shopping bags, on ceilings • Relatively expensive compared to other media	• Limited space: Finite space for messages; may be blocked by other shoppers, employees, etc. • Limited effects on new users, primarily reminds current users • Message exposure time very short • Consumer focused on their list

has become a key element of many media plans. In addition, individual stores advertise loyalty programs to make sure their store is the one most visited by customers (see Table 32.1).

Consumers can move seamlessly from in-store to online. The rise in smartphone penetration allows the consumer to research products on the go, access mobile coupons, and sometimes pay for their purchase via phone. People can check a store web site for promotional offers and information and the store can market themselves to consumers and potential consumers thus helping drive them to the store. In-store media, then, will be discussed for both the physical and digital shopping world.

TYPES OF MESSAGES

Three broad categories of in-store advertising are *mass messages, personal messages*, and *loyalty programs*. Mass in-store messages display the same information to all customers, whereas personal messages provide an interactive experience where the consumer can get information appropriate for an individual purchase decision. In a survey involving 5,400 respondents, 34% said they found out about new products present in the store, 40% found out about new products from friends and acquaintances, and 42% learned of new products by using search engines. Thus, a combination of online and instore advertising can be highly effective.

Table 32.2 shows some of the key vendors in the in-store market.

TABLE 32.2 Players in the in-store industry

Type of media	Key companies
In-store signage	Vericast, (CBS) Outernet, Floorgraphics
In-store coupons	Smartsource and Catalina Marketing
Shopping carts	Cart America
In-store video	PRN, Target Inhouse Video

MASS IN-STORE/ONLINE MESSAGES

In-store signs promote a single product (such as Heinz ketchup) or a group of products from the same manufacturer (such as Kellogg's cereals). These messages are placed in aisles near to the product(s) being promoted, providing a persuasive message close to the purchase decision. Within this category are:

- Shelf talkers: Small signs that point customers to products on shelves.
- Banners: Larger vertical signs that span two or three shelves.
- Floor signs: Large graphics placed on the aisle floor to point customers to products on lower shelves. There are 3-D graphics available for a grocery floor: A soda or snack that looks like it is placed on the floor. There are also see-through graphics available to cover the glass doors to soda and drink coolers.

Ads on shopping carts used by consumers as they shop provide messages on the cart. The ads are exposed both to the shopper with the cart and to the other shoppers as they roam the store. These include:

- A small sign on the child seat of the cart
- A larger ad on the side of the cart
- A complete wrap of the cart in an advertisement
- A touchscreen shopping list with coupons

Video advertisements provide messages on large screens near the checkout aisles or at other key locations in the store. The screens feature content from cable channels such as the Food Network, Discovery, *Entertainment Tonight*, and *Inside Edition*, and content is updated regularly. Advertisements are embedded into the programming. Unlike the screens near the checkout counters, which get a higher level of attention, screens throughout the store may be more influential on purchases. The Walmart smart TV network, Walmart Connect, provides advertisers with the opportunity to deliver television messages to their respective areas in Walmart stores where they have an audience of 150 million weekly customers.

Store websites and applications for tablet and mobile devices provide huge opportunities for brands. Store websites feature digital sale events and special deals for the online shopper. Applications for tablet and mobile devices allow the consumer to review products online and get in-store discounts by checking in through a location-based service such as Foursquare. The integration of social media platforms allows the consumer to share ideas with friends and get social media coupons. QSR codes also enable consumers to go directly to a web site and a coupon.

DIGITAL OUT-OF-HOME

Digital out-of-home advertising provides messages targeted at specific locations in the store at specific times. For example, prepared meals can be advertised at a grocery store after 5 P.M. to attract after-work shoppers. Digital signs also allow a store to sell ads to other businesses (a grocery store, for example, could sell a digital sign to the local auto repair shop or movie theater). More than one advertiser can be on the digital signage and the ads can rotate throughout the day.

Pepsi and Lays combined in store to create an immersive experience connected to the UEFA soccer championship. Store goers could enter through a recreation/replica of stadium tunnels. On screen, they could kick a soccer ball to other screens, which reached customers in four different cities. As the ball passed to 467 people on different screens, they set a Guinness World Record for the most people on an online chain video passing a football. Lights, sound, and action were created in store. There were displays of Pepsi and Lays on sale close to the screens, soccer stadium display, and interactive display.

INTERACTIVE KIOSKS

Interactive kiosks are stand-alone structures that allow consumers to access product information, recipes, and coupons. Kiosks can be placed near the front of the store or the promoted department to maximize customer exposure. Types of kiosks include:

- Leaflet dispensers that provide nutritional information and recipes to customers, often including shopping lists and meal-planning ideas to cross-promote products.
- On-shelf coupons, a small device attached to a shelf near a product, that allow a customer to print out their own coupon
- Self-service gift cards, a credit card-based device to vend gift cards to customers, freeing up sales associates for other tasks.
- Intel Magic Mirror is an interactive mirror display that shows consumers how they would look in clothing and jewelry they're considering buying without having to visit a dressing room. An LCD screen overlays a two-way holographic mirror display. Walmart has also set up touchscreen interactive beauty kiosks on which customers can browse different beauty products and style information as well as video tutorials. Brands such as L'Oréal, Maybelline, and CoverGirl are demonstrated.

REGISTER COUPONS

Couponing has embraced the digital world. Social media coupons and mobile coupons offer the consumer the ability to tap into coupons and offers that are relevant to them just by entering their shopping list. Large retailers such as Kroger have their own coupon application that allows the consumer to scan their smartphone at the register to get the latest manufacturer discounts.

Personalized register coupons are based on an individual's purchases. Checkout terminals can be programmed to print out price coupons on customer register receipts. The coupon may be either for a future purchase of a product just purchased or for a competitor's product. For example, the purchase of Iams dog food might generate a coupon for Kal Kan dog food.

LOYALTY PROGRAMS

Loyalty programs encourage loyal buying behavior by rewarding customers for their purchases and can help attract new customers. Loyalty programs issue a membership card – sometimes called a rewards card, a points card, or a club card – to an individual shopper. Cards typically have a bar code or magnetic strip that can be scanned easily to track an individual's purchases. Customers can usually also use their phone number to record and get loyalty rewards. After a certain number of purchases (say, 10 Boba teas) or a certain dollar amount spent on purchases ($200 worth of books at a bookstore), the shopper receives a reward – a free product, a discount, or some other benefit on a future purchase. To join a loyalty program, a customer provides a certain level of demographic information, which is then compared with her purchases, allowing for the collection of data that can be used to make marketing decisions. Sephora has a tiered point-based loyalty program called "Beauty Insider." Members earn one point for every dollar they spend in the store. More points equal a higher category of membership and offers. Points can be redeemed as discounts or store credit or for giveaways. Their "Rewards Bazaar" is an online shopping space where points can be redeemed for merchandise. The multiple options in their loyalty program aids top-of-mind awareness as well as helping build loyal return customers.

MEASUREMENT

Measurement of in-store media involves an assessment of both exposure to the message and reaction to the message. Three types of measurements can assess customer activity and thus gauge exposure:

- Traffic counters measure the actual number of people who enter a store. This can be done through technology such as a laser beam across a store entrance. The number can then help to generate the potential "reach" of an in-store vehicle, given that reach is defined as the opportunity to see the advertising in a given time frame.
- Video recognition systems such as wall-mounted cameras count the number of people who walk past a certain place in the store (generally the location of the in-store advertisement). This type of system can also track whether or not customers stopped to look at the message, for how long, and can generate the total exposures, or impressions, for a specific media vehicle during a defined time period.
- Ceiling-based cameras can assign a unique numerical ID to each customer who enters the store and track the movements of each customer through the store, creating a log of the customer's activity and exposure to advertisements.

Data provided by the Point of Purchase Advertising Institute allows reach and frequency to be calculated. The average supermarket in the United States hosts 6,000 shopping trips per week, and the average trip has 1.25 people doing the shopping. Thus, the average exposure of an in-store sign per week is 7,500. The average household shops 1.5 times per week, and the number of unique visitors to a supermarket is 5,000 per week, with an average frequency of 1.5.

Therefore, the average frequency for an in-store campaign can be calculated by multiplying 1.5 times the number of weeks the campaign runs.

Like gross rating points, in-store rating points are calculated by multiplying reach by frequency. This can be used to compare cost measures as well on both a cost-per-point and cost-per-thousand basis. Measurement of digital initiatives such as website, tablet, or mobile devices can be calculated by the number of unique visitors to each site and through engagement metrics on the length and depth of the visit. Transaction information can be obtained from the unique user as well.

The Point of Purchase Advertising Institute researches shopper trends and the influence in-store media has on purchase behavior. They conducted pre and post intercept interviews with shoppers as well as eye-tracking to measure behavior of 2,991 shoppers. So information is ascertained regarding shopper behavior as well as reach and frequency numbers. It remains to be seen if the Covid-19 pandemic has altered or will alter shopper behavior and number of average visits.

FUTURE OF IN-STORE MEDIA

Due to increased technological advances, we will be able to see more *personal* and less *mass* media in local stores in the years to come. Technology such as a shopping cart with a small computer attached to the handle is one example. The computers have cell phone-style navigation buttons on the handle and a self-scanning feature to use at checkout. The wording can also be in different languages as well as in English.

GPS systems can direct you from your house to the store, and now technology is allowing for "in-store" GPS. One supermarket chain launched a mobile app that provides a database of the entire store's offerings, showing customers where restrooms and customer service kiosks are located and directing consumers to the supermarket's most enticing promotional offers and sale items. It also reminds customers where they parked. The app takes advantage of multiple Wi-Fi hotspots in each store, since GPS is not very reliable indoors.

A lot of activity is being centered on the idea of SoLoMo – the convergence of social media, location-based services, and mobile devices. This combination is about helping the consumer engage with the brand regardless of the channel. Retailers are working feverishly to make the physical and digital experience as seamless as possible.

The Innovation Lab at the international agency IPG has developed a variety of new technologies that are being seen in the marketplace. Among them is a device that transforms the front window of a store into a giant touchscreen. Designed for use at retail clothing boutiques, it allows customers to interact with a screen to select outfits for a virtual avatar instead of looking at an outfit on a mannequin. A similar device developed by IPG is a mirror that enables a shopper to scan a dress and then project that clothing onto her body before going to the dressing room. The interactive screen allows the shopper to examine different colors of the clothing and find matching accessories. An image of the outfit can be posted on the shopper's Facebook page.

Retailing has become less about a battle between brick-and-mortar and online and more about integrating channels into a single experience. With mobile devices as a constant consumer companion, it is a matter of bringing that retail experience to engage consumers at home, on the go, and in the store. For example, Walmart is testing a livestream shopping platform on Twitter. Walmart customers can shop from Twitter as well as Walmart's other social platforms thus providing a form of in-store and digital shopping.

SUMMARY

In-store shoppers are captive audiences, and every day sees new opportunities in reaching them. The retail experience is becoming more and more challenging, and smart media planners will look for interesting and new ways to break through the clutter to showcase products in the store aisles.

Gender-neutral displays

By 2024, all retailers in California who sell toys and other children's products will need to provide a gender-neutral section or area of their store. The section must include a selection of items and toys, regardless of whether the items have traditionally been marketed to either exclusively girls or exclusively boys. The law reflects a policy put in place by the large retailer Target.

The law stemmed from consumer concerns that some marketers have charged different prices for what is essentially the same product, but with slight differences to appeal more to one gender rather than another. Often this is done through colors: For example, one retailer reportedly charged more than a third more for girls' roller skates than boys'. The only difference: The boys' were blue and the girls' were pink.

The goal of the law is to make it easier for consumers to identify these unjustified differences in similar products. It also helps to stem gendered perceptions of what types of toys and products are appropriate for girls and which are appropriate for boys.

The law allows for separate sections for boys' and girls' products, so the Barbie section is likely to remain intact. The law also does not apply to clothes.

Starbucks re-purposes coffee sleeves to bring in customers

Starbucks, the world's largest retail coffee shop, faced a challenge in its home market of Seattle. Competitors were crowding into downtown Seattle, undercutting Starbucks price and taking market share.

To combat the competition, Starbucks developed a unique solution. Marketers pondered this question: What goes best with coffee in the morning? The quick answer was the daily newspaper. However, newspapers were having a hard time selling, even in the heart of the downtown Seattle business district. Was there a way for Starbucks to make the coffee/paper connection during a downturn in newspaper readership?

Starbucks found one. They re-purposed their coffee sleeves to include a promotional incentive, and then developed a co-branded promotion with the local newspaper to distribute the coffee sleeves around their papers. Paper sales went through the roof and readers flooded to the downtown Starbucks to drink coffee and read the paper. Starbucks defended its turf and the newspaper found new readers. Rain in Seattle? Not at this Starbucks.

CHAPTER 33

Direct response

....

GETTING TO YES!

Every piece of advertising should elicit a response. So, what is the difference between direct-response media and just plain media? The industry is continually wrestling with this question, and there are many different opinions on the answer.

The Direct Marketing Association (DMA) has defined direct marketing as "any direct communication that is designed to generate a response in the form of an order, a request for further information and/or a visit to a store or other place of business for purchase of a specific product or service." Others view it as a measurable system of marketing that uses one or more advertising media to build transactions and a relationship database.

Direct response is different from other media in two areas. First, direct-response media is an interactive marketing system. It links the buyer and the seller directly. Most advertising campaigns use media to help persuade consumers to take action. Direct-response media is the conduit for action. Instead of asking you to go to a store to buy something, direct-response media provides an incentive that prompts immediate action. The second area where direct response is different from other media is in how it measures a store where you can buy something. Media are typically measured by how many people are reached and how often people are reached. The advertising measurement is gauged in the form of brand measures as well as sales measures. It assumes that advertising is one element of a broad array of tools for generating sales. Direct-response media has an immediate and measurable response. This response can take many forms, from responding to a mail offer, to calling on the phone, going to a website, or responding to an offer on social media. Apps are also enabling direct response for users. Direct-response media is measured based on the transaction rather than the reach.

DOI: 10.4324/9781003258162-33

LANDSCAPE OF DIRECT RESPONSE

Is it any wonder that direct-response media is well liked among marketing directors? Unlike much of the advertising world, direct response is accountable. Managers know what their return on investment (ROI) is. In a world where ROI reigns supreme, direct-response media is the champion. According to Statista, the United States is the leading direct-selling market in the world at 40%, followed by China at 19.18%.

eMarketer reports that 59% of digital advertising in the US is spent on direct response. The global customer relationship management (CRM) market is poised to reach about $113.46 billion by the end of 2027 (Globe Newswire, 2021) (Source: https://www.hubspot.com/marketing-statistics). It is clear that direct response is a significant sector of the media world. Some of the top direct-response agencies and agencies that have a strong direct response arm are Acxiom, Epsilon, Rapp, Merkle, and Ogilvy.

During the Covid-19 disruption, many large advertisers cut back on their spending on brand building. Direct-response advertisers increased advertising, encouraging consumers to take immediate action to download an app, purchase an online course, or order products. Some of the most popular direct-response products are detailed in Table 33.1.

https://www.cmo.com.au/blog/sales-strategies/2020/05/26/why-direct-response-advertising-is-winning-this-year/

https://www.statista.com/statistics/1171614/popular-direct-to-consumer-brands-usa-social-media/

ROLE OF DATABASE MARKETING

The rise of direct response is tied to the use of database marketing. Database marketers build and maintain a vast amount of information on current and prospective customers. With the increase in available personal information and the ability to aggregate this information via computer technology, marketers can communicate with individuals in a personal manner using a variety of media.

TABLE 33.1 Popular direct-to-consumer brands on social media

Rank	Brand	Actions taken (millions)
1	Kylie Cosmetics	194
2	KKW Beauty	25.8
3	Glossier	19.8
4	Food52	17.9
5	Stance	5.8
6	Farfetch	4.2
7	Fabletics	3.6
8	FabFitFun	3.5
9	Everlane	2.4
10	Hello Fresh	2.1

A good database enables marketers to profile and segment their customers and prospects. It provides them with the knowledge of who their customers and prospects are, when they have purchased, how much they have purchased, and how to best communicate with them.

This leads to the CRM programs to which direct response campaigns are tied. Direct response is associated with generating an initial sale, whereas a CRM program is associated with subsequent sales. In building more and more sales from the same customer, the marketer establishes a relationship with that customer. The more purchase history there is, the more the marketer can anticipate what the customer needs or wants. This is why direct response and CRM play such a large role in many communication plans.

By using the database as a learning tool, markets can constantly test different media, offers, and creative messages (creatives) to keep improving their ROI.

TYPES OF DIRECT RESPONSE

Advertising that asks the consumer to provide feedback directly to the sender is termed *direct-response advertising.* Any medium can be used for direct-response advertising. Whereas the most commonly used direct-response media are direct mail, catalogs, and television, an array of digital media that corresponds to each of their traditional counterparts is growing and changing continually.

Table 33.2 shows the traditional and digital direct-response media for the broadcast, print, mail, out-of-home, and directory categories. Let's discuss each category and how digital media have expanded the direct response universe.

BROADCAST

Most or all of us have seen an infomercial. Infomercials are those 30- or 60-minute paid programs on television that sell everything from fitness equipment to kitchen appliances to get-rich-quick schemes. Some of the better-known brands that use direct-response television as a key part of their marketing mix are, Flex Seal, Copper Fit socks, and Nutrisystem. Some more well-known and larger brands such as Procter & Gamble, AT&T, Geico, and L'Oréal use direct-response TV.

Radio is also a large direct-response medium. Like television, radio has paid programming that provides content and then sells a product. And radio is the home of announcers and commentators who pitch a wide variety of products.

TABLE 33.2 Traditional and digital media for direct response

Category	Traditional	Digital
Broadcast	DRTV & radio	Video/Audio podcasts
Print	FSI	iPad
Mail	Direct mail	E-mail
	Catalogs	E-commerce
Out-of-home	Take ones	Interactive kiosks
Directory	Telephone book	Search engine marketing

On the digital side, video and audio podcasts are popular ways to gain traction in the marketplace. A number of media outlets provide free content in video or audio podcasts as a means of enticing consumers to subscribe to their paid content. *The Wall Street Journal, The New York Times,* and *The New Yorker* provide regular podcasts as a means to gain subscribers. The social audio app Clubhouse has some speakers or rooms that are directly or indirectly selling their brands or services. And some brands, such as Budweiser and Taco Bell, are selling NFTs directly to consumers.

PRINT

Print has always had a number of direct-response advertisers that feature coupons or toll-free numbers as response mechanisms. Print is also the delivery mechanism for large-scale couponing efforts and product inserts.

The iPad and other tablet devices as well as smartphones enable dynamic direct-to-consumer print ads. People can click on a website within an ad or an app to purchase the product directly. The tablet is a convergent media delivery system that combines the best of brand media with direct response.

MAIL

Direct mail is the grandfather of direct-response advertising. Nearly a quarter of all direct-response advertising is spent on some form of direct mail, followed closely by catalogues, the next largest category of direct response. Marketing via catalogues is a huge business with nearly 11 billion catalogues hitting the mail every year in spite of increased paper and postal costs.

More digital alternatives to mail are available every year. Email marketing is easy to execute and extremely cost efficient. However, with the increase in spam and more sophisticated spam filters, nonpermission-based email is rapidly falling out of favor with marketers. However, permission-based email is one of the staples of a multiple-channel direct response plan. Just like traditional postal mail moving to email, paper catalogs are moving to digital catalogs and sophisticated e-commerce websites. Many retailers have an e-tail component to their business, which is driven by direct-response media.

OUT OF HOME

Most people think of billboards when they think of out-of-home media. But there are a number of direct-response mechanisms that are outside the home. The simple "take-ones" that are omnipresent at retailers and other public venues are an example of an out-of-home tactic. Billboards that feature a text response can be made into an effective direct-response vehicle.

Digitally, interactive kiosks found in shopping malls or at ballparks are examples of how electronic forms of an old medium can breathe new life into a direct response vehicle.

DIRECTORY

Direct response is not always the most glamorous media. And this is so true of the directory category. Telephone yellow pages and white pages are digital. According to the Yellow Pages company, more than 80 million people visit the YP.com site or use the Yellow Pages app. All paper directories are on the wane. Obviously, the most used direct response vehicle today is *search engine marketing* (SEM). Business searches on Google alone are a dominant form of direct response.

MEASUREMENT AND COST

Direct-response media has its own measurement system and currency. Most media are purchased based on cost-per-thousand (CPM). The media audience has a certain CPM value. Multiplying the audience by the CPM yields the *media unit cost*. The measure of efficiency, then, is how low the CPM is. The general idea of media plan efficiency is to reach the largest number of consumers in your audience for the least amount of money.

Direct-response media on the other hand is not based on CPM. It is based on a cost-per-response. That cost-per-response can be a cost-per-lead or it can be a cost-per-sale. The key concept, though, is that every media vehicle purchased is based on a behavioral cost.

Success in the direct response world is based on driving down the cost-per-lead or sale. Unlike other media, the idea of direct response is to get the most leads or sales for the least money. This may actually mean reaching fewer consumers overall – but reaching more active consumers.

Most direct-response campaigns have a test phase where the media buyer allocates funds to a variety of media or vehicles within a specific medium. Based on this initial investment, the media buyer then determines the optimum cost-per-lead or sale from which to benchmark future costs. Rather than negotiate with the media based on a CPM, the media buyer will negotiate based on a cost-per-lead or sale. The media partner is rewarded based on sales or activity rather than on total audience.

Table 33.3 provides an example of a direct response direct local television analysis for a fictitious product, the Easy Chair Stair Climber, priced at $50. As you can see, the media buyer purchased programs in a variety of dayparts.

Each program in those dayparts has a specific commercial unit cost. For example, the M–F 9 A.M.–7 P.M. daypart has a unit cost of $300. So, each time the commercial

TABLE 33.3 Direct response direct TV analysis for the $50 HYPO exercise product (fictitious company)

Daypart		Cost	Leads	CPL	Conversion (%)	Sales*	ROI (%)	Cost per sale
M–F	9 A.M.–7 P.M.	$300	30	$10	40	$600	100	$25.00
M–Su	5 P.M.–12 A.M.	$600	25	$24	50	$625	4	$48.00
M–Su	12 A.M.–12 P.M.	$200	25	$8	30	$375	88	$26.67
S/Su	10 A.M.–5 P.M.	$400	20	$20	50	$50	25	$40.00
		$1,500	100	$15	42	$2,100	40	$34.90

* Conversion $50

airs, it costs HYPO Exercise $300. The balance of the analysis is the response. Reading across, the M–F 9 A.M.–7 P.M. program generated 30 leads. By dividing the leads by the unit cost of $300, you get a cost-per-lead (CPL) of $10 ($300/30 = $10). The next column shows the percentage of those 30 consumers who purchased the product. In this case, it is 40 percent or 12 customers (30 ×.40 = 12). Those 12 customers each bought a $50 Easy Chair Stair Climber, making the total sale for this commercial in this daypart $600 ($50 × 12 = $600). The ROI is 100%. This is calculated first by subtracting the total cost of advertising by total sales and second by dividing the incremental sales by the cost of the advertising ($600-$300 = $300 and $300/$300 = 1 × 100 = 100%). Another way to evaluate it is that it cost $25 for every sale made.

So, this particular daypart was very successful. Contrast this with the next daypart, M–Su 5 P.M.–12 A.M. Here, the buyer paid $600 for a commercial yet only generated $625 of sales. In this case, the sales barely covered the cost of the media purchased. This particular media placement was obviously not efficient, especially if the media buyer knows the average cost-per-lead is $15. Forty-two percent of those leads convert to sales with the average cost-per-sale at $35. The media buyer may work with the media to set a benchmark on the cost-per-lead to be no greater than $15 or even lower. And the media buyer may tell the television media partner that because certain dayparts work much better than others, he or she will purchase more commercials in the better-performing dayparts.

This type of analysis and concept can be used with every medium. So, in the interactive area, it may be a cost-per-click and then a cost-per-sale. In the print area, it would be a cost-per-lead and then a cost-per-sale. Other media would also be the same. Direct-response advertisers view each media purchase in two ways. The first is the amount they made for each advertisement; the second is the learning gained from each media placement. Each placement opportunity is one step closer to optimizing their investment.

The push and pull of purchasing direct-response advertising is different from a brand or promotional message. In the case of the latter, the media placement is done at a specific time when the message is most relevant. For direct response, the placement is done based on making the most money regardless of the time. If that means scheduling all your broadcast ads after midnight, then so be it.

The direct-response media buyer evaluates media based on cost and response. If prices get too high on a highly responsive media vehicle, the media buyer will not agree to place the schedule. It is better to save the dollars rather than to purchase media inventory where you will not make a profit.

This type of media purchase strategy is the opposite of a brand strategy. In the brand strategy, you look to purchase media that is popular with consumers. This may be high-demand media where lots of advertisers are supporting the media vehicle. In direct response, you look to purchase media that has less advertising demand. The weaker the demand, the more likely you are to gain a favorable rate where you can make the most profit.

CREATIVE UNITS

As we have discussed, direct-response advertising is different from brand advertising. Brand advertising is designed to continue to build goodwill over time. It has a cumulative effect. Direct-response advertising needs to pay out each time it runs.

Because of these differences, direct response creative units are more involved than brand messages. It is unlikely that a direct-response advertiser can develop a compelling story and a call to action in a 15-second television commercial. Yet brand advertisers regularly use this length of unit to communicate brand differences.

Size may not necessarily make a difference in print advertising. A small space ad with a phone number or mailing address that is properly targeted may elicit as much response as a large full-page advertisement. Or a quarter-page ad with a coupon may generate as many takers as a full-page advertisement. Every brand and offer is unique.

Determining the optimum creative message, offer, and size or length are key variables that direct-response advertisers continually test. Combined with the media placement, these become the test cells for a direct-response campaign.

Where there are key creative unit implications for the media team is in the broadcast category. There are three types of creative units: short-form units, long-form units, and paid programming. *Short-form units* are commercials that are 30 or 60 seconds in length. These are commercial units that are also popular with brand messages. *Long-form units* are commercials that are 2 minutes, 5 minutes, or other lengths of time. They are longer than standard lengths but they are not paid programming. *Paid programming* is purchasing a 30-minute or an hour program of time in one chunk.

The logical extension of long-form commercials is an entire network devoted to direct selling. The Home Shopping Network and QVC are the two dominant networks that have provided a forum for product sales of all types over the past decade. Everything from jewelry to collectibles to general merchandise is sold on the airwaves.

The tenet of direct response is to continually look for opportunities where you can maximize the ROI. This means that both the media team and the creative team must constantly seek ways to improve performance.

FUTURE OF DIRECT RESPONSE

Direct response has moved from a specialty advertising area to a mainstream one. In the coming years, the growth of direct response should outpace that of brand advertising years. There are a few trends that are fueling that growth.

Convergence of media

There is no doubt that we are in the midst of a convergent media revolution. Devices combine the immersion of print, the emotion of broadcast, and the response of the Internet. All media types can be interactive. Print ads can be opened up directly to buy products on a website with a link or a QR code. Television programs will offer point-and-click technology for deeper dives and product purchase, especially with addressable TV or specific ads being offered to specific people. Radio will have voice-activated purchasing opportunities. So, direct response will morph into the call to action for much of what was traditional brand advertising.

Mobile and social media

Mobile media greatly enhances direct-response capabilities. By triangulating your location through your cell phone, marketers can push offers to you as you drive or walk by a store. With greater access to media content via mobile phones, the ability to add this geotargeting dimension to existing content is a marketer's dream come true.

Social media is a great frontier for direct-response advertisers. On social media platforms, pay-per-click direct-response advertisements are a part of the advertising landscape. Direct response brands are experimenting with their own social media platforms where they can sell their products and build a community of followers. As people have to opt in to receive messages from advertisers, even if the audience is smaller, they are more likely to pay attention to offers since they voluntarily opted in.

Mobile payment

The ability of consumers to pay for goods and services whenever or wherever they want is another boon to the direct-response world. As technology accelerates the accessibility coupled with the safety and privacy of electronic payments, the opportunity to make a sale is greatly enhanced. Electronic payment systems such as PayPal, and in some cases Venmo, help make payments easier. Comcast, Hulu, YouTube TV, and others have integrated PayPal as a gateway to payments for products and their services.

SUMMARY

Many different media can become direct response in the way it is bought, sold, and measured. Direct response is rapidly moving forward as a mainstream marketing method. As technology advances, there is no doubt that direct response will be a crucial part of every marketer's planning arsenal.

Panda Express and direct mail

Is direct mail – those coupons and flyers we get in our physical mailbox – an innovation? It is when it drives success. Panda Express had not used direct mail for 20 years. But when the pandemic caused people to stop going out to eat, the fast-food chain tried a direct-marketing campaign.

The mailing was timed to coincide with the creation of Panda Express delivery, which was implemented in all stores that didn't have drive-through windows. The campaign, which contained coupons and online ordering information, targeted homes within three miles of Panda Express locations.

The results? Redemption rates were as high as 33%, much higher than average redemption rates for the same types of promotions, which average 3–4%. Not only that, but Panda Express tracked sales from the mail coupon, which was double the amount compared to the regular digital promotions that they implemented.

CenterPoint Energy uses scratch and sniff to promote safety

You may be familiar with the concept of "scratch and sniff." Perhaps you've visited a cosmetics counter or purchased a magazine and got a small card with a sample of perfume or cologne embedded in it. Scratch and sniff printing is created by putting microscopic capsules of scent into a solution that is applied to some type of print cardstock. When these capsules are rubbed, they break and release the chosen scent.

Scratch and sniff isn't just for perfume. On Valentine's Day, the fast-food giant KFC produced Valentine's Day cards with a scratch and sniff panel that smelled like fried chicken.

Another innovative use of scratch and sniff was implemented by CenterPoint Energy, a large regional natural gas and electric utility in the US. Every year, CenterPoint is faced with the task of warning people about the potential dangers of natural gas flammability. This is particularly true of natural gas used in heating appliances or to heat your home. A natural gas leak in one's home can lead to a fire or an explosion, and people can get physically sick from the gas as well.

Rather than simply tell the message of how dangerous these leaks are, CenterPoint's agency wanted to demonstrate it. How do you demonstrate gas – something that is basically invisible? The insight was the smell. While natural gas is odorless, the smell of rotten eggs is added to natural gas so people know when the gas is leaking. This led the agency to borrow a tactic from perfume marketers and create the first scratch and sniff print ads for natural gas so people would recognize when a leak was happening. The pungent ad did the trick. Consumers were much more aware of what to look, or smell for, when around their natural gas heater.

CHAPTER 34

Gaming

....

"IT'S JUST A GAME" – OR IS IT?

Games are one of the most popular downloads for digital devices including computers, tablets, and mobile phones: according to Statista, 25% of all mobile apps in the Apple store are games; twice the next category of apps. People play games to take a break from other tasks, to compete with friends, and to entertain themselves when bored or on long trips. During the Covid-19 pandemic, gaming increased by 45% in the United States. The majority of games available for these devices are free, and most of these free games feature ads. Even paid games – games users need to purchase to play – may feature an advertisement. As the amount of time spent in gameplay has increased, players' exposure to ads has also grown with a total of 2.9 billion players worldwide.

GAMING DEMOGRAPHICS

Female gamers tend toward tablet and mobile games and males tend toward consoles; overall 45% of gamers are women. Of all American gamers, about 60% play games daily. The amount of money spent on video games rose to $49 billion in the United States in 2020, according to Statista.

Looking at the whole gamer market, 72% are over age 18 and the 18–34-year-olds comprise 38% of that percentage (Statista, gamesindustry.biz). Three-quarters of US households own a device that they use to play video games. Perhaps surprisingly, the average gamer isn't a 14-year-old high school boy, but is 34 years old, owns a house and has children; 67% of parents play video games with their children at least once per week. People ages 18–24 are the most likely to purchase a game.

Mobile gaming continues to grow; 74% of mobile phone owners use their device each month to play games. It's obvious that gaming now reaches a broad spectrum of people. The key is to look at the game and match it carefully with the audience.

DOI: 10.4324/9781003258162-34

GAME ADVERTISING PLACEMENT

Just as a media buyer works with a television network, there are game networks that allow media planners to place brand messages in a number of different games through a single network. Ad Exchange, Rubicon Project, and Select Media are examples of networks that work with a wide variety of advertisers. With networks such as these, games are selected for inclusion in the media plan based on different criteria, including gender and age demographics, application preferences, type of mobile device used, and carrier network type. Networks provide metrics that can include impressions, taps, tap-through rates, unique visits, and average time spent, for example. Ad Exchange can tie in with Google analytics to monitor how buys are performing. Pricing for these types of messages is similar to the pricing strategies of other companies that offer bidding and fixed costs for clicks and click-throughs. With so many games available, it is difficult to compare the value of a game to the value of an ad on Google. However, anecdotal information suggests that click- (or tap-) through rates are much higher for ads on games than for other types of ads. Companies like Microsoft and EA Sports can also create networks with the variety of the games they produce and own.

Companies that want to create a game around specific brand generally work directly with a game developer to do so.

DIFFERENT MODELS OF GAME ADS

1. **Freemium model**. Free to play ads are designed for specific audiences. Most ads are geared toward encouraging users to upgrade in the game (e.g. by purchasing items to enhance game play) but other ads can appear while people are still playing for free. If there are too many ads and players start to get annoyed, they either stop playing the game and find another free game or they can pay to upgrade to avoid ads. Thus, the key is to not overload the number of ads in these games.
2. **Static vs. Dynamic ads.** A static ad is similar to product placement in video content and is put in the game when it is being developed. Such ads cannot be updated in real time and need to be more generic in nature. They can appear as, for example, a billboard in a road race game and look as they would in real life. Even if these ads are not clicked on, there is brand exposure. Dynamic ads are more along the lines of web banners and can be different sizes and updated. These are more flexible and are more often seen and clicked on.
3. **Interstitial ads**. These ads usually appear in a break in the game. They most often are seen when moving from one level to the next or during a transition in a game storyline. So as the player pauses, they see the ad. These are basically pop-up ads and there is exposure to the brand whether someone clicks or not.
4. **Native banners.** This is one of the most common ad formats in games. They appear to be part of the game, and as such, often appear in a corner (for example, next to a scoreboard) and in no way interrupt the game.

5. **Contextual ads.** These are very common in mobile game apps. Characters in the game are pictured with products from the "real world," such as a character standing near a Starbucks or wearing a branded outfit.

6. **Ads as a reward**. Players often get a reward for earning a certain number of points in game challenges. These rewards can be points or coins or rewards can come from an advertiser. The rewards can be connected to opening a link to a brand website, following a brand on social media, or sharing a brand's post. These ads have a high click rate. In addition to the cost of the ad, though, the advertiser is responsible for the cost of the prize.

7. **Expandable ads.** These are immersive experiences. They can be a short video clip for a concert or movie trailer, for example. They can be very creative and entertaining to the viewer who clicked. The downside is some people click accidentally on these ads and are not too entertained by that.

8. **In-game video.** These can be 15 or 30 seconds or shorter increments. They need to be highly creative to reward the player as they pause the game, which is, of course, what they are there for.

9. **Advergaming**. These are games built to promote a brand or a product. The game is the ad and they build a strong connection with the brand. For example, Lexus has a racing game that involves their cars. This can help build a strong connection with people who align with the brand.

PRICING OF GAMES

Like all digital media, there are a variety of pricing models for advergames, including:

- Cost-per-thousand (CPM): inventory is purchased by the advertiser on the basis of the number of impressions delivered.
- Cost-per-click (CPC): the advertiser pays whenever the user clicks on the banner ad.
- Cost-per-action (CPA): the advertiser pays when the user or game player takes a desired action with the advertiser. For example, the advertiser pays a fee whenever the game player downloads or purchases a branded t-shirt. This is an example of a performance ad network.
- Cost-per-view (CPV): the advertiser pays when the user or game player clicks on a video.
- Cost-per-session (CPS): the advertiser pays for every gameplay session that features a large amount of brand integration.
- Sponsorship: the advertiser pays for every branded opportunity in a gameplaying environment.

As may be evident from this chapter, game advertising is not at all standardized, which can be a boon to some brands but may be challenging to more traditional brands that want to compare the costs of one type of experience to another. Additionally, there are unclear definitions as to what constitutes an impression in an in-game ad: Is it 10 seconds? Five seconds? What is optimal for a brand?

Also, there are challenges with cross-platform placements. With new platforms invented all the time and customers shifting among platforms, brands must constantly assess where the best space is for them to reach their audiences; creative executions must be adapted accordingly. It's important to remember that game audiences can be broader than other media. Because the audiences on games can be broader, deciding who the planner wants to reach on specific games has to be less analytically decided. Finally, because games can be played on so many different devices, e.g. tablet, smartphone, console, or PC, the ads can look very different on the different devices.

Advertisers must also be aware of problematic content, as some advertisers may not want to be associated with questionable violent or sexual content in video games. Some studies show that even though a brand may wish to be in a popular video game that features violence, many consumers have negative reactions to the brands appearing in such games. It is hypothesized that our natural negative reactions to blood and gore may transfer to the brand, which limits the effectiveness of the placement. There is also a backlash against branded games targeted to children, particularly games sponsored by foods that parents may not wish promoted to their children. Games can "age gate" trailers, for example, that are intended for ages 17+ or rated M. They can make sure younger audiences are not exposed to the material that is intended for a more mature audience the same way that YouTube does.

SUMMARY

Games are becoming omnipresent in the media marketplace today. There will continue to be a lot of discussion about what is most effective and what is most responsible as the number and types of video games continue to expand. Games in virtual reality on devices such as the Oculus Quest are opening new doors and ways to advertise and communicate with audiences. Hold on to your joysticks – gaming markets will continue to grow and shift and it's important for planners to keep on top of the evolving situation.

CHAPTER 35

Culturally specific media in a global world

·····················

IT'S A SMALL WORLD AFTER ALL

There is a variety of media channels used to reach people in the United States from different countries in languages other than English. The audiences may have a variety of different religious backgrounds, food choices, attire, and utilize the same media categories, but they are geared toward the different cultures. Understanding culturally specific media is a good way to understand the nuances of global media.

The Internet is certainly a global phenomenon, but it is important to note that just because everyone MAY be exposed to the same message, not everyone WILL be exposed to that message. At the same time, different types of people have different ways they prefer to access media content. Regardless of whether you're trying to reach Japanese people in Seattle, Washington or young women in Accra, Ghana, it's important to closely understand the nuances of where that group allocates their media time.

CULTURALLY SPECIFIC MEDIA

Culturally specific media are media that produce information or entertainment for a particular culturally specific group. New York is one of the most diverse cities in America. Global media in New York is an important part of the framework of the entire culture in the city. More than 60 different global groups writing in 42 languages populate the city. There is a variety of different media that cater to those audiences.

New York has the largest Asian population (8,175,133) followed by Los Angles (3,792,621). New York also has the largest Latino population (2,200,000) and Los Angeles is second again (1,800,000). However, there are many cities across the United States with many different ethnicities with different media that focus on the different cultures and interests. Exhibit 35.1 shows another challenge – that language use varies among populations.

DOI: 10.4324/9781003258162-35

EXHIBIT 35.1 LANGUAGE USED BY US HISPANIC ADULTS FOR CONSUMING CONTENT, MARCH 2020

	Internet	TV	Radio	Print
Spanish and English equally	36%	42%	41%	34%
English only	27%	20%	23%	26%
English mostly	24%	23%	19%	22%
Spanish mostly	8%	10%	12%	11%
Spanish only	5%	5%	5%	6%

Source: 9th Wonder and Think Now, "The 2020 Guide to Hispanic Digital Purchase Behavior," June 10, 2020

Television

Television remains a mass medium and is still a great medium for brand awareness, but it is fragmented for all audiences. TV content has grown and diversified as the audiences have diversified. Even what people refer to as "TV" has diversified. The fact that TV can be viewed on more devices at different times and in different locations has made it easier but more complicated to reach global audiences.

Hispanics represent the largest multicultural audience with roughly 61 million. Like all culturally specific markets, Hispanics are diverse as they may come from different Spanish-speaking countries or be second- or third-generation and use English more than in the past. They also may be in very different age, income, and education demographics. One-size-fits-all does not work with culturally specific or global media.

There are specialized networks and programing aimed at the Latino market. Univision has launched a free ad-supported streaming service called Prende TV. It has movies, comedy and drama shows, and sports from Univision and Televisa. People can jump up to a paid primum tier from there. ViacomCBS's Pluto TV Latino is a streaming network and NBC Universal's Peacock Latino airs programming from Telemundo, which is Univision's biggest rival. These streaming platforms reaching 79% of the Latinx audience aged 18–75 saw a two-hour increase in streaming since the beginning of the pandemic.

Currently, 46.8 million people in the United States identify as Black and that population is growing. They reflect a number of different ethnicities and racial identities due to different cultural backgrounds and intermarriages. It is a very diverse audience and that is reflected in media choices. At the same time the Black audience is growing, those who identify as Black or African American only are declining. And 63% of multiracial Black people were aged 22 or younger. Most (56%) of the Black population in the United States lives in the South.

Black representation in TV programming continues to grow with streaming services like Netflix being more representational.

Nearly 20 million people in the United States identify as Asian alone and another 4.1 million identify as Asian in combination with another racial group, making a total of 7.2% of the population. Like Hispanic and Latino and Black populations, Asian is a kind of misnomer. The Korean population is 2.3 million. There are 2.5 million Chinese in the United States, 1.5 million are Japanese and 1.7 people are Vietnamese. The Asian population also includes, Indian, Laotian, and others.

Urban areas in America have the largest populations of global representation, including New York, the Los Angeles metro area, San Francisco, Miami, and Chicago.

All this points toward programming that is written for these audiences and a sound media planning choice. However, these audiences are not watching programming aimed at their culture of origin exclusively. Few television stations in the United States broadcast in foreign languages, such as Korean, Japanese, and some Chinese dialects. At the same time, a growing number of programs are rebroadcast on YouTube and other streaming channels from different countries.

Regardless of one's ethnicity, about three-fourths of each group utilize digital media regularly.

Radio

It's less expensive to operate a radio station than it is to run a television station. The top reasons are that it requires fewer people and less equipment. As a result, there are many more radio stations in the United States than there are television stations that broadcast in a foreign language. There are also radio networks that contain a number of different formats including stations that are in languages other than English, e.g. Odyssey and iHeart radio. Table 35.1 shows that there are many more Hispanic stations in the United States than Asian stations.

In addition to foreign language radio stations broadcast in the United States, global radio programming is available to be streamed through apps. Some examples are Radio Garden, which is a free app. The listener can type in any country and connect to a number of stations in that country. French radio is available on http://www. rfi.fr/en. Indie music from Mexico is available on https://ibero909.fm/. And if that's not enough, you can find apps that play top music from Bogota, Colombia and aboriginal music from Australia. And the list goes on.

The media buyer is then challenged, as radio moves from being a local-market powerhouse to a global entity, to reach key audiences in the markets that are most important to the client and not pay for the markets that are not pertinent.

TABLE 35.1 Top examples of foreign-language radio stations in the United States

Hispanic	1075
Korean	16
Chinese	10

Newspapers

Foreign-language newspapers have been around since the earliest days of settling the Western hemisphere. Newspaper publishers in the United States continue to print papers in a wide variety of languages, including Arabic (six), Chinese (12), Danish (five), Dutch (one), French (14), German (three), Italian (four), Japanese (nine), Korean (one), Norwegian (nine), Portuguese (two), Polish (ten) Russian (two), Spanish (five), Swedish (three), and even Urdu (three).There are more than 100 Black and African-American newspapers in the United States. There are also newspapers published in different countries that are shipped to subscribers in the United States.

Most global and foreign-language newspapers earn the majority of their revenue from advertising, not from subscription. Additionally, the majority of these niche newspapers are published on a weekly basis, offering an added benefit for advertisers since the message will be available in the home for a week. As with other media mentioned, most of the foreign language newspapers are available digitally as well as in paper form. Each paper, whether a digital or paper version, will provide an explanation of the sizes and costs of ads in their publications.

Magazines

Some magazines, like other mass media, are also intended for specific groups.

There are also magazines published in the United States in foreign languages, but many magazines published in other countries are also shipped to the United States. With newspapers, the coverage is usually timely. With magazines, however, the coverage may focus on events that are less time-sensitive, or the editors may choose to run feature stories that have little – if any – time relevance. These factors make the importation of magazines more widespread than it is for newspapers.

Black African Americans read an average of 5.7 magazines per month, which is higher than the national average of 4.5. Magazines such as *The Root, Ebony, Black Enterprise Arts & Culture*, are three of the top 25 magazines published for that audience. *Latina, The Acentos Review,* and *Huizache* are three of the top Latino magazines. *Banana, Buah*, and *Mochi* are three very popular Asian magazines published in the United States.

As with other media, magazines are also often accessed digitally from other countries. From the media planner's standpoint, the magazines published in the United States usually offer the best possible opportunity for reaching the audiences this country.

Other media

In larger metropolitan areas especially, where the largest number of foreign-language speakers live, business signs often appear in different languages as well as in English. There are thousands of Internet sites originating in the United States that use languages other than English, and because the Internet is so accessible throughout the world, foreign-language websites are readily available to US residents where brands can reach different global audiences. The number of non-English podcasts has surpassed the number of English podcasts. Most of those podcasts carry brand messages. A variety of social media can also specifically reach specific audiences.

Like other digital advertising, advertising networks serving global and culturally specific audiences provide simple ways for advertisers to provide content to audiences through one media buy using the standard metrics of digital advertising. Some of these network opportunities are also cross-platform opportunities, which maximize reach and frequency to reach these audiences.

SUMMARY

It's important to note that every country is made up of a variety of people with a variety of media habits. There's no one-size-fits all to reach all Koreans in the United States just as there is no one-size-fits-all to reach all Koreans in South Korea. It's important to fully understand the nuances of each target audience you're trying to reach to do an optimum plan in this area.

CHAPTER 36

Business-to-business advertising

"BUSINESS PEOPLE ARE PEOPLE TOO" – TRACY WONG, FOUNDER OF WONG DOODY

Business-to-business (B2B) advertising is often deemed more informational, less relatable, or more boring than consumer advertising. On the other hand, according to a BrandZ value survey (available at https://www.kantar.com/campaigns/brandz/global), five of the top B2B brand's growth rate was higher than the top 100 global brands, which are mostly consumer brands. The related business decision can involve a more emotional purchase decision because there is more at stake. If we decide to go to a restaurant that doesn't deliver on its promise, we are out the cost of a meal and the time it took to eat. If we make the wrong purchase decision sparked by B2B advertising and then a sales pitch, it could mean a lot of money lost for the company, loss of a promotion, or even loss of a job. So, the people (or possibly person) we are trying to reach with B2B advertising are making a deeply emotional as well as rational decision.

Business to business advertising is used to help influence a decision-maker to choose a solution or product for their company over another solution or product. The media strategy can help influence the purchase decision before, during, and after the sale has been made. The company (the end consumer) can be exposed to messages that help them decide, then feel good about the choice they have made.

Almost any consumer category of product or service can market to a business in addition to a consumer. Pharmaceutical companies direct advertising to physician practices and hospitals. Financial services market to banks. In addition, hundreds of companies that make parts for products such as computers, automobiles, and appliances reach out to the manufacturers who make these items that we all use.

Let's compare some of the traditional aspects of a consumer plan, known as Business to Consumer (B2C) to a B2B plan.

DOI: 10.4324/9781003258162-36

OBJECTIVES

Similar to B2C, the media objectives support the marketing objectives as well as the advertising objectives.

AUDIENCE

In B2B advertising, we need to identify the audience just as we do with B2C media. However, in B2B, our audience could be one person or it could be a group of people. What is crucial is understanding who the key decision-makers are. If you are developing a plan for selling artificial intelligence (AI) widgets, then who is the person or persons who will decide which brand to buy? Understanding that may take some in-depth research.

A famous story involved the aluminum industry trying to convince auto manufacturers to use aluminum in cars rather than just steel. Salespeople were being ignored. The ad agency learned that the head of one of the auto manufacturers drove home a car that had been manufactured that day on the assembly line. They also learned that he turned on the radio on the drive home. So, the media planners bought ads for the aluminum industry on nearly every radio station in afternoon drive to support the creative elements advertising the use of aluminum in the manufacturing of autos. The CEO listened to the ad, and then was willing to listen to the sales pitch, which resulted in the auto manufacturer using aluminum in their cars. From a usual efficiency standpoint, it was not a cost-efficient buy. From a B2B standpoint, it turned out to be highly efficient. This is an extreme example of using consumer media to reach a business prospect. People don't automatically stop thinking about their business when they are away from work.

MEDIA CHANNELS

A business might use any medium, depending on who the audience is. Commonly used are paid trade media, social media, email marketing, and sometimes, earned media. Occasionally, outdoor might be used – but used in a different way than to reach consumers. Though outdoor is a high-reach medium, it might be used to reach only a handful of people who are the key decision-makers. Events, large and small, might be important channels. The events might include a way to demonstrate a product, or they might simply open the door for a sales rep to visit the company.

TIMING/SCHEDULING

The time between research, consideration, decision-making and purchase can be, and usually is, much longer than the consumer process. There may be previous contracts that have to expire, existent products that must be used up, or many discussions among the end users, management, and the purchasers of these AI widgets.

During the research process, planners can ascertain what stage of the buying process the audience is in. The media schedule must take all the stages of the purchase and use of the product into account to support the different stages of messaging.

One of the challenging aspects of B2B is considering the real value of the brand related to the customer experience. Did the brand or company deliver on the promise and is the service level in keeping with expectations. This is not as simple as returning an ill-fitting shirt to the store. Therefore, the media planner must stay informed about how the company they are advertising for performs. If there is some difficulty or, on the other hand, outstanding success, the plan may have to be altered to reflect or support these changes. The planner may also have to communicate with a public relations firm regarding what communication takes place.

BUDGET

In B2B, the budget will be scheduled in detail for the coming year, but there would also be an outline for the next two or even three years since the time for consideration to purchase can be much longer than with consumer products and brands. Usually, the budgeting and planning are usually not figured out that far in advance for B2C media.

FUTURE

Many B2C brands have some sub-brands that need B2B advertising and media. The skills and experience a media planner has can be transferable, which makes someone who is open to planning for B2B as well as B2C more valuable and sought after.

CHAPTER 37

Sales promotion

....

DRIVING THE MESSAGE HOME

Sales promotion isn't a medium. Nor is it a special method of buying a medium, such as direct response. Sales promotion is an activity to stimulate short and/or immediate demand for a product. Because most brands are under short-term pressure to perform, sales promotion activity is a large part of many brands' integrated marketing plans.

As a communication planner, you will be faced with planning, developing, and analyzing sales promotion activity. Even if you are not directly involved in that activity, the marketing director or brand manager will be weighing sales promotion activity and dollars versus that of alternative approaches to communication.

Sales promotion is a direct inducement that offers extra incentives anywhere along the marketing route to accelerate the product's movement. There are two types of sales promotion: *trade* and *consumer.*

TRADE PROMOTION

Trade promotion is called *push marketing.* It consists of activities designed to secure the cooperation of the retailer by the manufacturer, but the consumer also benefits.

In trade promotion, the manufacturer provides an incentive to the retailer to feature its products. This can be as simple as discounts or other dollar incentives to stock or sell the product. Many times, retailers will pass on all or part of this savings onto the consumer through a short-term sale or special. This is sometimes done through "co-op" advertising where the manufacturer helps pay the cost of the ad with the promotional offer.

Other trade incentives include advertising allowances either as a percentage of gross costs or as a fee, where the retailer can purchase advertising that features the brand as well as other retailers' private-label products.

DOI: 10.4324/9781003258162-37

CONSUMER PROMOTION

Consumer promotion is called *pull marketing.* It involves activities aimed at the consumer to entice them to buy or request your brand on the spot.

Consumer incentives can take a variety of forms. Normally, they involve an offer to make it easier to buy now or buy more, visit a store, request literature, or take some form of action. The promotional offers can be money, prizes, gifts, or many other offers and enticements.

The idea behind a consumer promotion is to move the product *now.* From a marketing standpoint, consumer promotions should accelerate the purchase process by one of two methods: (1) creating an incentive for current customers to stock up on a given product, or (2) convincing new customers to try the brand.

The planner needs to be aware of trade promotions because they compete for your marketing dollars. Nevertheless, the focus of this chapter is on consumer promotions. *Consumer promotions* can involve almost any medium or channel. Regardless of the type of promotion, the goal of sales promotion is to make sales happen in the short term. And sales promotions tend to work well: more than 75% of consumers said they were more likely to buy a product if there was a rebate offered. Another study found that 84% of consumers view rebates as an opportunity and more than half (42%) search out products with rebates or Buy-One-Get-One (free) offers. The danger with offering rebates and sales incentives is the manufacturer or brand can become dependent on them and find it difficult to return to their normal pricing.

Most advertising and public relations agencies do sales promotion activity, however there are some agencies that specialize in sales promotion. Some of these agencies also specialize in brand experiences and events. Several leading agencies are outlined in Table 37.1.

Each of these agencies takes a bit of a different view on what sales promotion is. GMR says, "Don't just make ads. Make memories." They focus on creating consumer experiences. George P. Johnson also views themselves as helping marketers create an experience. Their experiential marketing approach combines large-scale events with short-term promotional strategies. Carlson Marketing Group, on the other hand, combines customer relationship management with sales promotion activities so that they move into *brand engagement.*

The Integer Group is the type of agency most people imagine when they think of sales promotion agencies. It's an advertising agency that focuses on "retail experience

TABLE 37.1 Landscape of sales promotion

Agency	Website
GMR marketing	gmrmarketing.com
Integer Group	integer.com
Jack Morton	jackmorton.com
Carlson Marketing Group	carlsonmarketinggroup.com
George P. Johnson	gpj.com
Tracy Locke	tracylocke.com

design, retail marketing, ecommerce and social commerce." The Integer Group develops retail promotions for manufacturers to move products off the shelf and functions as a marketing partner within a brand organization.

As you look at other names on this list, you will find that sales promotion is a catchall for a variety of marketing communication activities. Every company defines its specific niche in its own way. Sales promotion does overlap with direct-response advertising and event marketing. Because promotions are designed to elicit a response, there are elements of direct response used in sales promotion. Many times, these responses yield customer names, so there can be a database component to sales promotion. And because promotions can take on large-scale events as a catalyst for consumer interaction, there can be an event component to sales promotion as well.

These varied companies are a reflection of the wide array of sales promotion activities available to today's marketer. Let's examine the most popular types of sales promotions.

TYPES OF SALES PROMOTION

The types of sales promotions available to a marketer are based on fulfilling several distinctive objectives: to gain consumer trial of the product, to reward brand loyalty, to encourage a consumer to trade up, and to stimulate the consumer to buy more of the brand. These are all offensive marketing strategies. Defensively, a marketer might use promotional tactics so that other brands don't steal share when they are also implementing promotions. The sections discussed next cover the key promotional strategies that fulfil these objectives.

The role of media planning in sales promotion strategies may be to find the best medium to deliver the strategy and to find a media partner who can best execute a promotional strategy. Much of the sales promotion media strategy is to determine the role of retailer or in-store versus advertising in various media.

COUPONING

Sales promotion is sometimes defined by *couponing*. A coupon is a certificate that provides a value that, when presented to a retailer, will offer a discount on the specific product purchased.

The media role in providing coupon support is to find the most effective means of distributing the coupons. This may be through a wide variety of media. Traditionally, newspapers, magazines, door-to-door, package placement, and direct mail are all options for coupon distribution. However, for the first time, digital coupon usage in 2020 surpassed the use of paper coupons. Online shopping sites such as Rakuten, Ibotta, Groupon, and coupon.com are but a few of the large number of websites where consumers can get coupons. According to Statista, the top searched coupon categories are household items, restaurant, grocery, electronics, apparel, and beauty. It's not surprising that Millennials are more likely to use digital coupons than Baby Boomers. In 2020, 88% of Millennials used paperless promotional coupons versus only 64% of Baby Boomers. Coupons can be found on store websites, in social media, and in apps. Mobile couponing enables the customer to use their mobile phone to scan the bar code of the products they are purchasing.

There are a number of coupon methods that involve in-store media. Many supermarkets have interactive touch-screen kiosks where consumers can load up their store membership card with electronic coupons. Coupon dispensers can be put at the point of purchase so that consumers can simply hit a button and a coupon will be available as they buy the product. Consumers can also find coupon offers on the back of their receipts in some stores.

Companies such as Groupon offer a twist on discount coupons. Groupon promotes deep-discount coupons triggered when a specific number of consumers agree to accept the coupon promotion. This crowd-sourced couponing is another way that retailers and brands help generate consumer excitement for their brands.

Coupon incentives are a large and complex part of sales promotion. There are media specialists who focus solely on this area of media planning and buying. Each coupon method has its pros and cons. And each has a number of cost components, which we will discuss later in this chapter.

SAMPLING

Salespeople and companies can be found offering free samples – it's a common marketing technique. You can't make it through the cosmetics aisle of a department store or turn a corner in a grocery store or Costco without running into someone offering you a smell or taste of something.

Sampling can be a very costly way to incentivize someone to use your brand. However, it is one of the most effective methods for new products because it offers consumers a free trial in hopes of converting them to become loyal customers.

Just like coupons, samples can be distributed by mail, via coupon advertising, or in person at the store. Because sampling is so expensive, marketers are always looking for targeted methods to ensure that their samples reach their specific audience.

One method of doing this is through *polybagging* in selected print media. In polybagging, samples are delivered in a plastic bag along with the specific newspaper or magazine or by mail. This allows marketers to refine their audience either by reader type or by geography or both. It is also a benefit to the newspaper or magazine because it is giving that reader something of value at no charge. However, the environmental issue of using plastic bags has reduced the use of this method.

Another method of sampling is to develop *sampling events* that are promoted by the media. Examples include sponsoring a concert, a race, or a community event where you provide free samples to the audience. Sampling events involve organizing a relevant event for your audience and then promoting it through the media. Although this type of promotion can be complex logistically, it offers the brand exposure through the media along with the opportunity.

Event sampling programs are often driven by the media themselves. To encourage advertisers to buy their media, many media brands extend their reach by developing tie-ins with brands. Magnum ice cream tied in with Netflix to promote the Sweet Goodbye co-promotion for the last episode of the series *Money Heist*. Lucky fans could win a Magnum Money Heist bundle; a box filled with Magnum ice creams and instructions that enable the winner to unlock a special "Sweet Goodbye" message from *La Banda* – the criminal group trying to pull off the largest heist in history. So both the product, Magnum, and the series, *Money Heist*, received a great deal of attention in mobile and online. A limited number of pixels were released each day, leading up to the series end. Winners got a large package to sample of Magnum's ice cream bars.

Sampling, like couponing, can be simple or complex. It can be done in-store, through the media, or by developing an event.

MEDIA CELEBRITY TIE IN

Just as the media are looking to extend their brand through events, they offer an advertiser the opportunity to leverage their on-air or editorial talent. Giving you the opportunity to *tie in* with a media property and to use their talent to promote your brand can be an attractive method of sales promotion.

One common way that local retailers or auto dealers develop short-term promotional excitement is by having a radio station schedule an *on-site promotional event*. In radio parlance, this is called "scheduling a radio remote." This remote, or event, features one of the station's on-air personalities, who provides prizes and other incentives to get his or her listeners to stop by the local retailer's location for a limited-time event. The remote usually has a short time limit, so there is an incentive for consumers to act quickly. These events were curtailed by the pandemic but will restart again due to their local success.

Another variation on this theme is sponsoring a tour that features, for example, entertainers from a popular show and opportunities for fans to attend and participate in the show. For example, the show *Taste of Home Live* is an interactive national cooking show that highlights dishes from their popular national cooking magazine. Tours based on different types of food allow audiences to learn about and eat foods from the test kitchen.

As media planners work with a media vehicle, they are on the lookout not only for how to find the proper advertising fit, but also for how to use personalities within the media to further promote the brand.

SWEEPSTAKES

Sweepstakes offer prizes based on a chance drawing of an entrant's name. They offer a valuable opportunity for an advertiser to stimulate some excitement about the brand and to build a database of prospective buyers. *Sweepstakes* is a catchall term for games, contests, and sweepstakes (drawings). Games are similar to sweepstakes but are usually conducted over longer periods of time. A sweepstake is a one-time event, whereas a game may be played out over the course of months. The advantage of a game is that consumers must continue to engage with the brand or the retailer, so it leads to repeat purchases or visits. A contest technically offers prizes based on an entrant's skill. Contests are another way that customers engage with a brand.

Media play a huge role in sweepstakes, games, and contests. HGTV has a "Dream Home Giveaway" People can enter twice daily on HGTV and once a day on Food Network to win a dream home and $250,000 from Rocket Mortgage as well as a new Jeep Grand Wagoneer.

Sweepstakes must be promoted aggressively by advertising to be effective. And a sweepstake program must be well thought out from the business perspective. It is important that the manufacturer/retailer/business and the media all work together to ensure success.

Contests are a popular way to engage with loyal consumers. Doritos once held a contest for its consumers to make a Super Bowl commercial. The winning entry got to produce their television commercial, which aired during the game. CBS ran a contest on all their digital assets. Users used a QR code, which took them to a site where users could win 20% off their subscription costs.

COST AND MEASUREMENT

Promotions can be extremely successful for stimulating short-term sales of a brand. However, the more successful the sales promotion, typically the more money a brand or company needs to spend. So, sales promotion can become a double-edged sword. You want it to be successful, yet you want to ensure that you don't make it so successful that you can't afford it.

All this means that when you plan sales promotion media, you need to consider more than just the media cost. You need to understand the impact of the discount as well. Table 37.2 provides an example of a sales promotion cost analysis for Jelly Belly jelly beans.

In this example, there was a media support for a $1.00 coupon incentive. The media total included broadcast media, print media, and online media. The total paid media

TABLE 37.2 Jelly Belly jelly beans

Sales Promotion Cost Analysis	
Item promotional media	Percentage of cost ($ million)
Broadcast	3.0
Print	1.0
Online	0.5
TTL Media	4.5
Incentive redemption	
$1.00 incentive at 1% redemption rate	2.0
Processing fee	0.2
Misredemption contingency	0.4
Total redemption cost	2.6
Total cost	7.1

was $4.5 million. Two million consumers used the $1.00 discount, so the cost of the coupon redemption was $2 million. Processing the coupons from the retailer to the manufacturer cost an additional $200,000. The marketer also budgeted $400,000 for the possibility of misredemption of coupons. All told, this program cost $7.1 million, yet the media total was only $4.5 million.

The lesson in this example is that if the media planner had only factored in the paid media for the budget instead of estimating the outcome of the promotion, there would be a $2.6 million budget discrepancy.

As sales promotion programs are developed, the media team must budget for media while simultaneously estimating the success rate of the promotion. Success for the promotion is usually measured by the number of consumers who take advantage of the offer. Future success of the promotion is based on those consumers who return to buy the brand without the offer.

Sales promotion costs include a number of items outside that of traditional paid media. We have just mentioned that one big aspect is the actual redemption rate or consumer response. Other costs that may be included are talent charges if the plan uses a celebrity. And there can be legal charges for developing the rules of a contest to ensure that it meets federal guidelines, along with myriad processing and handling or logistics charges.

FUTURE OF SALES PROMOTION

It is safe to say that marketers will always have a need to drive short-term sales. It is equally as safe to say that consumers are always receptive to a discount or a deal. Those two factors combine to make sales promotion a consistent force for businesses and brands.

Just like direct response, sales promotion has been impacted by digital media and the growing sophistication of database marketing. However, paper coupons are still popular. Print coupons comprise 44% of the coupon market. The majority of coupons redeemed at major retailers are still paper coupons. Coupon use increased during the Covid-19 pandemic (Vericast).

MOBILE INCENTIVES

The use of mobile coupons will continue to expand. Programs with retailers and grocers enable the consumer to present a coupon on their phone at checkout. Coupons can also be pushed to the consumer who has opted in. Specific businesses such as a coffee shop or restaurant can have a coupon offer texted for their business when the customer is close by. Snipp interactive (snipp.com) works with companies and brands to develop shopper promotions, reward programs, and coupon/rebate programs (https://www.facebook.com/SnippInc/videos). Consumers can submit their receipt by text, mail, or email. Then they can choose their reward of cash, a certificate, Paypal deposit, etc. The brand then has data on the consumer whom they can interact with later.

CONVERGENCE

Just as you see with the leading sales promotion agencies, there is convergence in terms of direct response and sales promotion. The ability to link incentives to store-loyalty programs is rapidly gaining steam. Developing incentives that are both new customer and loyal customer-centric, and that are tied to an ongoing program, will continue to develop through apps and through other methods as the technology continues to advance.

The interaction with Pokémon Go drove players to local business; 84% of players visited a business while playing. Restaurants, coffee shops, convenience, grocery stores, and other businesses were able to tie in and boost sales by being near a "PokéStop."

MEGA-EVENTS

With 88% of the United States using some form of coupon and more than 80% involved in at least one store-loyalty program, it is difficult for marketers to break established purchase cycles. This leads to mega-events, where marketers go over the top to provide an experience that leads to a trial. The pandemic has forced marketers to develop hybrid events; digital and in person. These hybrid events will continue to develop and be refined for maximum engagement. To quote the Head of Strategy at Imagination, Christophe Castagnera, "This is a new paradigm and it will become the gold standard where virtual and physical experiences will live in parallel and emerging new technology ignites more creativity." So, events will be held both in person and online and both may be held at the same time.

Mucinex held a first-of-its-kind fashion line and over-the-counter brand collaboration: they collaborated with fashion icons Steven Alan and The Great Eros' Christina Viviani to create Sickwear, a six-piece, gender-neutral collection that helped consumers feel better and more comfortable while they were not feeling well. This was a direct-to-consumer YouTube livestream event. Consumers could then buy the "sickwear," which sold out in less than 24 hours. Product sales of Mucinex increased 236% over the same year average week.

SUMMARY

In summary, sales promotion is far more than just a media purchase. It is an inducement to buy a product based on a time-limited incentive. These incentive programs can take many shapes and forms from simple couponing to elaborate sweepstakes to timely events. Sales promotion is a crucial part of the marketing and media mix.

CHAPTER 38

Perspectives on international and global media planning

....

GIVE US A CHAPTER, AND WE'LL GIVE YOU THE WORLD

The world continues to change in unexpected ways economically, politically, and environmentally. Therefore, it should not be surprising that media usage continues to change around the world also. Globally, people consume more media than ever before, quite simply because there is more media than ever to consume. During the Covid-19 pandemic, all media was up, but some far more than others. For example, newspaper readership was up 5% worldwide. The top country was Italy with 6%, China was second with a 5% increase, and several countries saw a 4% hike, including the United States, United Kingdom (UK), and Singapore. Reading more magazines was up 6% worldwide. Watching more broadcast TV was up 20% worldwide, with the Philippines showing a 37% increase and Japan a 32% increase. TV viewership in the United States, was up 24%. Streaming services, (e.g. Netflix) viewership was up 27% worldwide. The Philippines was up 36%, China was up 31%. and the United States was up 34%. Japan increased streaming site usage 13%, again, the differential of broadcast TV (up 32%), being indicative of the graying society.

Media multitasking, or using multiple digital devices simultaneously, is evident on a global scale. People are connected to friends or businesses around the world throughout the day. Most of global communication is digital. The top five visited websites are Google, YouTube, Facebook, Twitter, and Instagram. Roughly 45% of global Internet users use social networks at least once per month when they want information about products or services they are interested in. Mobile use worldwide is above a four-hours-per-day average and 92% of that time is spent using individual apps. More than 55% of web traffic worldwide is served to browsers on mobile phones. Africa and parts of Asia have the highest usage of mobile web traffic.

DOI: 10.4324/9781003258162-38

GLOBAL AND INTERNATIONAL STRATEGIES

In 1983, a marketing professor named Ted Levitt suggested that people are becoming globally homogenized despite deep-rooted cultural differences. He suggested that all products be standardized so the same product is sold everywhere around the world to take advantage of huge economies of scale in both production (manufacturing the product) and distribution (providing access to the product), in addition to economies of scale in developing and producing a single campaign around the world. This would result in low prices for consumers and high sales volumes and market shares for brands. Additionally, consumers would be exposed to a consistent brand message wherever they went. Levitt's idea is considered a global strategy. Global and international advertising are communication strategies that companies use to drive demand for goods and services in markets outside their home markets.

However, the two terms, *global* and *international*, are not always used interchangeably. *International advertising* strategies are tailored to reflect regional, national, and local market cultural differences and preferences. For example, Pepsi used the phrase "The Pepsi Generation" in the United States and "The Pepsi Revolution" in Brazil, selected words that best express the idea of a "movement" in each place. Global advertising strategy includes several different regions around the world with the intent of coordinating the messaging across each country involved. The brand is positioned the same way and has the same audience. Microsoft, Coca-Cola, and McDonald's are companies using a global strategy.

Most brands that are marketed in multiple countries use an international strategy that considers unique aspects of culture in advertising executions. There are differences in how people view themselves relative to others in the country and differences in economic structures that affect what consumers purchase and how often. Countries such as Japan and Korea culturally focus on society first and the individual a distant second. The United States focuses on the individual first. This can make a difference in the messaging and the media. Different countries also have different laws about what products can and cannot be advertised, and there are time and place restrictions on media placement in some categories as well. The UK is banning fast-food advertising online before 9 P.M. on TV. France has laws that stipulate food ads must be accompanied by messages on the benefits of a balanced diet.

Facebook and Instagram do not allow advertising for tobacco or vaping products, so a global media campaign would need to consider that. There is a variety of policy regarding cigarette advertising worldwide from outright bans such as in Singapore, Taiwan, and South Africa to restricted advertising in Pakistan and Mexico. The advertising of alcohol products is also restricted differently in different countries. Global strategies work best in categories where the trend toward global integration is strong and local cultural influences are weak, such as the consumer electronics market. With the growth of digital media, brands are looking to leverage local strengths while achieving some level of consistency across regions and media platforms. Many agency executives say that global planning is fueled by the globalization of brands brought about via partnerships with global digital players such as Google, Microsoft,

YouTube, and Facebook. A global planning agency might produce TV or digital content to air on YouTube and look for other media outlets on a market-by-market or country-by-country basis.

GLOBAL ADVERTISING

Many multinational marketers embrace a compromise between global and international advertising, known as *glocal* advertising, where brands "think global and act local." Glocal marketers standardize certain core elements of the advertising strategy while incorporating local cultural influences into advertising executions. The strategy combines a global appeal that recognizes a consistent audience motivation – but with tactics that take local nuances into account. Most media planning prior to the digital age was done based on a local analysis of a country or market. Before the Internet, it was impossible for an American to watch a British television advertisement outside the UK. It's important for the planner to remember that the way TV commercials are aired is different in different countries. In the United States, for example, ads air usually in two-minute pods that interrupt the programming with an average of 17 minutes of commercials in an hour of programming; in the UK, commercials air for nine minutes per hour of programming. The UK and Korea switched from running commercials before and after programs to the American style of interrupting the programming with commercials.

Global media are channels and forms of mass communication that expand across the world. That could be TV, radio, or YouTube, Twitter, and Instagram. Most media are geared to specific areas of the world, but can be accessible anywhere, thus, making many different media a global medium. Planners need to look carefully at the culture and media usage to understand those differences. Not only can the percentage of commercials allowed on TV vary by country but logically, gross rating point (GRP) levels would be different or would run over longer or shorter periods of time. In a global situation, there may be a core message that is distributed via global media, along with country-specific media plans to address the local consumers' media usage patterns.

With the growth of digital media, brands are looking to leverage local strengths while achieving some level of consistency across regions and media platforms. Many agency executives say that global planning is fueled by the globalization of brands brought about via partnerships with global digital players such as Google, Microsoft, YouTube, and Facebook.

Almost 87% of YouTube traffic is now from outside of the United States. India has 26% of the total YouTube traffic, putting it as a clear number one in usage. Incidentally, more than 70% of the videos on YouTube are watched on mobile devices.

Social media is affecting media planning and buying. Worldwide, more than 4 billion people are participating in online social networks – and in many cases, individuals outside the United States have access to the exact same online offerings that people in the US have. Marketers are struggling to find ways to both manage and engage global audiences with their social media marketing efforts. Marketers must make decisions about whether they'll have a single brand profile or multiple brand profiles for every country, and at the same time, they must maintain consistency in brand messaging, design, and the overall voice. Social content and communications must make sense to people in a particular region but must also match your brand's identity.

A global social media strategy takes more than just translating Tweets into different languages. Many marketers are surprised to find that the United States is not the center of the social media universe. Social media site users around the world all have different preferences when it comes to platforms. Media planners need to research which social media channels are most used by audiences in the countries where they will be advertising. For example, among younger audiences in Taiwan, Line, Instagram, and YouTube are most popular, and TikTok, Xiaohongshu, and Telegram continue to grow in popularity. Facebook is declining in popularity among younger people in both Taiwan and Korea. Instagram is most popular in Korea and TikTok use continues to grow. Line and Twitter are most popular among younger audiences in Japan and WeChat is by far the most popular in China as it is a combination of TikTok, Venmo, Instagram, and other functions. When planning global media, a first step is to put aside the idea that any one site is always the best site for engagement and look at other social media sites that might be more appropriate for the countries where you are advertising.

People in different countries are likely to express themselves uniquely and share different kinds of content and uses for the same medium. For instance, Germans have tended to use Facebook primarily to arrange group or friend meet-ups, whereas in the United States it has been used to post pictures of various personal activities.

SUMMARY

There's no single way to plan a global brand or account, just as there is no single way to plan any type of brand. However, media planners who want a global career are well advised to become experts in the media in many different countries. There are many opportunities for global employment for savvy media planners and buyers. Media agencies like MediaMonks, Horizon Media, or Spark Foundry and others have international media planning and buying capabilities. Media planners that truly grasp the concept of global media planning have a great path to success.

CHAPTER 39

Preparing a communication plan

....

PREPARATION LEADS TO INSPIRATION

The steps in a communication plan are straightforward. Most plans use a format similar to the one illustrated in Exhibit 39.1.

In this chapter we will elaborate on the elements of a communication plan that were originally introduced in Chapter 7.

OVERVIEW OR EXECUTIVE SUMMARY

As we do with most business reports and proposals, we start with an *overview*, often called an *executive summary,* in which major recommendations are summarized. This summary should not be used to rehash things that are already known about a company or a brand. Instead, this section should be a summary of the media recommendations that are contained in the body of the report.

Use the executive summary to preview what is to come. With this advance knowledge, you can read and make more sense of the actual proposed communication plan. Some top executives may read only this summary, but the brand manager needs to read and study the entire proposal, using the overview to provide background information and expectations before getting into the heart of the communications plan.

Even though the executive summary is the first section of the communication plan, it cannot be written until the rest of the plan is completed because it provides a review of the entire proposal.

COMPETITIVE ANALYSIS

Complete analysis of your major competitors should be detailed in your communications plan, along with the competitors' marketing and advertising efforts and their audience and media used. It is essential that the competition be analyzed thoroughly

DOI: 10.4324/9781003258162-39

EXHIBIT 39.1 OUTLINE OF A MEDIA PLAN

An advertising media plan may take more than one approach and there is no industry-wide outline that is always used. The organization below includes the necessary topics and can serve as a guide to prepare a media proposal for an advertising campaign.

Overview/executive summary
Competitive analysis
Market situation
Objectives and goals
    Marketing objectives
    Communication objectives
    Advertising objectives
    Media objectives
Media strategies
    Audiences
    Markets
      Groups
      Specific Audience
    Media types
Media tactics
    Media vehicles
    Media units
Media promotions
Media logistics
Continuity plans
Schedule/Calendar
Budget
Events

---

and completely before getting into the objectives. Because some of the objectives will likely deal with understanding and besting the competition, the competitive analysis is an important input to those objectives.

MARKET SITUATION

If the marketplace is complex and its analysis cannot be covered in the competitive analysis, it will require a separate section. Again, information needs to be analyzed prior to the formation of objectives. This information can deal with aspects of the culture surrounding the audience and their interaction in that society and culture. The analysis might also deal with economic issues that might influence branding or sales.

OBJECTIVES AND GOALS

Next come the actual objectives – what you will try to accomplish with the advertising communication plan. There are usually at least three categories of objectives: *overall marketing objectives, advertising objectives*, and *media objectives.*

Marketing objectives

The *marketing objectives* deal with the overall selling goals. They may be established at the corporate or company level, or at the marketing level. The advertising staff may be involved in establishing the marketing objectives, but oftentimes the objectives have already been set by the time the advertising media planner gets them, leaving little chance for input or adjustment to these goals. Communication objectives support the marketing objectives as discussed in Chapter 8.

Advertising objectives

The *advertising objectives* are essential for several reasons. They support the overall marketing objectives and clarify the advertising effort. They help focus research, message, visual, and media phases of the advertising campaign. The media planner may be given these advertising objectives based on marketing goals and strategic input. Ideally, the media planner has a chance to provide input and can influence the formation of the advertising objectives

As is the case for all objectives, the advertising objectives need to be spelled out in detail, with thorough justification provided for each one.

Media objectives

Media objectives define what we want the media to accomplish. The media objectives must be consistent with and support the overall advertising objectives, which in turn must complement the overriding marketing objectives. Sometimes the marketing and advertising objectives are summarized here, providing lead-ins to and references for the media objectives. Look back at Chapter 3 for examples of the various topics that might be included under each type of objective.

MEDIA STRATEGIES

Remember that strategies are plans regarding what you are going to do, so this section contains the actual plans that are proposed to meet the media objectives.

Markets

This could refer to the actual geographic markets where the media will run or it could refer to the people that the media is geared to reach.

Audience groups

What are the people like that the plan is trying to reach? This could be in demographic and/or psychographic terms. There isn't one medium that reaches "everyone." Nor do most brands expect or want to reach "everyone." There are also people other than the specifically intended audience that will be reached by a medium. Thus, the different media audiences are often discussed and defined.

Media types

Advertising media are ways of achieving specific ends – they are not objectives in and of themselves. That is why the media to be used are included as strategies rather than goals. The selection of each advertising medium proposed for a campaign must be fully justified. In addition, other advertising media that were considered and not selected can also be listed, along with the reasons for not using them.

MEDIA TACTICS

The tactics are the implementation of the plan – the specifics of the advertising campaign being carried out. Even though the tactics do not come into play until the proposed media plan is approved, there still should be some discussion at this point of the tactics to be used and complete justification of each one. That discussion can include strategy people, writers, and designers as well as media people.

Media vehicles

It is likely that the media channels will be spelled out in the strategies section. A media channel is a category of media such as magazine or social. Individual media vehicles will likely not be discussed at the time. A media vehicle is a specific medium such as *The New Yorker* magazine or TikTok. Under *tactics*, each specific media vehicle selection should be discussed and justified.

Media units

A detailed description of media units is essential, such as the length of broadcast commercials, size of print advertisements and specifications such as the use of bleed or color, or the type of digital ads. In other words, clarification of the specifics for each medium should be specified here, again with justification.

MEDIA PROMOTIONS OR EVENTS

If the use of nonadvertising promotions or events connected with the plan are not discussed anywhere else, it should be included here. Although its proposed use may come in an earlier section, it is most likely to appear in the tactical stage.

MEDIA SCHEDULE/CALENDAR

The advertising campaign schedule may be discussed in the advertising objectives, or it may be set earlier. Still, there should be some detail on the proposed timing of the advertising, including start and stop dates, flight and hiatus plans, levels of advertising, coordination of scheduling across the various media, and recognition of the selling calendar and other timing factors. This schedule should also be displayed in a flow chart of some sort. For example, in an Excel chart with each medium on the left axis and months and weeks across the top of the chart. Anyone should be able to see at a glance when and where the media is running. Again, justification is required.

CONTINGENCY PLANS

The contingency plans should be complete enough to be used if they are actually needed. If something in the original campaign must be changed, it will likely be on short notice, leaving little opportunity to develop complete plans in a high-pressure situation. Contingency plans can kick in for a variety of reasons, such as when the originally planned media is not available, if there is an unexpected large cost increase, or if there is a problem with production being available or approved.

See the detailed discussion of contingency plans back in Chapter 8.

BUDGET

What the plan will cost? The costs are best shown as the total cost for each medium unless the actual costs have been negotiated and agreed upon ahead of time with the media. That way, there are usually no big surprises in case there are changes in costs. Other costs will also be shown in the budget sheet, such as promotional costs, promotional item costs, or event costs. It's important to include the rationale for costs and the percent of allocations.

SUMMARY

A solid communication plan needs justification and rationale at every stage, along with a logical progression from objectives through strategies to tactics and outcomes. Check back to make sure that the media objectives are clear and can be accomplished.

Media planners should keep in mind that a media plan is crucial to bringing a successful conclusion to your advertising and marketing efforts.

CHAPTER 40

Media and campaign measurement

···

GETTING WHAT YOU PAY FOR, DELIVERING WHAT YOU PROMISE

The brand strategic communication plan has been developed. It is now being executed in the marketplace. Now, how do we know if it worked? It's a question that has plagued advertisers for years. As the famous department store guru John Wanamaker once said, "I know that half of my advertising is wasted. I just don't know which half."

Media measurement, part of the broader *campaign measurement,* seeks to answer the questions, did the plan reach its intended audience? And did the plan have an impact? Campaign measurement, on the other hand, seeks to answer the question, what was the attitudinal or behavior impact of the plan on the audience? Let's examine each of these areas across the paid, earned, and owned media framework of the brand strategic communication plan.

PAID MEDIA MEASUREMENT AND POST-ANALYSIS

Media professionals typically develop a paid media post-buy analysis that looks at how the paid media aspect of the plan performed in the marketplace. The following are key points addressed in a post-analysis:

- Did the media run as planned? Did the actual media units run as they were ordered?
- Did the media reach its intended audience? Was the level of the projected audience in the media plan or purchase actually achieved?
- Was the media on budget?

Media post-buys are a combination of accounting and media audience analysis, examining the paid media costs of the cost of the media and an explanation of what you received for that cost. While media can vary on their billing procedures, this

DOI: 10.4324/9781003258162-40

forms the basics of accounting. The following are the accounting basics for the majority of paid media categories:

- For broadcast, you'll need monthly bills that provide an affidavit of the time, day, and creative unit for each commercial aired, along with the cost of each commercial unit. This information is then compared to the original buy to determine if there is a discrepancy. If a discrepancy exists, the buyer asks the station for additional commercial units or *make-goods*.
- For print, you'll need monthly bills that provide the day, creative unit, and cost for each advertisement. Buyers also request a copy of the publication or a tear sheet (copy of the ad within the print publication) to review placement and reproduction of the advertisement.
- For out-of-home media, you'll need monthly bills that provide the number of units, creative costs, and cost per unit. Buyers also request pictures of the outdoor units for examination. In some cases, a buyer may want to see the unit in person.
- For online display and paid social media, you'll need monthly bills that provide an affidavit of time, day, creative unit, and cost per unit. Both of these media areas are tracked on an ongoing basis. The accounting is done on a monthly basis.
- For search engine marketing (SEM) or pay-per-click campaigns, the advertiser either budgets a set amount per month or pays based on the total activity per month. SEM campaigns can be tracked daily to understand the number of actions taken.

For media other than SEM, the second step in the process is to understand the media audience that has been reached. Each medium has its own nuances regarding this type of post-buy analysis.

- For broadcast, a media buyer will compare the forecast of the audience they agreed to purchase with the latest measurement through Nielsen or Arbitron rating information.
- For print, a media buyer will compare the circulation of the publication that formed the basis for their purchase with the latest circulation audit conducted by the Audit Bureau of Circulation (ABC), a third-party auditing firm that verifies the number of copies published by various newspapers and magazines.
- For out-of-home, a media buyer may request a traffic count or an eyes-on-the-board analysis from the Traffic Audit Bureau (TAB), which historically has measured the number of cars that drive past an outdoor board. More recently, they have developed a research panel that provides a measure of the actual viewership of each billboard. This approach has helped elevate the industry measures so that they are more comparable to other media.
- For online display, a media buyer can track their audience through accessing Nielsen and/or Comscore audience information. These two companies provide audience measures for thousands of consumer online media properties.

- For online campaigns, ad serving companies such as DoubleClick provide deep measures of audience engagement, interaction, and interaction time.
- For social media campaigns, the specific social media platform provides detailed information based on their digital user base.
- For SEM campaigns, tracking can be constant. SEM professionals focus on understanding the top performing keywords, the average position of the keywords, and the optimum bid level for those keywords.

By combining the accounting of the media schedule with the post-buy media audience analysis, a media planner can evaluate the marketplace performance of the media plan. The latter post-buy analysis is designed to measure the paid media schedule.

OWNED MEDIA ANALYSIS

What about any earned media? A media planner or perhaps a public relations professional may be in charge of developing this analysis. The first step is to determine the total reach of the earned media program.

- For traditional publicity, press releases and other campaigns aim to gain journalists to promote their information. Those articles or mentions can be tracked and recorded and measured for audience reach.
- For an influencer campaign, the size of the influencer's audience can be measured along with the number of activities mentioned for the brand.
- The same can be said for any digital content that is shared on behalf of the brand. The audience size is easily measured, similar to that of paid media.
- Where earned media can be more telling is the impact of the program. In the digital space, posts/content can be measured for engagement with downloads, likes, and shares. All of these activities can be quantified.

From a budget standpoint, earned media exposure is free. The cost is the fees paid to the communication agency running the program or any internal resources. There is also the possibility of fees being paid to influencers.

OWNED MEDIA AND TOTALS

Adding the paid media to the earned and owned media schedule provides the brand with an accounting of the communication plan in terms of dollars invested and impressions generated.

Owned media may have internal costs associated with personnel but no other outside costs. From an analysis perspective, owned media can be central to the return on investment (ROI) of the entire brand communication campaign.

- If the campaign is directing consumers to the brand's website, there are many metrics that can be tracked. The number of people coming to the site, where they are coming from, and when they are coming can all be tracked.

- The website itself has measures of engagement such as time spent and how deep a consumer goes into the site. And perhaps the most important metric is some form of conversion. This can be a sale, signing up for more information, or providing information – some form of behavior that can be tracked. From tracking behavior, the brand can develop some form of ROI analysis.
- Just like other parts of the earned media campaign, the brand's owned social media can be tracked for engagement metrics.
- If the brand owns other media properties such as an event, or a media program, the same analysis that paid media provides can be done here.

When you roll up paid, earned, and owned media, the brand has a complete view of their strategic communication program. This offers those who are ultimately in charge of the program to provide senior management with tangible results across all media channels.

CAMPAIGN MEDIA MEASUREMENT

We now have an accounting of the media schedule and an understanding of the amount of people reached. Our next goal is to understand behavior. Were there specific effects that the media brought about? Some key media-related behaviors include:

- Coupon redemption
- Request for information
- Leads generated
- Traffic generated
- Sales

If the communication campaign is designed to have the consumer take a specific action, then that action can be tracked. Many advertisers tailor coupon offers, requests for information, and lead-generation devices (printed and digital) to a specific media vehicle. By doing this, each media vehicle can be analyzed for a specific ROI. For example, if you invest $100,000 in a paid media campaign and generate 1,000 leads, you could develop a cost-per-lead analysis. In this case, it would be $100,000/1,000 = $100 per lead. Compare that to an event that costs $10,000 and generated 500 leads. This yields a cost-per-lead of $20 ($10,000/500 = 20). You could conclude that an event is five times the value of paid media in generating leads.

It is relatively easy to track a coupon redeemed or a request for information. When measuring traffic – consumers coming into a store or going online – it's not as simple to peg this action to a specific media tactic. Traffic generation is a broader activity that, in aggregate, is easy to measure but difficult to apply to the specifics of a plan.

Digital media offer a wealth of opportunity to measure behavior. Digital media can be tracked to measure forms of engagement (how long someone has viewed an ad), action (clicked on or visited a website), and even purchase or requests for information. That is one of the most attractive features of digital media: the ability to finitely measure the impact.

Digital media were initially viewed as direct response vehicles. Measurement largely drove this perception. Since you were able to measure an action (when a consumer clicked on an ad), advertisers viewed this as a digital version of direct marketing. As online display ads have matured, click-through rates have consistently gone down. This has led advertisers and digital media owners to look for new ways to measure online impact.

One way that advertisers, agencies, and the media are viewing online behavior is based on detailed research about the online campaign. Research companies such as Dynamic Logic, a Millward Brown company, use a standard/control exposed methodology. Two online groups are surveyed. One has been exposed to the communication campaign and the other group has not. The results of each group are then compared to understand the impact of the campaign. Measures more commonly found in broad-based brand studies have been incorporated into this methodology. So, advertisers can review brand metrics such as awareness, favorability, and purchase intent on a comparative basis between those exposed and not exposed to the campaign.

The ultimate goal for a commercial company/brand is to increase revenue. If buying something online is an option for the consumer, then sales can be easily tracked and assigned to specific aspects of the strategic communication campaign.

CAMPAIGN MEASUREMENT

Most brands measure their overall success through some form of *awareness, attitude, and usage* (AA&U) research study. These research studies form the foundation for defining the problem that advertising must solve, as well as providing a benchmark for how well the total integrated marketing communication campaign performs.

Such research is usually referred to as a *tracking study.* The purpose of the study is to monitor the consumer perceptions of the brand. Awareness refers to the amount of knowledge the consumer has of the brand. This feeds into the top of the brand purchase funnel. Attitude refers to the consumer perception of the brand. This is usually where the advertising problem comes from. Usage refers to consideration, purchase, and loyalty of the brand. This feeds into the lower part of the purchase funnel. With all these measures, an AA&U study is a fundamental piece of brand research.

There are two basic ways to conduct an AA&U study. One method is to conduct a *premeasure* and *postmeasure study.* A study is conducted prior to a campaign's launch. Then, a second study is conducted after the program has been in the marketplace. The two studies are compared to measure the differences or movement of key objectives. Brand managers can determine if the campaign did indeed increase awareness, improve perceptions of the brand, and increase brand consideration, purchase, and/ or loyalty.

Most marketers conduct AA&U research studies annually, semi-annually, or quarterly. These point-in-time measures have their drawbacks. At any given point in time, there can be marketplace disruptions from outside forces, such as a competitor or the economy, that can influence the results of the study. This brings us to the second method of conducting an AA&U study: the *continuous tracking method.* Rather than picking a point in time to conduct research, the brand continually measures consumer sentiment on a weekly basis. Typically, the brand aggregates the weekly information into a monthly report. By always having a research measure in the market, the brand manager can analyze what may be affecting the brand in the short term and adjust the campaign accordingly.

Another benefit of a continuous tracking AA&U study is the possible analysis of these consumer perception measures with weekly sales. If sales are tracked on a frequent basis, then sales plus AA&U can be combined to create a very powerful diagnostic tool. Through advanced statistical analysis, a brand manager can correlate the impact of the campaign with actual marketplace sales. This is the holy grail of campaign measurement.

With the increased ability to access granular data, there has been a recent push for full loop measurement where marketers can determine the return on investment of individual aspects of their plan as it is being rolled out. Companies such as Adobe have been aggressively aggregating measurement companies to provide real time views of the impact of a campaign in both the consumer and business-to-business space.

SUMMARY

Strategic communication planning and plan execution is a continual loop process. A plan is developed. It is executed in the marketplace. It is tracked in the marketplace. Then it is updated. The process begins again. With increased frequency of media audience measurement and consumer behavior analysis, brand managers and media planners are in a better position to learn the impact of the media schedule. Monitoring the media schedule is a crucial aspect of maintaining the integrity of the media plan. It is important to place as much emphasis on execution as on the plan itself. As the saying goes, "A mediocre strategy well executed is better than a great strategy poorly executed."

CHAPTER 41

Presenting the plan

Developing the narrative

....

TELL ME A STORY!

Hours of work have gone into the development of your brand communication plan. Long hours, tons of analysis, checking and re-checking the details. It is finished. But is it?

Developing a brand communication plan is just the beginning. Now you have to persuade others that it is the best plan. That requires presenting. It likely requires not just presenting once but many times to many different stakeholders. Each one of these stakeholders may have a different agenda. And while your plan likely is extremely detailed, the majority of those to whom you present will not dive deeply into each decision that you have made.

Presenting a brand communication plan can be a very difficult task for even a seasoned media planning professional. Understanding how to communicate the plan in simple, non-jargon language by itself is daunting. Add in the complexities of a variety of media types each with their own idiosyncrasies on top of myriad media analyses and you have the recipe for a confusing presentation.

Yet, the outcome of the brand's ability to engage with its intended audience rests on your ability to develop a compelling plan. Plus your plan may include investing millions of dollars, which can get the attention of senior management.

Being able to present a plan is crucial to both the success of the plan and your personal success. In this unit, we offer guidance on how you should approach presenting a plan. It revolves around a few key concepts:

- Developing a narrative
- Tailoring to the audience
- Providing context
- Developing a simple format

DOI: 10.4324/9781003258162-41

As you continue to read, try to imagine yourself as the one who is tasked with presenting the plan.

DEVELOPING THE NARRATIVE

Your plan is part of a series of broader plans. Your plan is tied to brand or organization's goals, which are translated into a marketing plan, which is translated into the strategic communication plan in which your plan is housed. Understanding that your plan is part of a greater whole will help you shape the overall narrative for your plan.

The idea of a narrative is to develop a statement or idea that drives your plan. This idea can come from the brand itself, the advertising messaging, a new audience or disruptive campaign, or a competitive situation. The following are some examples of potential plan narratives for each of these.

One narrative for your plan could be based on the brand's mission or benefit. For example, if you were providing a plan for Coca-Cola, your theme may revolve around the idea that Coke's mission is "to inspire moments of optimism and happiness." That mission led you to develop a plan that tailors the message to those specific moments and content that may inspire them.

When Dove launched their "campaign for real beauty," the message idea was to disrupt conventional thinking about who is considered a beautiful woman. That message idea was carried forward in the plan that engaged women by asking them what makes them beautiful. The plan was built around "asking for feedback" rather than telling them about Dove. Asking versus telling became the narrative for the plan.

Competitive context can become the foundation for the plan narratives. Finding ways to stand out from the competition may be the thrust of the campaign. For example, Subway began its successful run by positioning the brand as a healthy alternative to fast food. The plan to carry that message forward was built on the insight that consumers wanted balance in their lives. If they overindulged on the weekend (think eating a huge burger and fries), they were apt to look for alternatives early in the week. This insight led to focusing messaging on Sunday–Wednesday to stand out from the traditional Thursday–Saturday fast-food promotional window. The idea of being able to dominate a medium, timeframe, or concept are very common narratives for media plans.

Regardless of the background, the idea of building a simple narrative is to help you quickly connect the overall idea of your plan to your audience. If it is the same plan as last year, then it is "maintaining the moment." Think about how you would describe the overall strategy of the plan.

TAILORING TO THE AUDIENCE

The narrative comes in handy because it is highly likely that you will present your plan to a wide variety of audiences. You need to maintain a consistent message while tailoring your presentation to the needs of the audience.

Let's assume that you are the media strategist at a media agency with the task of presenting your plan to the client. Your first presentation may be to your boss. And then to their boss. These are people with great technical knowledge and the responsibility of maintaining the client relationship. Their interest will lie in if your plan is technically sound, is innovative, and meets the client's objectives. They want to see if your plan represents the agency's work as well as how it meets the client's goals. In such internal presentations to senior management, the management's role is to challenge you to defend your plan. Management will want to see if you have convictions about your plan and have considered a wide variety of alternatives. If they are convinced that you have conviction and that the plan meets the goals, then it is onward to the client.

In large companies, there is a hierarchy of management for whom you will present your plan. You may start with an advertising manager or brand manager. They are responsible for providing you with direction for developing the plan. So, the plan now takes on a trail of ownership. The manager level of the organization is the primary ownership of your plan. They will be extremely detailed in reviewing the plan plus they will want to help you "sell" it to the higher-ups in their organization. As a result, they will need to be able to speak to your plan. In this case, you need to tailor your remarks to this audience so that they can convey them throughout the organization.

The next step in the process may be to a marketing director who oversees a variety of managers. The marketing director could be the chief marketing officer (CMO) who is a member of the executive committee responsible for all marketing activity for the organization. They will be keenly interested in how innovative your plan is. And they will be highly sensitive to its ability to achieve marketing goals because they are ultimately responsible for the plan. If your plan fails, they will fail.

The final step of the process may be a presentation to the executive committee or the C-Suite. This could be the chief executive officer, chief operating office, chief financial officer, and the CMO. It could also include board members of the organization. This group will rely on the CMO for expertise in the details of the plan. Their interest will begin with how much you are spending. Is it the right amount? Too much? Too little? How does it compare to others in the industry. The C-Suite may be under pressure from Wall Street, if they are a publicly traded company, to be more cost efficient. Your plan may impact their presentation to security analysts on overall capital spending. For this audience, you will need to be able to tailor your remarks to how your plan fits with their overall business strategy, which includes but is not limited to marketing.

Thought you were done presenting? Not yet. Let's say that you have made it past all these hurdles. Senior management has blessed your plan. Now you need to present it to the rest of the organization. This could mean sales people, franchisees, or frontline workers. This audience cares about how your plan impacts their daily lives. For example, if your plan is for a fast-food restaurant chain, the local franchisee may be most interested in the timing of your plan so that they can staff appropriately. A sales person may need to alert a retail store to stock up on their products based on the timing of your plan. Others may want to know specifics about your plan so that they can see/hear the commercials.

As you can see, each person you present to views your plan through their own lens. This is why it is so important to have an overall theme or narrative that you can adapt to the situation. Think about how you can tie your plan together while adjusting the content to fit each of your audience's needs.

PROVIDING CONTEXT: WHAT IS NEW?

No matter to whom you are presenting, a key part of your presentation should be centered on the thought of "what is new." Unless you are presenting for a new company/ product/service, your plan is going to the next plan in a series of historical plans. If you are working on an established company or brand, this could be plan number 30. Providing context on what is new about your plan will help you convince others that it is the best plan for the immediate situation.

From your SWOT (strengths, weaknesses, opportunities, and threats) analysis, you can pick up the key items that may impact your plan. Internally, you may be faced with a change in budget, a new campaign, a new audience, or new marketing challenge.

Externally, you may be faced with a change in the environment, such as a cultural shift, a natural disaster, or a new government regulation. It could be the emergence of a new media category or specific media alternative. Any outside force that is new could impact your plan. The other key outside force is the competition. A change in their strategy may force a change in your strategy.

Providing context to your plan is important as you present your recommendation. It provides the "reason why" or backdrop to your plan and your media choices.

As you develop your presentation, you may want to use some comparative charts or analysis to draw out those points. For example, a simple chart demonstrating how you allocated dollars last year versus this year offers a quick snapshot on how the overall plan compares from one year to the next. A simple listing of retained-versus-new media choices quickly highlights what is new about your plan.

Context is especially important as you build your overall narrative. A key change from year to year may be the impetus for your plan's narrative. For example, a number of new competitors may force a brand to "defend their markets." As a result, your plan may seek to reinforce the brand's benefits with its core audience.

Thinking about what's new will help you craft the proper narrative that can lead to a compelling presentation.

PRESENTATION TIPS

Presenting a media plan can be a tough task. On one side, you need to be creative and innovative and on the other you need to be extremely detailed and buttoned up. Here are a few tips to help you along the way.

- **Keep it simple:** use simple language when possible. Try to make complex concepts easily understandable. There is a tendency in media to use lots of jargon. Try to avoid this if at all possible.
- **Be confident:** you know your plan better than anyone else, so be confident in your presentation. The more confidence you express, the more likely your audience will be persuaded.

- **Be excited:** you should be excited to present your work. Show passion. Be excited about what new thinking you are delivering to the brand. Excitement is contagious. If you are excited, others will be as well.
- **Be brief:** less is more. That is particularly true in presenting media. It is easy to get caught up in the litany of details that surround a media plan. Your plan has all the details. Your presentation is designed to highlight the plan's benefits and not to rehash all the details.
- **Compelling graphics:** a picture is worth a thousand words. Just as you keep your language simple, you should keep your graphics simple as well. Even though a media plan may contain lots of analysis and budget numbers, try to keep rows and rows of numbers to a minimum.

The last tip is to be yourself. Everyone has their own unique style. You can borrow from others. Take a review of great speakers. In the end, make it your own and have fun with it.

SUMMARY

Learning how to present is the most important skill for your career. It does take time and practice. It begins with writing your presentation and then learning how to convey your message in a compelling manner.

Focus on building an overall narrative for your plan. Then describing how your plan builds on that narrative. Finally, close with how your plan meets the overall goals of the business/marketing and communication program.

Take the time to work on your presentation skills. You will find that it will pay off.

CHAPTER 42

Developing test plans

....

EVERY PLAN IS A TEST!

Every brand is looking for the optimum way to allocate its funds. Some brands spend a lot on advertising, others don't. Some use television, others use print. Because every brand is unique, it is important to develop a base of knowledge that, over time, guides the brand's support. That's why many brands develop test plans – it is a relatively safe and low-cost way to learn what works and what doesn't for your brand.

Test marketing is the use of controlled tests in one or more geographic areas to gather information about the brand, its customers, and its competitors. There are two basic reasons to test market: the first is to gain knowledge about a new product or line extension in a limited area before rolling it out nationally. The second is to test different marketing-mix strategies for an existing brand. These strategies can include a media-weight test, a media-mix test, a comparison of different copy strategies, or a test of a different blend of advertising-to-trade support.

Test marketing gives the brand management a lot of opportunities to fine-tune the brand strategy. It helps reduce the odds of failure for a future strategy, and it can lead the brand to a bolder strategy. Success depends on setting up an effective and representative test-market situation.

Establishing a worthwhile test-market scenario requires the proper research structure, appropriate test markets, and the ability to act on the information on a broad scale.

GUIDELINES FOR TEST MARKETING

It's a terrible thing when you believe you have an appropriate test but later find that something has muddied the waters, rendering the results unreadable or unreliable. It is important to set up the proper structure for having test markets that are reliable and projectable, with the ability to broadcast to a broader area.

DOI: 10.4324/9781003258162-42

TABLE 42.1 Test marketing standards

2+ Test markets
1+ Control market
Geographically dispersed
Demographically representative of the United States
Test length at least 6 months
Weight levels tests at 50%±

There are no hard-and-fast rules about what makes for a proper test, but there are some standards that, over the years, have served brand managers well. Table 42.1 lists the standards that are recommended for test marketing. Ideally, there should be a minimum of two test markets in addition to a control market; if you are introducing a new brand, however, you would likely want three or four test markets to protect yourself from a regional bias.

Be sure to select markets that are geographically dispersed. If you concentrate your entire test in a certain region and the regional economy tanks, then you have an unreadable test.

Markets should be representative of the United States unless there is a specific ethnic or demographic skew to your brand. Then you would want markets that mirror the category in which you compete. You also want the markets that you select to cover 3% or more of the country, so you'll have a sizable population base that has good projectability.

Most tests should run for at least six months. For most brands that have a four-week purchase cycle, a six-month test would allow for six complete purchase cycles and 26 individual data points that allow for statistical comparison to a baseline. If possible, it is desirable to schedule a test for 12 months to offer greater numbers of data points so that your test period can be statistically validated. If you have a product with a longer purchase cycle than four weeks, then you should consider testing for longer than a year to be able to read and trust the results.

If you are testing media-weight levels, you should look to increase or decrease the weight level by a minimum of 50%. If you adjust it less than this amount, you run the risk of not having data on which you can rely.

SELECTING TEST MARKETS

One of the most important elements in test marketing is selecting the right markets in which to test. For example, if you are testing a new baby formula and pick Fort Myers, Florida, where more than 50% of the population is over the age of 55, that might not pan out for you. The market must reflect the population of the United States or whatever the population base is in which your brand operates.

The second aspect to a test market is to select a market that is neither too small nor too big. Typically, a test market should be no less than 0.2% but no more than

TABLE 42.2 Examples of top test markets

Designated market area	Market rank	Percentage of United States
Oklahoma City, OK	45	0.597
Louisville, KY	50	0.574
Tulsa, OK	60	0.466
Toledo, OH	68	0.406
Des Moines, IA	72	0.376
Omaha, NE	78	0.363
Syracuse, NY	80	0.352
Rochester, NY	77	0.364
Spokane, WA	79	0.357
Madison, WI	86	0.327
Colorado Springs, CO	94	0.284

Source: Nielsen Media Research. U.S. TV Household Estimates.

2.0% of the United States. This usually translates to markets that range from 30 to 150 of the top 210 designated market areas. Table 42.2 shows some of the more popular test markets.

If you select a market that is too small, it might not have the appropriate number of media outlets to translate your test plan. If it is too big, it is not very cost efficient. Who wants to test a plan in New York, where media rates are sky high? As we discussed before, once you are in a few of the top 10 markets, you may have the media equivalent of a national brand.

MEDIA REQUIREMENTS

A test market must have a variety of media outlets available. It should be representative of the normal market. A market should have at least four television stations – basically the Big Four networks. Cable penetration should be no more than 10% above or below the national average; if it is outside this range, then you run the risk of a skewed viewing environment. The market should have a good range of radio stations covering a variety of formats. It should also have a dominant local newspaper that includes a daily and a Sunday edition. The Sunday newspaper should contain Sunday supplements and free-standing inserts. It is essential that the medium you want to test is contained in the test market.

Another aspect of test markets is their degree of media isolation. For example, San Angelo, Texas, receives more than 20% of its television viewing from Dallas/Fort Worth. You wouldn't want to purchase both San Angelo and Dallas stations for a test market. This is known as *spill-in*, when television signals from one market may be seen in another market.

Conversely, you don't want to air your commercials in one market and have them seen in another market where consumers can't get your product. You don't want to have consumers coming to your future retailing partner looking for a product that is not on the shelf. Television spill-in or spill-out should be restricted to less than 15%.

MARKETING CRITERIA

If you are developing a test market for an existing product, you will want to find markets in which it makes sense to test. First, you want a market where you have solid distribution; it makes little sense to do a heavy spend test if you are not in 50% of the distribution outlets in the market. Once you have the proper distribution, then you should find markets that have average sales characteristics. If you have a 70% market share, the chance of pushing it up 20%, to 84% market share, is a lot less likely than if you picked a market where you start with only a 20% market share.

Use your brand and category development indexes (BDI and CDI) to help establish the criteria. For a test market, you should keep within a range of 115 to 85, or ±15 percentage points, from the average. The goal is to keep the markets as typical as possible, assuming that your test is designed to be rolled out nationally.

BEHAVIORSCAN MARKETS

For consumer packaged goods (CPG) brands, one popular method of test marketing is to use Information Resources Inc.'s BehaviorScan test-marketing method. BehaviorScan uses a household panel in discrete designated marketing areas to measure the impact of advertising and actual product-sales movement of the test brand.

Respondents in the panel use a wand to scan their grocery and drug purchases. These same respondents also have their television viewing metered so you can understand their viewing behavior. In addition, respondents are profiled regarding their other media habits as well as their purchase behavior.

BehaviorScan has markets that cut across the country. You can choose from markets such as Cedar Rapids, Iowa; Midland, Texas; and Pittsfield, Massachusetts. When you choose to use a BehaviorScan test, obviously the test-market criteria are already taken care of. If you elect to do your own study, then stick to the criteria in the previous section.

TEST-MARKET TRANSLATIONS

When you are developing a test plan, you should start with how the plan will ultimately be executed. For example, testing a plan that might translate to a $50 million national plan is a waste of time if you know you can't afford such a plan. If your goal is to be a national brand, start with the objective of how you would execute the tested plan on a national basis; if your goal is to be a regional brand, focus on executing the plan on a system-wide basis.

Assuming that your goal is to be a national brand, or to implement your test nationally, let's review the techniques for doing just that. There are two commonly used techniques for translating national media plans into local test plans. The two techniques are called "Little USA" and "As It Falls."

"Little USA," sometimes called "Little America," assigns each test market the average national rating-point level. This technique assumes that the local market will behave similarly to the whole United States. If a national media plan calls for 100 network television rating points and 100 magazine rating points, then each test market would be assigned those weight levels. The plan at the local level is a replication of the plan at the national level.

The "As It Falls" method is a bit different from the "Little USA" approach. In the "As It Falls" method, each test market's media delivery is based on what that delivery would be if the plan were to be implemented nationally. If the national plan calls for 100 network television rating points and your test market normally delivers 10% above the average in terms of network delivery, then the test market would receive 110 rating points. The purpose of the "As It Falls" method is to replicate as precisely as possible the actual national plan that would be implemented.

There are reasons to select one method over the other. "Little USA" is best used when the advertiser is testing a new brand and has no benchmark category sales data available on a local market level. In this case, you want to understand the performance of the product and not necessarily the media variation. On the other hand, if a brand has a good amount of historical sales data, then the "As It Falls" method is preferable because it is closer to what will actually happen once the plan is implemented nationally. You may want to compromise if you find that the "As It Falls" test markets produce abnormally low or high rating-point delivery compared to the national plan. Then you either go to a "Little USA" method or reexamine your test markets.

TRANSLATING NATIONAL MEDIA TO THE LOCAL LEVEL

You've figured out what you want to test. The media group has developed the perfect national plan. You've selected your test markets. Now you have to take that hypothetical national media plan and execute it in the test markets. In doing so, you need to make some media decisions. Unfortunately, the process is not as simple as taking one plan and executing it. National media and local media are different. Each medium has its own nuances. Getting the stars to align takes some work. Let's examine the four major national media, starting with network television.

In scheduling commercials, the biggest difference between network television and spot or local television is that network purchases are usually made within an actual program whereas spot purchases are made between the programs. For example, if you use CBS's *Survivor*, your commercial will run within the actual program, either at the 10-minute or 20-minute commercial break after the show begins. Spot television, on the other hand, offers commercials at the program break, so your commercial would air between *Survivor* and the following program. Why is this important? Research shows that retention of commercials at the between-program break drops 20 to 30% compared to commercials within a program. Therefore, you may want to boost your test plan to compensate for this inequity.

Unlike network television, 15-second commercials are immediately preemptible in spot television. This means that unless a local station has another advertiser running a 15-second unit during the same program that you are, your commercial will not air. There are few natural breaks for 15-second commercials on a local basis, so the chances of your commercial not running can be great. With that in mind, you may want to schedule 30-second commercials on a spot basis to guard against being bumped off the air.

Cable television is difficult to translate to a local market. Many local cable operators sell advertising only on selected channels, which may not be the ones you would purchase. Even on those channels that they do sell, they may offer only broad rotation schedules so you cannot pick the time you want. In some areas, local cable operators may not sell advertising. Local cable is problematic at best. If national cable is a part of an overall plan, you should consider purchasing that test weight on over-the-air television. Local early fringe, late fringe, and/or weekend times can be good substitutes for cable weight.

Network radio translates well to the local level. In radio, it is important to ensure that whatever station format you plan on using nationally, you end up purchasing locally. The only other nuance to radio is the cost implications of 60-second commercials versus 30-second commercials. Usually, :30s are half the price of :60s nationally, yet many local stations charge the same for :60s and :30s locally.

Magazine placement has its own set of issues as well. Depending upon the publication, it may not have a large enough circulation to offer a test-market edition. Most large circulation publications such as *Good Housekeeping, Time*, and *TV Guide* offer very detailed local editions. But if your strategy is to be in more of a "niche" publication such as *Chili Pepper*, then you are going to run into problems. All you can do is to find publications that are similar in nature to what you plan on scheduling.

The other major issue with magazines is the type of unit that can be scheduled in a test-market edition of a national publication. Because publications must actually make a mechanical plate change in the printing process to accommodate your advertisement, they usually allow only full-page advertisements to be in a test-market edition. If your test plan calls for checkerboard advertisements or a fractional unit, you may want to rethink your test. A checkerboard is scheduling quarter-page ads in each of the four corners of a two-page spread; fractional units are anything less than a full page, such as a two-thirds-page or half-page unit. Regardless of your creative wishes, you must use some practical sense when testing in magazines.

Developing test plans takes some serious thought. You need to have your objectives honed with the understanding that what you test can actually be rolled out. Then, select the proper test markets and develop your test translation. Finally, work the local plan so that it fits the national plan as closely as possible.

TACTICAL TESTING

This chapter has focused on developing classical test-market plans typically used with CPG brands. The basic tenets of this type of planning can apply to any brand situation regardless of category. However, you don't have to develop classic test-market scenarios to have a valid test.

As a brand manager, you should always look at ways to improve your advertising and media program. Learning what works or doesn't work provides a golden opportunity to further your brand's cause in the marketplace. There are plenty of areas to do small tactical tests that can reap big rewards: all you have to do is isolate the variable to be tested and have test and control markets.

For example, suppose that you are a retail brand that relies on weekly inserts to drive traffic to your store. You could test if you want your ad to be inserted in the weekday or Sunday newspaper. Or you could see if paid newspapers outperformed free distribution papers. A home accessories retail chain recently ran a test where they changed their insert drop from Sunday to Thursday. They found that their sales had no change by moving the date, but they saved nearly 30% on their media costs since the Sunday paper had a higher cost-per-thousand than the daily, plus it distributed more copies. By doing this small tactical test, this retailer saved millions of dollars for the company.

The same is true for business-to-business (B2B) marketing. You can isolate a market or a particular job title to do a test. One B2B marketer had a publication sort his database with their circulation. For the customers that they had in common, he sent one message; to the prospects, he sent another. This led to an increase in both new customer acquisition as well as the retention of existing customers.

If you have an online component to your marketing plan, you are in a constant state of testing. Most online campaigns are built similar to direct-marketing campaigns with message, creative, offer, and media testing all available. It is like being in a test kitchen for a restaurant chain. Just about anything that can be thought of can be tested in the online arena. Online media can be an effective laboratory to test ideas before rolling them out to offline media.

SUMMARY

Whether you are developing classic test-market scenarios or you want to understand how one media vehicle performs, test marketing should be a part of any media plan. As a brand manager, you want to continually add to the brand's knowledgebase. Test marketing is one consistent method of doing just that.

CHAPTER 43

Evaluating an advertising media plan

....

DEVELOPING YOUR OWN SEAL OF APPROVAL

Like so many professional tasks, evaluating a proposed brand strategic communication plan requires experience and knowledge. Such evaluations are much easier after you have seen a few others, and they are even better once you have been exposed to dozens of them.

Even if you do not have a high degree of experience, there are still some major and minor factors to watch for, examine carefully, and use to determine whether the plan seems to be "on track" or is just a random collection of haphazard ideas. This chapter provides a checklist for evaluating the plan whether you are responsible for developing it or are the one in charge of approving it.

FORMAT

The format of a good plan should be clear, logical, and easy to read and follow. It should take you through the entire process, from the background information on which the plan was based to the current situation, and on through the hoped-for goals and objectives. Then it should move from objectives into strategies and plans – the methods that will be used to achieve the goals and objectives, including a recap of paid, earned, and owned media. The plan also describes the tactics to implement the plans, which might include paid media vehicles and units. A final section that involves the necessary support activities – research, production, checking, and the like – may be included as well

Any media plan will be judged more favorably if it is well designed and easy to read. Just as in real estate or in meeting new people, first impressions are important, and a sloppy plan that is not carefully crafted and assembled will likely receive a poor evaluation. Is there a table of contents with page numbers included in the plan? Does that table of contents make logical sense, and does it match up with the actual pages on which the corresponding materials appear? Are the pages numbered and

DOI: 10.4324/9781003258162-43

assembled in proper order? An upside-down or backward page creates the impression of poor planning and hurried thinking.

Starting each new section of the plan on a new page, using double-spacing, including graphics and tables, and providing full explanations of each point you wish to make will also create a better impression in the evaluation.

OVERVIEW

The overview or executive summary should be the first element in the plan, even though it cannot be written until all the other sections have been completed. The overview lets the reader see what is coming, so that he or she is not forced to read through it all twice. For the senior executive, the overview gives the essential information and answers the questions: who are we trying to reach with our message? Where are they located? What media methods will be used to reach them?

It is important not to give too much information in the overview. For example, including the history of the client firm is unnecessary; after all, the client will know this history better than an agency media strategist ever could.

CURRENT SITUATION AND COMPETITION

There should be some treatment of the current marketing situation – the problem that this plan is attempting to solve.

In addition, there must be detailed information about the competition. It is not possible to establish the marketing or strategic communication objectives without first considering the competition. This section should include not just general competitive information but also detailed insights into the competitors' uses of all aspects of strategic communication. And all competitors should be included, not just the major ones.

OBJECTIVES

It is essential that objectives are set early and followed throughout the rest of the plan. The objectives and goals must be explained, with complete rationale and justification.

Too often, strategies such as the types of media to be used are included in the objectives. It is important that this section include only what is to be accomplished – the goals – and that the strategies to achieve them be held back. Paid media, for example, are strategies, not objectives. Using television or social media is not a goal; the goal is to sell, to convince, to change opinions, to inform, and to communicate, and the various aspects of strategic communication are strategies that will be used in the plans to achieve these ends.

Brand communication objectives should be specific rather than vague. The best objectives will be quantified with actual goal numbers stated, so it is clear at the end of the campaign whether the objectives have been reached.

TARGETS: UNDERSTANDING WHO YOU ARE ATTEMPTING TO REACH

There should be three kinds of targets: *target markets*, which are the geographic areas and cities where advertising will be focused; *target groups* or publics, who are the kinds of people you will attempt to reach; and *target audiences*, who are the people who can actually be reached through advertising in the mass media.

For example, advertising for the Hyundai Accent automobile may be aimed at cost-conscious young adults who are seeking a high-performance car and live in a large metropolitan area. The problem is that there may be no one advertising medium that reaches those persons, only those persons, and all of those persons; therefore, the target audience may be slightly different from the target group and target market.

Targets are sometimes given as part of the objectives, although it may make more sense for the targets to be included with strategies and plans, because they are a means of accomplishing the goals and objectives.

Targets are typically described in prose in the plan, but they should also include a numerical component. How many people (in thousands and as a percentage) are you aiming for, and how often will they be reached? Do these numbers make sense, and do they match up with the numerical targets?

Like every other section of the plan, the targets should be fully explained and justified. They are important and deserve complete attention and treatment. Why these particular targets and not others? How were these decisions made and why?

In addition, there should be a clear delineation of targets for paid, earned, and owned aspects of the plan. For example, paid media may be directed at potential new customers while earned and owned media may be directed more toward existing customers. Or there could be specific niche audiences that may be addressed in one category and not the others. This is especially true of global brands, where the brand may be perceived differently in different countries. For example, Pizza Hut is perceived as largely a take-out or delivery pizza chain in the United States yet in China, Pizza Hut is much more of a casual dining establishment.

STRATEGIES

Strategies are plans – the plans that will be used to achieve the campaign objectives. As mentioned earlier, these strategies may include the targets. And the strategies will certainly include the media choices that are being recommended for inclusion in the campaign.

These media cannot possibly be selected before the objectives and the targets have been detailed. After all, a medium is by definition a go-between, so it must be clear what the goal is before any medium or go-between can be determined. Similarly, the target must be clearly defined before media can be selected, because it is not possible to know which media will reach those targets until the targets are clear.

The reasons for using each medium must be spelled out in detail. In addition, and just as important, is one fact that is too often overlooked: the reasons for not using other media. It should be clear that all possible media were considered and judged fairly in their applicability to the situation, to the campaign objectives, and to the targets to be reached.

It is not enough simply to list media types. For the media being recommended, what are the specifics being recommended? Is it a specific social media platform such as Snapchat or an audio platform such as Spotify? Is it a specific influencer or a specific set of bloggers to try to ramp up earned media? How is owned media being treated? And, as always, there must be compelling reasons to justify every decision, strategy, and tactic.

BUDGET

Now comes the money, an essential element in any campaign. Is there enough money to do an adequate job? Are the monies being spread too thinly across too many targets or too many media? Is there enough money to do an adequate job in each medium and against each target group?

Money will need to be thoughtfully allocated to each medium. In the case of local market plan, the media selected should be tailored to that specific geographic market. It makes no sense to allocate money outside those markets. On the other hand, a plan that is more national in scope for an entire country may include some additional local market support beyond the national plan if an analysis indicates that is a wise decision.

Allocations to media and markets should be explained and justified in the plan. The budget should be given in a coordinated budgetary overview, and the allocation of funds to various types of media should be determined prior to the tactical phase of the plan.

CONTINGENCY PLAN AND TEST PLANS

Toward the end of the plan, there should be a contingency plan, with details on what will be done if the proposed plan is not working as anticipated. Contingency plans are often too brief and oversimplified to be of any real use. In an emergency, there is no time to come up with alternative plans, so the contingency plan is vital.

The same can be said for developing test plans. We covered the various test options in the Chapter 42. A test plan may be a separate document. It should be referenced in the overall plan so there is no confusion over the role of testing and budgeting. If the budget comes from the overall plan or a separate fund, this is a good place to reference it.

SCHEDULE

There also needs to be a schedule or calendar showing which activities will be scheduled during each phase of the campaign. This schedule is often given in the form of a flowchart because it can combine the media to be used, the weights for each medium, the time span, and the overlapping uses of various media. A presentation of the calendar in a flowchart or some other visually appealing graphic makes this information easier to communicate and easier to understand. (See Exhibits 43.1–43.5 for media checklists.)

EXHIBIT 43.1 MEDIA CHECKLIST

I. Marketing goals
   A. Is the plan designed to:
      1. increase usage from existing user base?
      2. increase usage from lighter users?
      3. increase trial among nonusers?
      4. protect current user base from erosion?
II. Communication goals
   A. Is the plan designed to:
      1. increase awareness among the target?
      2. change perception of the target(s)?
      3. generate an immediate response?
      4. generate an inquiry?
III. Timing
   A. Do you know the fiscal year?
   B. Is there a specific start date?
   C. What is the plan period?
IV. Target audience
   A. For consumer goods, have you defined the target(s)?
      1. Usage (heavy, medium, light)
      2. Demographics
      3. PRIZM clusters
      4. Need-based segments
      5. Drawn-out specific target segments with names
      6. Looked at MRI, media audit
      7. Looked at Spectra for packaged goods
      8. Purchaser versus user
      9. Purchaser influencer
   B. For business-to-business (B2B) clients, have you defined target(s)?
      1. Standard industrialization classification code
      2. Job description
      3. Demographics
      4. Need-based segments
      5. Influencers in decision chain
V. Seasonality
   A. Have you looked at the following:
      1. Sales by month or week?
      2. Category sales versus brand sales?
      3. Competitive activity versus sales?
VI. Geography
   A. Is the plan national, international, or local?
      1. Do you have sales by markets?

   2. Do you have category sales by market?

   3. Have you calculated brand and category development indexes (BDI/CDI)?

      a. Do you know distribution by market?

      b. All commodity volume (ACV) for packaged goods?

      c. Number of stores/units for retailers?

VII. Creative considerations

  A. Are there creative considerations for the plan?

    1. Are there creative advertising units produced?

    2. Are the creative units in sync with the communication goals and budget?

    3. Are there other paid, earned, or owned programs that are ongoing?

VIII. Budget

  A. Do you know the total budget?

  B. What is the media budget?

  C. Is it net or gross?

  D. How does it compare to last year?

  E. How does it compare to the competition?

  F. Have you calculated share of market (SOM) to share of spending (SOS)?

  G. What is the ad-to-sales ratio?

IX. Mandatories

  A. Are there any sacred cows?

  B. Has the client purchased anything on his or her own?

  C. Should earned and owned media be a part of the plan?

X. Communications goals

  A. Have you set up specific communications goals?

    1. Reach/frequency

      a. Is there an effective frequency level?

    2. Have you used the matrix?

    3. Is there a continuity goal?

    4. Is continuity more important than higher weight levels?

XI. Media strategies

  A. Do your media strategies include:

    1. which media mix is best? Paid, earned, and owned?

    2. how to best use each medium?

XII. Media tactics

  A. Do your tactics include:

    1. what is the best vehicle and why?

    2. a cost analysis?

    3. a target audience analysis?

  B. Can you own a vehicle?

  C. Did you include a flowchart?

  D. Did you include a budget recap?

E. Did you compare this year to last year?

F. Do you have alternative plans?

XIII. Test options

A. Is there the option of testing?

1. Higher spend level?

2. Alternative media mix?

3. Different target?

4. Different buying strategy?

Source: FKM.

EXHIBIT 43.2 RETAIL CHECKLIST

1. Do you know what the comp store sales goal is?

2. Do you have daily sales and know when key holidays are?
   - How have holidays changed versus one year ago?

3. Do you know how sales are by channel such as stores versus online?
   - Have you defined a store trading radius (e.g. three miles)?

4. Is the target audience different by sales channel or by market?
   - Are there pockets of consumer opportunity?

5. Do you know how short-term promotions are planned?
   - What dates are the sales promotions?

6. How was media planned year-to-year?
   - Many retailers comp on a weekly basis.

7. Competition is crucial for retail. Do you have a handle on when and where the competition spend? Do you know their sales channel strengths and weaknesses?

Source: Compilation of Agencies

EXHIBIT 43.3 MEDIA CHECKLIST: PACKAGED GOODS

1. Do you know the source of volume for marketing mix?
   - Has a marketing-mix study been done?

2. Do you have volume and incremental volume goals?

3. Do you have target definitions from MRI and Spectra?

4. Do you have BDI/CDI for markets?

5. Are the markets listed IRI or Nielsen markets? (If so, do you have appropriate designated market areas [DMAs] for these markets?)

6. Do you have ACV by market?

7. Do you know when consumer promotions are scheduled?

8. Do you know if there are any limited-time offers that are time specific?
9. Do you have category versus brand seasonal sales and have you compared both to spending?
10. Have you done alternative plans on media mixes?
11. What is the role of advertising with the trade?
12. Is there a test component to the plan?
13. Do you know purchaser versus user?
    - mom versus kids

EXHIBIT 43.4 MEDIA CHECKLIST: B2B (BUSINESS-TO-BUSINESS)

1. Do you have a clear understanding of the target?
   - The right standard industrial classification code?
   - The right job position?
   - The decision process?
2. When are decisions made?
   - Are they ongoing or at a specific time of year?
3. Do they have a customer database of current and prospective customers?
   - Should there be a retention program?
4. Do you have the industry or job universes to better understand coverage of media?
5. Are there any key trade shows to support or consider?
6. Is direct marketing part of the program?
7. How does your customer relationship management (CRM) program fit as part of the mix?
8. Are there any vehicles you can own?
9. Are there opportunities for senior management to gain industry visibility?
10. What is the role of owned media? Is it to provide more information or to secure a sale?
11. Is there anything that should be tested?

EXHIBIT 43.5 BUDGET CHECKLIST

1. Is the budget adequate? Is there enough money to accomplish all the objectives?
2. Does the target audience size make sense? Will it account for a sizeable portion of the target groups?
3. Are there enough communication methods to cover a diverse audience?
4. Are enough markets used to cover most of the country or most of the region in question?
5. Is there enough media weight to achieve sales goals? Enough markets? Adequate portion of coverage?

6. Are larger markets getting more of the media allocations?
7. Over the course of the campaign (e.g. for the coming year), will the frequency be sufficient?
8. Are the advertising creative units affordable and sensible?
9. Are reach, frequency, and impact balanced? For example, expensive units (bigger print advertisements, longer broadcast commercials, using digital page take-overs) cost more, which leaves less for reach and frequency. The corollary is that less expensive units will provide more money for more reach and frequency.
10. Are reach and frequency sensibly balanced?
11. Are expensive media (e.g., television) slated to receive larger budgetary allocations than less expensive media (e.g., outdoor)?

MEDIA CHECKLIST: RETAIL

Retail advertising can be slightly more complicated than other advertising, and it is often different even when it is not more complicated. Exhibit 43.2 details a checklist for retail advertising media plans; use this checklist in addition Exhibit 43.1, the checklist used for all advertising media plans.

PAY ATTENTION TO THE NUMBERS

In any analysis of a proposed media plan, it is crucial to pay attention to the numbers – to determine whether they make sense and to see if they all add up correctly. This retail checklist may be of help.

SUMMARY AND OVERALL APPROACH

General standards to consider include the following:

1. When information or data are provided, the sources of those facts should also be provided so the reader can judge the quality and reliability of the information.
2. When tables or figures or similar data are included, they should be related to the plans and objectives rather than simply dropped in with little apparent connection to the plan.
3. When various terms are used, they should be clearly defined. Not everybody agrees on the meaning of every specialized term or expression.
4. The plan should not be too general or oversimplified. The more information and detail included, the better.
5. If a plan starts strongly and then becomes much more general or just falls apart at the end, it is usually an indication that the planner started too late and ran out of time to complete the job.
6. Writing is important, too, so the written plan should use good grammar and correct spelling, with no typographical or punctuation errors. It might also be

a good idea to avoid slang and abbreviations in formal business reports. Write from the brand's perspective, not your own; after all, this is the brand's plan and money.

7. Finally, as stressed earlier, justification is key to any successful plan. A communication budget may involve large sums of money, and the proposed expenditure of those funds needs to be sound.

Just like a good story, a plan needs a narrative. The plan should be something that anyone can quickly grasp and communicate to someone else. Clear, concise, and compelling communication is what makes a successful plan.

Index

Note: Page references in *italics* denote figures and in **bold** tables.

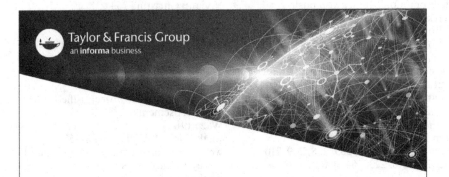

Printed in the United States
by Baker & Taylor Publisher Services